SUNY Series in Classical Studies
John Peradotto, Editor

OLD AGE

in

GREEK *and* LATIN

LITERATURE

Edited by

Thomas M. Falkner & Judith de Luce

STATE UNIVERSITY OF NEW YORK PRESS

Published by
State University of New York Press, Albany

©1989 State University of New York

All rights reserved

Printed in the United States of America

For information, address State University of New York
Press, State University Plaza, Albany, N.Y., 12246

Library of Congress Cataloging-in-Publication Data

Old age in Greek and Latin literature/edited by Thomas M. Falkner
  and Judith de Luce.
      p.   cm.—(SUNY series in classical studies)
  Bibliography: p.
  Includes index.
  ISBN 0-7914-0030-1.   ISBN 0-7914-0031-X (pbk.)
  1. Classical literature—History and criticism. 2. Old age in
literature. 3. Aged in literature. I. Falkner, Thomas M., 1947-.
II. De Luce, Judith, 1946- . III. Series.
PA3015. 043043 1989
880'.09'3520565—dc19

                                                      88-29358
                                                      CIP

10 9 8 7 6 5 4 3 2 1

Contents

Preface

"If we do not know what we are going to be, we cannot know what we are: let us recognize ourselves in this old man or in that old woman. It must be done if we are to take upon ourselves the entirety of our human state."
                    —Simone de Beauvoir, *The Coming of Age*[1]

When de Beauvoir published her ambitious study of old age in 1970, it was in the recognition that old age constituted not only a biological but a cultural fact, whose meaning in contemporary society could only be appreciated by an exhaustive comparison with other societies and times. Neither her study, nor any single work, could hope to achieve that end. But the attempt itself reflected an increasing awareness among intellectuals in general, as well as those with a specific interest in gerontology, that the nature and meaning of old age was a subject of concern not only to the life sciences and social sciences but to a broader range of disciplines, including the humanities. Old age is at once a cultural and a personal event; because concepts of age necessarily participate in larger cultural systems of value, their representation in the many forms of human expression provides a window on a culture as a whole. Apart from its relevance and application to contemporary problems, the subject of old age is of intrinsic interest and is crucial to a complete understanding of any culture, historical or modern.

While in 1970 there was little published research or even interest among humanists in issues related to old age, the years since have witnessed a minor explosion of studies of old age and the elderly in literature, art, religion, philosophy, political thought and history.[2] It is therefore especially ironic that so little work has been done in studying old age in relation to Greek and Latin literature, a tradition in which discussion of old age and images of the elderly are so abundant as to suggest a cultural preoccupation with the subject. The current volume represents a variety of recent efforts to undercut the silence about old age in Greece and Rome and to understand its significance in ancient literature, not just in relation to other textual or historical concerns but as a cultural and intellectual reality of central importance to understanding the works themselves.

The introductory essay, "The Elderly in Classical Antiquity" by the late M.I. Finley, admirably sketches the social background for the subject, addressing the demographic and physiological aspects of the question and correcting a number of popular misconceptions about old age in antiquity. At the same time it shows the problems, in some cases insurmountable, that face historical analysis in the absence of the necessary data and in view of the differences in basic social structure—labor, class, economy and family—between ancient institutions and our own. By acknowledging that many social aspects of the subject are and will remain largely *terra incognita,* it alerts us to the danger of imposing modern ideas about old age on the ancient world, and turns us with fresh eyes to the only extensive sources available—the literary tradition itself.

The nine chapters that follow address in breadth and depth a central aspect of the subject: the representations of the elderly we find in Greek and Roman literature, and the concepts of and attitudes toward old age embodied within them. The essays span a number of central authors and texts: Homer, the Homeric Hymns, Aristophanes, Euripides, Sophocles, Horace, Virgil, Ovid and others. The diversity of the texts is paralleled by the range of methodologies, disciplinary perspectives, and interpretive tools—literary, historical, anthropological, psychological, biographical, structuralist, philological—brought to bear on the subject. All share an appreciation of the social and historical background of the texts; their unity consists in their common emphasis on the literary nature of these treatments of old age, and in their recognition that these are representations whose meaning cannot be evaluated apart from their place in the larger economy of the work, the corpus, or the literary tradition as a whole. In one sense, each of the essays attempts to answer the same question: what factors, whether in the text, the tradition, or the creative process itself, determine the character of a particular representation of old age?

The first two chapters look at old age in early Greek poetry. In "Ἐπὶ γήραος οὐδῷ: Homeric Heroism, Old Age and the End of the

Odyssey," the author suggests a conflict within the heroic attitude to old age, reflected in the ambivalence of the representation of the elderly in both epics and linguistically in their situation "on the threshold of old age." The issue is of special concern to the story of Odysseus, the hero who is destined to a "sleek old age." In Laertes, the poet explores the problematical nature of old age in a heroic society, and finds in Laertes' work in the orchard a model of old age appropriate to the post-heroic world ushered in by the poem. In "Tithonos and the Tettix," Helen King examines the idea of old age in the myth of Eos and Tithonos, who wins immortality without the complement of eternal youth. King's structural analysis supplements the familiar version in the *Homeric Hymn to Aphrodite* with versions that include Tithonos' transformation into a cicada (a being at once beast and god, young and old) and finds in the myth a positive valuation of the human condition: the "destructive old age" of mortals mediates the full immortality of the gods and the endless old age of Tithonos.

The three following chapters deal with Greek drama. Thomas K. Hubbard, in "Old Men in the Youthful Plays of Aristophanes," challenges the notion that the elderly characters and choruses in the playwright's early work are simple expressions of nostalgia for the virtues of Athens' past. The elderly serve in a larger capacity as representatives of the Athenian audience and of the values increasingly under assault by new political and intellectual leaders, by whom the elderly are in fact often seduced and manipulated. Aristophanes uses these old men to define his artistic relationship to the city, and by rallying the community against the dangers of the new orthodoxies he renews it, in some cases literally. In "The Wrath of Alcmene: Gender, Authority and Old Age in Euripides' *Children of Heracles*," the author looks at one of the few detailed representations we have of elderly women in Greek tragedy and examines the contrast between male and female old age as the poet develops it in Iolaus and Alcmene. Her assertiveness in old age is developed throughout in negative terms, and her brutal behavior at the end of the play points to a larger stereotype of the "vengeful old woman" with its own literary tradition. In " 'Do Not Go Gently . . .' *Oedipus at Colonus* and the Psychology of Aging," Thomas van Nortwick studies Oedipus the aging hero and Sophocles the aged playwright in the light of recent research on the psychology of aging, and sees some of its troubling features as reflections of the problems confronting Oedipus as an old man facing death. Van Nortwick sees in Oedipus' movement from weakness to strength a psychological and artistic response to a universal problem for aging men: how to preserve self-esteem and personal prestige in the face of diminished physical capacities and decreased social and political effectiveness.

Two chapters discuss the relationship between sexuality and old age in Greek and Roman literature. In "The Ashes and the Flame: Passion and Aging in Classical Poetry," Stephen Bertman reviews poetic representations of old age from Homer to Ausonius, and traces a common theme through many of the authors and passages analyzed in detail elsewhere in the collection. Citing the traditional association of loss of youth with loss of beauty and hence of desirability, he considers a variety of poetic responses to the idea of ardor in old age. Bertman's concern for the different consequences of old age for men and women and for the literary silence about old women is shared by Carol Clemeau Esler in "Horace's Old Girls: Evolution of a Topos." Esler sees Horace weaving together the strands of poetic convention in three distinct poems to aging women, and identifies a movement from the harshness of the Lydia poem (*Odes* 1.25), to the more muted tones and metaphor of the Chloris ode (3.15), to *Odes* 4.13, in which Lyce becomes not so much an object of ridicule as of pity, a symbol of human mortality. She concludes by questioning why Horace does not extend to aging women the enduring intellectual pleasures he grants to old men.

The material on Horace is complemented by studies of two of his Augustan contemporaries, Virgil and Ovid. In "The Old Man in the Garden: *Georgic* 4.116-148," Jenny Strauss Clay sees this alleged digression as the central panel of the fourth poem, with the independent, isolated old man standing midway between the uncontrolled animal passion of the preceding poems and the unerotic bees of the fourth. The old Corycian represents a central human impulse, which moves beyond utility and instinct to beauty for its own sake. Clay's old Corycian is not himself an artist but prepares us for another old man living in isolation who is. In "Ovid as an Idiographic Study of Creativity and Old Age," the author looks at the relationship between aging and creativity by comparing the earliest and latest poems of Ovid. Drawing on recent work on the psychology of aging and on creativity, she suggests that the echoes of the earlier poems found in the exilic poetry, as well as the transformations of earlier motifs, reflect in part the influence of the poet's age. This chapter raises questions about continuity and change in creativity over time and suggests future directions for the examination of creativity.

What emerges from the collection as a whole is a number of overlapping frames of reference in which the images and concepts of old age in classical literature can be studied. Some look at the images in relation to the social and psychological realities of old age, the institutional realia of the lives of the elderly or the cultural and attitudinal environment in which they participate. Others assume a relationship between representations of age and the life stage of the author, particularly in the case of "old-age art," to use Kenneth Clark's unglamorous phrase, which is so abundant in the classical tradition. Other essays view the representation of old age as primarily metaphorical and symbolic, as poetic vehicles for ethical qualities and values—strength and weakness, wisdom and foolishness, autonomy and dependence, and so-forth—and see its character as determined primarily in relation to other textual concerns. All in turn appreciate the relation between these images of old age and the generic conventions that govern their respective literary worlds.

Several of the essays in the collection draw upon the extensive gerontological literature developed in the social sciences: Falkner and Van Nortwick, for instance, on the cross-cultural gerontology of David Gutmann, and de Luce on the life-review theories of Robert Butler. Can the work of a classicist be genuinely informed by gerontology, or are we destined to make only occasional nods at that developing field? In the afterword "When Fields Collide or A View from Gerontology," Mildred M. Seltzer, a professional gerontologist, considers more fruitful collaborations between the traditional methods of the humanist and the social scientist, drawing important distinctions and connections between them and warning against the phenomenon of the "instant gerontologist." The concerns she raises and the core of readings in gerontology she recommends generate an agenda and set a high standard for those who would risk a collision with a set of assumptions, goals and methods quite alien to those of their professional training.

In the annotated select bibliography, Emiel Eyben reviews the significant research within classics on the life course in general and old age in particular. Eyben's bibliography includes materials relevant to the literary representation of old age and extends to the physiology and psychology of old age, to the social and legal condition of the elderly, and to changes in the concepts and imagery of old age that come with Christianity.

The current volume clearly is not intended to be the definitive exploration of old age in classical antiquity, nor does it pretend to offer an exhaustive survey of literary images of old age. Taken together, the materials suggest the range of issues and methods by which one might examine the experience of old age in Greece and Rome and the artistic expressions of that experience. But the essays here raise as many questions as they answer and suggest agenda for future research. Important authors and texts are not represented in this collection, and many aspects of the subject will be better explored across authors, genres and cultures. And more work needs to be done on elderly women. Much of the work to date focuses on old men—this is true even of the current volume—although there is considerable evidence that old men and women do not experience aging in the same way. As such, the current volume is as important for what it leaves out as for what it includes, and for the interest it provokes in others to follow different paths of inquiry perhaps to different ends.

A word on the circumstances of the collection, which was inspired by a panel "Aging and the Aged in some Greek and Latin writers" at the Classical Association of the Middle West and South in 1985, by the Virginia Humanities Conference "Humanistic Perspectives on Aging" at the College of William and Mary in 1986, and that same year by the panel on "Old Age in Ancient Literature and Society" at the meeting of the American Philological Association. Several of the essays here were first aired at these meetings, and we wish to thank the host organizations and others who, whether represented in the collection or not, pursued the subject, traded ideas, and in other ways encouraged the appearance of this collection. We are grateful to Oxford University Press and *Greece and Rome* for permission to reprint the essay by M.I. Finley and likewise to *Arethusa* for the essays by Helen King and Jenny Strauss Clay. Particular thanks are due to Judith P. Hallett, for her lively support of our work in the field of aging, and to John Peradotto, general editor of the SUNY Press Series in Classical Studies, who from the outset encouraged the volume and helped bring it to reality.

We wish to express our gratitude for the institutional support that enabled us to complete the project: Falkner to the College of Wooster for a research leave for 1987-1988 and various forms of support from Faculty Development, as well as to the Department of Classics at Cornell University, where the leave year was spent; de Luce to Miami University and the Department of Classics for a semester's assigned research appointment in 1987 for the opportunity to continue work in this area.

Finally, we wish to dedicate this volume to our parents, Ruth and Norbert Falkner and Martha Hudson and Hollinshead de Luce, less as a gift than as a kind of academic version of the *threptēria*. It seems fitting that we repay those who nurtured our spirits as well as our bodies with an offering of words and ideas. We are pleased to observe that they provide happier paradigms of old age than many of the images that follow.

The Editors

Notes

1. Trans. Patrick O'Brian, New York 1972 (orig. publ. *La Vieillesse*, Paris 1970) 5.

2. For collections of such efforts across the disciplines, see, for instance: *Aging and the Elderly. Humanistic Perspectives in Gerontology,* edited by Stuart F. Spicker, Kathleen M. Woodward and David D. Van Tassel (Atlantic Highlands, NJ, 1978); *Aging in Literature,* edited by Laurel Porter and Laurence M. Porter (Troy, MI, 1984); *Memory and Desire. Aging-Literature-Psychoanalysis,* edited by Kathleen Woodward and Murray M. Schwartz (Bloomington, IN, 1986). For a general bibliography, see *Where Do We Come From? What Are We? Where Are We Going? An Annotated Bibliography of Aging and the Humanities,* by Donna Polisar, Larry Wyant, Thomas Cole and Cielo Perdomo, published by the Gerontological Society of America (Washington, 1989).

Acknowledgments

"The Elderly in Classical Antiquity" by M.I. Finley originally appeared in *Greece and Rome* 28 (1981): 156-71, and is copyrighted by Oxford University Press.

"The Old Man in the Garden: *Georgic* 4.116-148," by Jenny Strauss Clay, originally appeared in *Arethusa* 14 (1981): 57-65, and "Tithonos and the Tettix" by Helen King appeared in *Arethusa* 19 (1986): 15-35; copyrights are held by the Department of Classics of the State University of New York at Buffalo.

"The Ashes and the Flame: Passion and Aging in Classical Poetry" is copyright 1989 by Stephen Bertman.

All other material ©1989 by SUNY Press.

Standard abbreviations for ancient authors and texts are according to the *Oxford Classical Dictionary*. In most instances, the abbreviations of periodicals are those used by *L'Année Philologique*.

Introduction
The Elderly In Classical Antiquity[1]

M.I. Finley

We begin with an obvious but not simple question: Who are, or were, the elderly? There is, of course, a vague biological boundary-line, but the "concept of aging is a statistical one, and no valid means of measuring it in the individual are available."[2] Statistically, today as in antiquity, the agreed points at which to draw the line in general terms seem to be either sixty or sixty-five. In concrete terms, however, there are many lines, determined by social, economic, and political considerations, for which biology provides no more than crude limits. For example, in England today a woman qualifies as an old-age pensioner at sixty, a man at sixty-five. Retirement is normal in the civil service at sixty, compulsory in the universities at sixty-five or sixty-seven, depending on a vote taken in individual institutions more than twenty-five years ago, but in Scotland at seventy. Members of parliament and until recently judges, in contrast, are allowed to go on until they drop if they so choose, and many do so choose. That these variations are directly linked with political influence, pensions, the desire to spread employment, access to lucrative post-retirement employment, ideology, and so on, not with biology, is self-evident.

In ancient Greece and Rome, hardly any of these considerations applied. To begin with, women did not enter into any calculation or policy. Nor did slaves. They were ubiquitous and of the greatest importance, but for the present discussion they were part of the background rather than of the subject. Then, there were no pensions, no benefits, none of the questions arising from conditions of employment or unemployment, no formalized or institutionalized concept of retirement. Political and administrative rulings about retirement were therefore restricted almost entirely to the army. When the army was a citizen-militia, and that was the case in Greek history down to the conquest of Alexander and in Roman history to

1

nearly the close of the Republic, the formal obligation of military service did not end until a man reached the age of sixty. The actual call-up of specific age-classes depended on the military manpower needs at any given moment; 'emergencies' were frequent enough to put men in their fifties at risk, particularly for defensive duties when a city was under direct attack. The exceptions were the generals in Greece, for whom there was no age limit: Pericles was still a general at his death, aged about sixty-six, in the early years of the Peloponnesian War, though it must be confessed that his active duty was restricted to engagements near Athens in which no serious fighting was anticipated; half a century later King Agesilaus of Sparta died on his return from mercenary service in Egypt, aged eighty-four.

Individual cases tell us little, though that little may be significant as we shall see. The prior question is, how many aged were there? What proportion of the total population? Today that proportion is so large and is increasing so steadily that the aged have become a major social issue in all western societies. It has been estimated that if present trends continue, twenty percent of the total population of the United Kingdom will be sixty or over by the end of the century. No comparable figures are available from antiquity: various attempts to calculate have all been futile because the only documentation consists of tombstones, which as a group are too selective to provide a proper sample of the population.[3] However, there can be no doubt that infant mortality was far higher than today, that the average life expectancy of those who survived infancy was far lower. Sir Martin Roth has formulated the profound difference dramatically: "Most ten-year old children can now expect to have two grandparents alive, to mature into adulthood, to marry, have children and survive through a working life to retirement and enjoyment of grandchildren. Such an outcome could not have been dreamt of a century ago,"[4] and certainly not, I may add, twenty centuries ago. Whatever the percentage of the over-sixties in antiquity, the certainty is that it was very much lower than today's figure.

It is important to stress that we are dealing with a fundamentally unchanging demographic situation throughout Greek and Roman history that was beyond human controls. Even medical science, we must remember, contributed little before our own century to the great modern demographic change. Our justified admiration of the best of the ancient doctors, the Hippocratic school, Galen, and the others, applies to their contribution to the knowledge of anatomy and physiology, to their skills with fractures and some surgery, to their concern for alleviating pain and comforting patients, to their 'rationalism', most famously expressed in the little Hippocratic treatise called *The Sacred Disease* with its argument that epilepsy was as natural as any other disease though its cause was inexplicable at the time; but our respect should not cover up the fact that they could not cure or extend the life of a patient with an infectious disease, a cardiovascular defect, a cancer, and so on through the whole list of potentially fatal ailments. Hence, for example, the ease and frequency with which allegations of poisoning were made and believed. Hence, too, the absence of serious discussion of aging in the ancient medical literature. Before the discovery of bacteria and of modern cytology, what could they discuss? They knew that pulse rates changed with age, for example, that the elderly tended to catarrh, failing sight, and deafness, or that age was a consideration in surgical cases, but beyond that they were absolutely blocked. One entry in the Hippocratic collection of *Aphorisms* (1.14) will suffice: "Old men have little warmth and they need little food which produces warmth; too much only extinguishes the warmth they have. For this reason, fevers are not so acute in old people, for then the body is cold."

No doubt there were some variations, in both time and place, caused either by contingent factors or by socio-economic factors. Among the latter, one has precedence: the poor had a more uncertain food supply and less sanitary living conditions than the rich. Of the former I offer an example that may seem esoteric but is not frivolous.[5] The Greeks and Romans were great consumers of wine. As a preservative, the Greeks used a resin additive (hence contemporary retsina), the Romans a syrup they called *sapa* or *defrutum* (which also gave a pleasant colouring and a sweet flavour to the wine, as in modern Marsala). *Sapa* was prepared by simmering must over a slow fire—in a leaden vessel. A recent calculation that the result was about 20 mg of lead per litre of wine means that the Romans were systematically giving themselves lead poisoning for centuries, with a consequent increase in mortality and decrease in fertility. We therefore have the right to assume, though we can neither quantify nor demonstrate, that in the retsina regions of the ancient world there was a somewhat

3

higher life expectancy (and therefore a somewhat higher percentage of the elderly) than in the *sapa* regions.

The ancients did not draw up demographic tables, graphs, and curves, but they would have been fully aware of their high infant mortality and the considerable chance of death at any age, spasmodically increased by epidemics and wars. Unlike us, they had no experience or knowledge of qualitatively different demographic patterns against which to measure and judge their own: utopian visions of an age of Methuselahs were a protest against the inevitable brevity of life, not a goal to be sought. Therefore their expectations were equally constant. I do not refer particularly to the personal expectation of imminent death, as I see no reason to think that in this respect their psychology was radically different from our own. In her brilliant though flawed book on old age, the only synoptic work of its kind that I know, Simone de Beauvoir quotes Marcel Proust with approval for his perception that "of all realities", old age is perhaps the one "of which we retain a purely abstract notion longest in our lives."[6] She goes on to note that it is the one state of an individual's life for which there is no rite of passage, no initiation ceremony. Proust's comment also holds for the average individual's "purely abstract" notion of his own eventual death, in antiquity as today, I believe.

The expectations to which I refer lie in another direction. I quote Simone de Beauvoir again: "For the old it is a never-ending grief to lose those who are younger than themselves . . ., above all if they are their children . . . : the death of a child, of a small child, is the sudden ruin of a whole undertaking; it means that all the hopes and sacrifices centered upon him are pointless, utterly in vain."[7] We can all agree, but we must also acknowledge the presence of an exclusively modern element in the psychology. Historically, there is an inverse of the expectation of any contemporary ten-year-old child today as I quoted them earlier in Roth's formulation. Any Greek or Roman who reached the age of marriage could look forward to burying one or more children, often very small ones, and to burying a young wife or rather less young husband and to remarrying with the same unhappy prospects. I do not suggest that Greeks and Romans buried their children and spouses without a sense of loss; or that, for example, the sixty-one-year-old Cicero's well documented grief over the death of his daughter Tullia was not genuine and deeply felt: she died in her early thirties, the only member of his family whom he loved. What I do suggest is that in a world in which such early deaths and burials were routine, so to speak, the intensity and duration of the emotional responses were unlike modern reactions, though I confess that I know no way to measure or even to identify the differences.

Closely linked is a radical difference—this one is easily identifiable—in the attitudes of children and childhood, and in the practice. Childhood in antiquity was a prepatory stage for adulthood, to be traversed as rapidly as was biologically reasonable, and nothing more. There was no glorification of childhood, a product of modern romanticism, and even less of such more recent developments as the American discovery (or should I say invention?) of the teen-ager or the increasing tendency, tied to the complexities of the modern labour market, to prolong social adolescence into the late twenties. There were toys and nannies for the very young, of course, but no children's books, no special legislation concerning children apart from laws protecting their property rights, which take us into the different realm of concern for preservation of the family and therefore of family property.

The dividing line between childhood and adulthood varied according to sex and class. Girls were married off at an early age—among the Romans twelve was not uncommon, fifteen and a half the average, at least in the more prosperous classes about whom alone we are informed[8]—and they then disappear from our present horizon. Administratively, a qualified adulthood began for boys at the age of seventeen or eighteen. That is to say, that was the age of entry into the citizen militia, for those who had the requisite property qualification (which excluded something like half the citizen male population); that was also the age of entry into the list of voters, in communities which gave at least partial political rights to all citizens regardless of birth or wealth.

But man does not live by war and politics alone. Among the peasants, who always constituted the majority of the Greco-Roman population, and among the self-employed craftsmen and shopkeepers in the towns, sons began to work as early as they still do in many parts of the world. Those who were apprenticed to others in order to learn a trade seem to have set off on their new lives between the ages of twelve and fourteen. For all practical purposes their childhood ended then.

5

The more prosperous preserved their pre-adult standing for a few more years, at least formally, until they were called up for military training. And thereafter? Those who chose and were able to participate in public life, in cultural activities or in such economic activities as were appropriate to their social status, tended to make a start at a much earlier age than we are accustomed to. Aristophanes produced his first play at eighteen or nineteen, a bit on the young side; Cicero did not plead his first law case until he was twenty-five, but he appears to have held back deliberately because of the then unsettled and dangerous political conditions. An early start was the inevitable consequence of the life expectancy and of their awareness of it. There were many, on the other hand, who did not choose such careers, for whom adulthood meant a life of idleness centered round the gymnasia, the palaestras, and the less reputable centres of entertainment. The ambience of Petronius' *Satyricon* is not all fiction.

Class distinctions did not end there. For those who had to earn their livelihood with their hands and who lacked the necessary conditions or qualifications for active participation in public affairs, as office-holders and political leaders, there was no further, non-biological, dividing-line between the time when they began to work and the time they ceased, the latter determined either by death or by physical incapacity. The same was true of the cultural figures, the writers, philosophers, jurists, and artists, scions of the leisured classes with negligible expectations. In both categories the decision whether to continue or to stop was essentially a personal one, physiological and psychological, socially conditioned but not legally imposed.

We are uninformed about the first category, the working population. Among the second group, however, the evidence of creative activity in old age, even great age, is plentiful and dramatic. For example, Sophocles wrote his last play, *Oedipus at Colonus,* when he was about ninety, Euripides his *Bacchae* and *Iphigenia at Aulis* at about eighty; no one will claim to see signs of flagging power or creativity in those tragedies, and if the *Oedipus* can be read as a play about old age in one sense, the *Bacchae* and *Iphigenia* certainly cannot. Plato completed his last and much his longest work, the *Laws,* shortly before his death at eighty-one; his contemporary and great rival in the field of educational theory, the rhetorician and political pamphleteer Isocrates, went on in full spate until ninety-eight: one of his major treatises, the *Panathen-*

aicus, was completed the year before his death. The elder Cato lived to be eighty-five; among the early Church Fathers, Athanasius, author of the Nicene Creed, lived to seventy-eight, St. Augustine to seventy-six, Tertullian to about eighty.

I have not gone out of my way to hunt for a handful of rare exceptions; I have merely selected a few of the most familiar names from a large list, whose dates are authentic, not legendary. (Roman examples appear to be notably fewer and I have no explanation.) My impression is that the Verdis, Picassos, and Bertrand Russells of (at least Greek) antiquity constituted a larger proportion of that class of men than their modern counterparts. Yet a much smaller percentage of men survived into old age; therefore one may infer that the survivors were a highly selected assemblage, men who possessed both great luck and great toughness, physiological and psychological, which is no longer the case as the number of over-sixties moves towards twenty percent of the total population. There are parallels even in a field in which the risks were greatest, military activity and regal power. Three of Alexander's generals went on to found monarchies and to live to a ripe old age. Antigonus in Macedonia to eighty or eighty-one, Ptolemy in Egypt to perhaps eighty-five, Seleucus in Syria to more than seventy-five. Augustus, founder of the Roman Empire, began his career in his late teens and died as the first Roman emperor at the age of seventy-two.

Peacefulness, it should be stressed, was not a mark of any of those reigns, internally or externally. Nor, in a rather metaphorical sense, was peacefulness characteristic of the lives of the cultural leaders whom I have just mentioned. On the contrary, competition, tension, combativeness were built into their activity and their careers: Greek playwrights literally competed for the award of the prize by a jury chosen from the audience, while philosophers, moralists, theologians, pagan or Christian, fought each other for the highest prize of all, the souls of men. May an unqualified layman suggest as an hypothesis that it was precisely this creative activity under tension, with the rewards of achievement, honour, and fame, that kept men in full mental and psychological vigour in their seventies, eighties, even nineties, although I believe that there is at present no scientific evidence to support such a proposition? I suggest further that this tension was of a different quality, so to speak, from the ceaseless tension of those who struggled daily for sheer survival, which exacerbated their anyway inferior physical conditions of life.

The Agesilauses, Platos and Augustines of that world were spared the psychological damage caused by the (to us) familiar cult of youthfulness. Youth meant a healthy physique, beauty, and sexual attraction. That was a fact of life which could no more be ignored in antiquity than in any other epoch. But older men and women were not goaded into seeking the fountain of youth or, worse, into pretending that they had found it. Those who did were figures of derision. That is not to say that Greco-Roman antiquity was immune from the conflict of generations. In so far as the conflict was over the sowing of wild oats, sexual excess, or pecuniary extravagance, it was transitory and of no great significance, certainly not in a consideration of the elderly in society. But there were also larger social and political issues involved, gravitating round the belief that the young were not to be trusted with public affairs, that they were easily 'corrupted' intellectually and morally and therefore a threat not only to themselves but to society at large. In Sparta men were required to live in their barracks until the age of thirty; only then were they considered sufficiently moulded to be allowed to assume a normal, private family life. "One of the finest of your laws," said the elderly Athenian to the elderly Spartan in Plato's last work (*Laws* 643D), "is the one absolutely prohibiting any of the young men from inquiring whether any of the laws is good or not."

Neither Sparta nor Plato can be cited as typical, to be sure; one of the main elements of the Spartan government machinery was a Council of Elders, comprised of two kings and of twenty-eight others, all over the age of sixty and elected for life, an institutionalized make-weight of the elderly that was uncommon in antiquity. Not even the Roman Senate was fully comparable, as it had a small but continuous input of new members, commonly aged about thirty. But it was in Athens, the most democratic, innovative, some would say volatile, of all ancient communities, that Socrates was indicted in 399 B.C. for "corrupting the young," and however we understand that rather nebulous change, the fact is that it impressed enough jurors to lead to a verdict of guilty. In Athens the minimum age for membership in the Council and the jury-courts and for the holding of public office was thirty; for membership on the board of arbitrators to whom most legal disputes were referred in the first instance, it was sixty. In Republican Rome, ten years' military service was ·a necessary justification for the quaestorship, the first in the normal sequence of higher magistracies culminating in the consulship.

Socrates was seventy years old when he was tried and executed for corrupting the young. A quarter of a millennium later, in 155 B.C., the heads of the great Athenian philosophical schools were sent to Rome by Athens on an official political mission. They took the opportunity to give some public lectures in philosophy, the success of which appalled the guardians of Roman morality, and they were expelled from the city on the initiative of Cato the Censor. "Let them return to their schools," Cato is alleged to have said in the Senate, "and practise their dialectic with the sons of the Greeks, while Roman youth obey the laws and the magistrates as before."[9] Old Cato was then seventy-nine, whereas the chief villain, Carneades, head of the Academy, was a youngster at fifty-eight or fifty-nine, the Stoic spokesman Diogenes of Babylon a mere eighty-five. What we have here is not a conflict of generations, but a conflict within the ranks of the old and the very old for control of the young, for their education, their moulding. "Corrupting the young" has been a familiar accusation, in one form of words or another, throughout history. The reverse, "corrupting the old," is unknown; naturally, because the old, or at least the older, are always in the commanding position, as fathers, teachers, judges, senators, censors. At issue is the future course of society, of its values and its institutions.

That is all too obvious; I mention it nonetheless because there is an implication that seems not to be sufficiently noticed, namely, the doubts it casts over the oft repeated banality about the wisdom of the old, the fruits of experience, and so on *ad infinitum*. One can produce an anthology of passages from ancient writers along these lines that will match a similar collection from any other era, and modern writers have not failed to do just that. It has been observed, for example, that in Greek art and poetry prophets, seers, and soothsayers are old men. A modern commentator explains: "Apollo chose the elderly as his vessels because of their venerability and consequent credibility."[10] But they were normally also irascible and unpleasant, they were not rarely blind, and their prophecies repeatedly went unheeded, with dire results. These aspects also require explanation, and "venerable therefore credible" cannot be sufficient; indeed, I doubt if it is of any use. Prophecy was a gift of the gods to a small number of individuals, in

9

each instance for a particular reason which had nothing to do with age or venerability.

The most famous of the blind seers of antiquity was Tiresias, best known from the *Oedipus the King* of Sophocles, a figure of myth, not of history, whose prophecies were regularly disbelieved. Accounts of Tiresias spread over hundreds of years fall into three main versions with a dozen variations. He had undergone a sex change at least once and was therefore the logical person for Zeus and Hera to appeal to when they disagreed as to whether the man or the woman derived more pleasure from sexual intercourse. Tiresias' verdict was the woman, by a ratio of no less than nine to one. Hera, always quick to heated anger, blinded him in punishment, but Zeus then gave him not only the gift of prophecy but seven lives. Or he was blinded by Athena because he had seen her bathing, and then, at his mother's intervention, the goddess gave him the gift of prophecy through observation of the flight of birds. Or, in reverse, he was blinded by the gods for revealing divine secrets.[11] Such stories reveal much about ancient thinking, as in the neat structural opposition between blindness and inner vision, but I suggest that they tell us less than nothing about old age and the elderly in ordinary human life.

Notably the Tiresiases, about whom so much is written, were all products of mythical thought and literary imagination, exemplifying Laslett's warning "to be wary of all inferences from literary and plastic evidence" on this subject "unless it can be checked from evidence outside itself."[12] For antiquity the warning bell must be sounded even more clearly because of the absence of the novel among the literary genres. If one searches through the surviving poetry, drama, histories, political and forensic speeches, philosophical treatises and essays, one will find, not at all surprisingly, passages running the gamut of possible attitudes and conceptions of the elderly. Quotations are available to support almost any judgment. At one extreme there is the wise old voice of experience; Homer's Nestor is the prototype—his name has become a common noun in all modern western languages. (Parenthetically, it should be noted that the Homeric portrait of Nestor is not without its nuances: he is garrulous to the point of boredom, and, more important, his endless talk was designed, through the recall of past incidents, to bolster morale or to cool tempers, not to provide arguments from experience in favour of one or another alternative course of action). At the other extreme are the jokes about the aged that fill comedy and satire; the *Wasps* of Aristophanes alone contains a sufficient quarry to keep a music-hall comedian in material for a season. The jokes become especially brutal when they touch on the sexual desires of older women, as in the two last surviving plays of Aristophanes.[13] I know of no more unrelieved cruelty in Greek or Roman literature than the scene in *The Assembly of Women* in which three old women squabble as they each try to compel a young man, who was lusting after a girl, to have sexual relations with them first, as required by a new law that had just been passed by the women of Athens who had seized control of the machinery of government; a scene that lasts for 235 lines, one quarter of the entire play.

I do not suggest that the varied attitudes are not 'realistic', including those in comedies. Why should they not have been? Why should we assume that Greeks and Romans were less prone than we are to hold ambiguous or mutually contradictory attitudes about the elderly? The trouble with this evidence lies in other directions. In the first place, to be informed that some people held some attitudes—much of which we could safely have guessed without any texts—does not advance our knowledge of the society very much, does not help us see the patterns of behaviour, the realities of the life of the elderly. In the second place, in so far as the literature touches on these realities, it is incurably partial. A central thesis of Simone de Beauvoir's book is that class distinctions "govern the manner in which old age takes hold of a man," that "any statement that claims to deal with old age as a whole must be challenged, for it tends to hide this chasm."[14] That is beyond dispute. So is the fact that ancient literature does precisely that. In his essay on old age, the *De senectute,* Cicero concedes (3.8) that "old age cannot be easy in extreme poverty"—in the Latin nine throwaway words in which Cicero has not the slightest interest and to which he never recurs while he proceeds at considerable length with massive platitudes to applaud the blessings of all passion spent and the inner resources of the wise man of sufficient wealth. Yet even the nine throwaway words are notable for their rarity.

That is why I have postponed for so long a consideration of the central themes that dominate the burgeoning sociological and psychiatric literature of the past thirty or thirty-five years about the elderly— housing, isolation and loneliness, mental illness, and the rest, summed up in the current jargon under the rubrics of 'allocation of social roles and resources' or 'social integration of the older person'. The ancient historian is driven to making bricks without straw. I do not wholly despair, but I am necessarily restricted to general statements based as much on broad sociological considerations as on ancient documentation.

I have to be particularly schematic about certain aspects of the essential background of our subject, about which we know significantly more than about the subject itself.[15] To begin with, it is necessary to underscore the very much smaller scale of this world. Our best estimate of the total population of the Roman Empire at its peak, at the beginning of the Christian era, is of the order of sixty million, no more than the present population of Britain spread out over nearly the whole of Europe, western Asia, and northern Africa. The majority were rural rather than urban, but both those adjectives require specification. The rural population lived in hamlets, villages, and small towns rather than in isolated homestead farms. The urban sector included hardly any really large cities. Only under the Roman Empire did a few—Rome itself, Alexandria, Antioch, Carthage—reach half a million or more. Antioch is known to have been rather an agglomeration of villages than a metropolis; Alexandria and Carthage may also have been that for all we know. The city of Rome, with its flimsy, dilapidated, unsanitary slum blocks of flats for the poor, was therefore the one and only place in antiquity to which the negative picture of large-scale slum poverty, loneliness, and reduced life expectancy can be transferred with certainty. Not many cities even reached one hundred thousand: Pompeii with its twenty thousand was nearer the norm for a town, as distinct from a village or hamlet.

Furthermore, the heartland of the Greco-Roman world, the Mediterranean basin, had a common life-style in at least two respects: first, the climate greatly reduced the basic requirements of clothing, housing, and heating; second, people tended to spend much of their time out of doors and in at least superficial contact with each other. Even the great theatres and political assembly places were out of doors, and the town squares—the Greek agora and the Roman forum—were always crowded with people in non-working as in working hours, as were the temples, shrines, and sanctuaries. Although I do not share the romantic nostalgia for village life and I do not underestimate the horrors of rural poverty, I submit, at least as a hypothesis, that this smallness of scale and Mediterranean life-style could have saved the aged from certain consequences of modern urban complexes with their lonely bedsitters and their doss-houses on the one hand, and from the starvation and hopelessness of the Calabrian or Appalachian highlands on the other hand.

The free poor were divided into the class of more or less independent tenants, craftsmen, and shopkeepers and the class of casual labourers in agriculture or in the towns. As usual, no statistics are available but I believe the signs point to the former, the self-employed, as having been much the larger class, except perhaps for the city of Rome and maybe Alexandria. Several consequences followed. There was no significant separation between residence and place of work: the family was the unit and the locus, so to speak, of both. There was also little geographical mobility: the exceptions, such as the wandering philosophers and artists, or the transplantations of people in periods of colonization, do not weaken that generalization. Finally, there was in a profound sense no labour market; hired labour was casual labour; slaves constituted the normal labour force in both rural and urban establishments that were too large for a family to man, and slaves were a commodity, standing outside the complex of problems we are considering. Old Cato, in his manual on farming (2.7), recommended in his penny-pinching way selling off surplus grain, old or blemished work oxen, worn-out tools and wagons, and sick or aged slaves. Not everyone agreed; some ancient moralists even criticized him for his hardness. I have no idea as to the norm; many slaves would anyway not have reached a sufficiently old age, those in the mines, for example, or the gladiators.

The complicated history of modern concern for, and legislation about, the elderly cannot be separated from the laws and arrangements for the poor or from the problems of the labour market, of wage rates and employment possibilities. That was almost exclusively the case from the sixteenth century to the end of the nineteenth; it is still the case now, though a new dimension has been introduced by the demographic situation, the sheer numbers of elderly, and no doubt also by a change in social attitudes. The contrast with antiquity could not be greater: then the concern, in so far as there was one, was with the preservation of the family, or more precisely the household—*oikos* in Greek, *familia* in Latin. The law everywhere (though with variations in

13

the nuances) required sons to provide for the support of their parents and grandparents. We have no idea of the scale of the problem, not even among the wealthier sector, but we can locate the concern within its larger context. In classical Athens, the ten archons, the annually rotated higher magistrates selected by lot, were subjected to an examination into their moral fitness before they could assume office (Aristotle, *Constitution of Athens* 55.2-3). One of the questions was whether they treated their parents well, preceded by the question whether they looked after the family tomb properly. Continuity of the family was the concern, not the elderly. Frequent resort to adoption (among the rich at any rate) is a further illustration of the same concern. As a plaintiff in an Athenian inheritance case explained (Isaeus 4.30), childless men fearing the approach of death took steps "that their households should not become extinct and that there should be someone to perform the sacrifices and the customary rites over them." So they adopted adult males, usually kinsmen; females could not help because they moved to other households on marriage, children were of no use because of the low life expectancy.

The final proof of the centrality of family considerations is the total absence of interest in the poor or the elderly outside the narrow kinship circle. No doubt there were many kindly people who showed pity or gave alms to beggars. That is not the point. There is not one text, to my knowledge, attesting either private or governmental action to assist the elderly—no charities, no pensions, no almshouses, poorhouses or old-age homes, nothing. Even the moralists did not go beyond an appeal for decent treatment and respect. Sons were held responsible for the maintenance of their parents and grandparents, and that was the end of the matter. And if they failed or were unable to do so, or if they predeceased their parents, what then? The answer is that we simply have no idea, and I see no virtue in idle guesses.

One large area of the modern discussion is thus ruled out. A second, retirement, warrants brief consideration: it has neatly, and rather brutally, been described as "exit from the labour force,"[16] which is another way of saying that retirement is a phenomenon of modern industrial society, more precisely of the twentieth century. In antiquity philosophers sometimes retired, as Carneades did from the headship of the Academy at the age of seventy-seven; men sometimes retired from political activity; aging domestics were sometimes "pensioned off'' in a will; a prosperous landowner sometimes turned the control of his estates over to a son or sons. Attested cases are rare, however, and anyway these are not examples of the labour force, the fourth type particularly not, for, in Paul Veyne's epigrammatic formulation, in antiquity land ownership on a sufficient scale marked "the absence of any occupation."[17] The only exit from the genuine labour force, free or slave, self-employed or hired by others, was through physical incapacity or death.

It ought to be unnecessary to say any more on the subject, but it is worth eliminating the confusion created by the still strong, and to me incredible, hold of Cicero's *De senectute*. As a prelude, let us pause for another famous work, Xenophon's *Memoirs of Socrates* (and put aside the question of how authentically Socratic any of it is in fact). Socrates meets a friend who is doing manual labour for hire but who is getting on in years and will soon be unable to continue. The philosopher's advice is for him to find an owner of a large estate to whom to offer his services as a steward (7.8). One may well ask what chances a manual labourer had in such a quest, but the question is irrelevant; the man was no labourer but a once-wealthy gentleman who had owned a large property abroad which he had lost because of war and who had then returned to Athens propertyless and penniless. Not, I submit, a very good illustration of how working Athenians overcame the incapacity of old age. And now to Cicero. The two pleasures of old age that he dilates upon are study and farming: the latter is "the nearest thing to the life of a wise man" (15.51). True, the essay is presented in the name of old Cato, author of the famous manual on farming, but neither contemporaries nor subsequent generations doubted that it was Cicero who was talking throughout. And never was he more disingenuous: "farming" meant the pottering about of an aging gentleman, and one can search Cicero's voluminous correspondence in vain for a single trace of pleasure in that; on the contrary, he complained and fretted whenever he had to visit his estates in order to sort out the accounts of his tenants or bailiffs, and he could not wait to return to the world of great affairs, as he did during the year and a half following the writing of the *De senectute*, thereby bringing about his assassination on the orders of Marc Antony.

The *De senectute* was addressed to Cicero's oldest and closest friend, Atticus, who survived Cicero by ten years. At the age of seventy-seven, having enjoyed excellent health for decades, Atticus came down with an incurable disease, perhaps cancer of the bowel or the rectum, and committed suicide by fasting for five days (Nepos, *Atticus* 21-2). He was a serious student and devotee of Epicureanism, and a fair number of cases are reported of philosophers (of various schools) who quietly and deliberately did as Atticus did, by various methods, including, if one is willing to believe the sources, self-asphyxiation by holding the breath. Otherwise the not infrequent suicides recorded in the literature fall largely into two categories, those in response to dishonour, and those chosen or offered, especially in the early Roman Empire, as an alternative to execution (often to torture and execution). There is continuing discussion of suicide among philosophers and moralists, and then by Christian writers, almost always condemnatory, but I am unable to find in this literature any useful clues about suicide among the elderly.[18]

Nor can I find the standard modern coroner's euphemism, suicide "while the balance of his mind was disturbed," apart from a casual statement or two. Although mental illness appears often enough in the ancient sources, the texts tell us more about ideas and doctrines, notably the theory of the four humours, than about the realities.[19] Thus, we know that the law invalidated contracts and other legal acts performed by anyone suffering from mental incapacity, *paranoia* in Greek, *furor* (also *dementia* and *insania*) in Latin. The archaic Roman law "code," the Twelve Tables of the mid-fifth century B.C., already provided that a *furiosus* should be placed under the guardianship of his kinsmen. We know, too, that the law did not define madness but left that to courts to determine, no doubt with the same resultant confusion that modern courts have created.[20] Not surprisingly, the most frequent cases centered around disputes over family property, notably inheritances. Unfortunately we lack detailed accounts of actual proceedings, which might at least have provided a picture of what was commonly held to be evidence of mental illness. There is an apocryphal story, which does not get us far, that the son of the ninety-year old Sophocles claimed that his father had become senile and asked the court to be declared guardian, and that the old playwright easily won the case by reciting some of his *Oedipus at Colonus,* which he had just writen. The tale was cited in the second century A.D. by Apuleius, author of the *Golden Ass,* in his *Apologia* (37.1-3), purportedly his address to the

16

court in a case in which he was the successful defendant. The trouble arose from his marriage when he was in his early thirties to a rich widow, who was in her mid-forties on his version, about sixty according to the plaintiff. The specific charge was the employment of magic in order to seduce the lady, and it points to the link in the popular mind between madness and magic, and consequently with poison.

The better medical writers of course rejected that in principle, in favour of a strictly physiological causation of mental illness, for which a remarkable battery of cuppings, pummelings, massages, purgatives, and diets was prescribed by one doctor or another.[21] (Fortunately for them, only a few victims could afford the costs of treatment.) I cannot go into the subject, except to make one point, namely, that I can find hardly any reference specific to mental illness in old age, and then only of the most casual kind. In the Hippocratic *Aphorisms,* there is a brief section enumerating the diseases characteristic of each age-group; the list for the old includes catarrhal coughs, arthritis, nephritis, apoplexy, insomnia, failing sight, deafness, and a few others, but not dementia or anything else that they (or we) would recognize as mental illness. I do not conclude from this silence that senile dementia was non-existent in antiquity, but I know no way to penetrate the almost total silence.

I do not wish to close on that negative note (and there have been too many negative notes in this essay). One conclusion seems to me to emerge from this survey that is not negative, though it may appear rather abstract and perhaps a bit perverse. On the one hand, modern medicine has made enormous leaps, not only in understanding the biological mechanisms of aging but also in therapy, though I believe what we laymen call senile dementia still resists stubbornly. It is no denigration of the ancient doctors to stress the immeasurable scale of the progress. On the other hand, whereas the sociological literature gives the illusion of comparable progress, the practice does not. The great demographic change that has occurred has been clearly and fully formulated and it is also sufficiently understood, but the serious problems that have arisen, not only as a result of that change, remain intractable. Partly this is a matter of the failure of social scientists to agree on most major issues—a situation that is familiar throughout the social sciences—but primarily the failure lies in the implementation of their findings and recommendations, especially with respect to the aged poor. The reason is that the elderly are not an isolated or isolable segment of society; they are integral to it, their situation and their needs are indissolubly meshed into the basic structure of society, some of the elements of which I have tried to consider—the economy, the labour market, the nature of the family and of the larger community. The basic structure of Graeco-Roman society was qualitatively different in all its elements. One lesson of history, therefore, is that a study of how other eras coped, or failed to cope, with analogous problems may be an aid to reflection, but that we cannot find usable practical answers to our problems in the past.

Notes

1. This is a slightly revised version of a public lecture given at the University of Nottingham on 5 March 1981. I am grateful to Keith Hopkins, Geoffrey Lloyd, Simon Price and Sir Martin Roth for advice and comment.

2. Roth 1980.5.

3. Hopkins 1966.

4. Synopsis and concluding remarks, Roth 1979.

5. What follows is based on Eisinger 1982.

6. de Beauvoir 1972.4.

7. de Beauvoir 1972.366-67.

8. Hopkins 1965.

9. Suetonius, *De grammaticis et rhetoribus* 25.1.

10. Kirk 1971.123.

11. See Brisson 1976.

12. Laslett 1974.

13. *Assembly of Women,* 877-1111; *Plutus,* 959-1095.

14. de Beauvoir 1972.10.

15. I refer to my *Ancient Economy* 1973.

16. Sheppard 1974.287.

17. Veyne 1961.238-39.

18. See Hirzel 1966.

19. See Flashar 1966.

20. Eventually, although perhaps not before the end of the second century A.D., the Roman lawyers held that madness could legally exist without violent agitation and crisis, but they did not pursue the distinction further: Renier 1950.

21. See Drabkin 1955. This is a programmatic article deploring the present state of knowledge of the subject and laying down a detailed research programme. Hardly a word needs to be changed today.

References

Beauvoir, S. de 1972. *Old Age,* tr. P. O'Brian. London.

Brisson, L. 1976. *Le mythe de Tirésias.* Leiden.

Drabkin, I.E. 1955. "Remarks on Ancient Psychopathology," *Isis* 46.223-34.

Eisinger, J. 1982. "Lead and Wine," *Medical History* 26.279-302.

Finley, M. 1973. *Ancient Economy.* Berkeley and London.

Flashar, H. 1966. *Melancholie und Melancholiker in den medizinischen Theorien der Antike.* Berlin.

Hirzel, R. 1966. *Der Selbstsmord.* Darmstadt (reprint from 1908, *Arch. f. Religionswiss.* 11).

Hopkins, K. 1966. "On the Probable Age Structure of the Roman Population," *Population Studies* 20.245-64.

Hopkins, M.K. 1965. "The Age of Roman Girls at Marriage," *Population Studies* 18.309-27.

Kirk, G.S. 1971. "Old Age and Maturity in Ancient Greece," *Eranos-Jb* 40.123-58.

Laslett, P. 1974. "Societal Development and Aging" in *Handbook of Aging and the Social Sciences,* eds. R.H. Binstock and E. Shanas. New York. 87-116.

Renier, E. 1950. "Observations sur la terminologie de l'alienation mentale," *Rev. int. des. droits de l'antiquité* 5.429-55.

Roth, M. 1979. *Bayer-Symposium VII, Brain Function in Old Age.* Berlin. 501-17.
_____. 1980. *Aging of the Brain and Dementia,* ed. C. Amnaducci et al. New York.

Sheppard, H.L. 1974. *Handbook of Aging and the Social Sciences,* eds. R.H. Binstock and E. Shanas. New York. 286-309.

Veyne, P. 1961. "Vie de Trimalcion," *Annales, E.S.C.* 16. 213-47.

1

Ἐπὶ γήραος οὐδῷ: Homeric Heroism, Old Age and the End of the *Odyssey*

Thomas M. Falkner

"... as the *Iliad* was written when his genius was at its height, he
made the whole body of the poem lively and dramatic, but that of
the *Odyssey* he made primarily narrative, which is characteristic
of old age."

—"Longinus," *On the Sublime*, 9.13

*A*ncient scholars and grammarians were fond of debating the chronology of the Homeric epics, but to the author of *On the Sublime*
there was no question about the order of their composition: the *Iliad*
was as clearly the product of inspired maturity as was the *Odyssey* that
of decadent old age. "Longinus'" evaluation of the poems may be
typical of the biographical and moralistic bias of ancient criticism, but
it also grows out of some sound aesthetic impressions about the
differences between the two poems and an intuition shared by others
since that the *Odyssey* was composed, if not necessarily after the *Iliad*,
somehow in response to it—"Longinus" calls it τῆς Ἰλιάδος
ἐπίλογος.[1] The world of the *Odyssey* is one in which the adventures in
Troy have already found a place in history and song, where the only
new materials from Troy are those left over (λείψανα) from the *Iliad*
and where, as Aristotle remarks, the simplicity and intensity of the
Iliad yield to a story of greater narrative subtlety and ethical interest
(*Poet.* 1459b). The *Odyssey* is, to use our expression, post-heroic, and
our fascination with it derives in part from the disparity between its
epic hero and a world that is scaled down enormously from the one he
has left. As one study captures the difference, the *Odyssey* takes us back
to the world of the similes of the *Iliad*.[2]

The kinds of differences "Longinus" found worthy of censure are epitomized in the Laertes episode of Book 24: its fantastic narrative, its orchards and stone walls and domesticated world of farmhands and humble servants. In its representation of the aged Laertes and in the interrelation of ethos and narrative we can locate the poem's distinctive approach to character. Where the *Iliad* portrays character, as it were, in the aorist, suggesting a heroic essence in a series of dramatic confrontations, the *Odyssey* depicts character in the progressive and against the steady movement of time. The *Odyssey,* from the first line of its proem, requires us to conceive of time in terms of human life, βίος,[3] in its temporality and in the sequentiality of the stages that constitute it.[4] While Odysseus is in full maturity at the time of the poem, the *Odyssey* provides in its span the impression of the whole of a life: we glimpse him as an infant and newly come of age in the tale of the scar, as a somewhat younger man at Troy in the recollections of Nestor, Helen and Menelaus, and in old age and death in the prophecy of Tiresias. Unlike Achilles, whose heroism seeks to transcend time and change, we come to see Odysseus as a hero fully engaged in the world of time. Where the *Iliad* compresses the Trojan conflict into its limited time frame, so the *Odyssey* provides in its compass a portrait of the hero larger than the events the poem describes.[5]

The poem achieves a similar effect in its use of generations. In Telemachus, Odysseus and Laertes, three life stages are represented synchronically and against the steady movement of time. Just as we see Telemachus in terms of his coming of age,[6] or Laertes edging precariously closer to death, we see Odysseus similarly in transition, moving toward the old age prophesied to him and away from his heroic past. One of the functions of the Laertes episode is to relate the hero's movement in time to a world that has changed along with him, and to provide an accommodation between him and a world at a distance from the heroic arena of his youth and maturity.

In what follows I will discuss the function of the episode by way of some observations about the nature of old age in Homeric society generally and in particular in relation to the end of the *Odyssey*.[7] The importance of the theme there is underscored by the diction, where references to old age and to the elderly abound,[8] and by its elderly cast of characters: Laertes himself, the Sicilian γρηύς who tends him, the farmhand Dolius, Eupeithes the father of Antinous, Halitherses the γέρων ἥρως, and Athena herself, who takes on one last time the guise of Mentor. I will suggest that the Homeric representation of old age is richer and more complex than has been appreciated, and that the character of Laertes is developed at two levels: (1) as a paradigm through which the poem explores what I will refer to as the problematic of old age — the nature of old age and its complications in the heroic and martial world of the *Iliad* and *Odyssey*; and (2) as a conclusion to the story of Odysseus, the hero himself destined to old age, which takes him irretrievably beyond the heroic world and locates him in one that is post-Iliadic and post-heroic. The two purposes are closely related, and the poem cannot do the second without also doing the first — that is, Odysseus cannot survive into old age unless it is in some sense redefined and its problematic resolved.

It is obvious that I am assuming the essential unity of the *Odyssey* and the coherence of what Page and others baldly reject as the "Continuation."[9] The Alexandrians Aristophanes and Aristarchus believed, perhaps, that the poem ended at 23.296, but others have argued on internal evidence that the *Odyssey* cannot conclude with the reunion with Penelope, and that the *nostos* as we have come to understand it must include a reunion of the hero with his father and a settlement with the families of the suitors.[10] What follows is not a defense of the episode per se but an inquiry as to why Homer (or, for that matter, an intelligent redactor) would end the *Odyssey* as it does. At least part of the answer lies in the tension between a hero destined to old age and the characterization of old age in heroic culture generally. A proper closure requires that both be in some sense rehabilitated.

Old Age in Traditional Societies

There is no society that does not have a concept of old age and give it expression within its system of life stages or age grades.[11] But while old age may be universal at the level of form, its content is culturally relative and can be constructed in fundamentally different ways. Old age is, to some extent, problematic in any society, since the long-term physiological changes that accompany it necessarily entail social changes, but the role of the elderly and societal attitudes to them differ greatly from culture to culture. For elderly persons in many modern societies, old age initiates a process of "disengagement" from one's earlier social role and from meaningful social interaction.[12] In such cultures, especially those in which personal worth is derived from occupational work and retirement is institutionalized, the opportunities for the elderly are limited and their status is often diminished.

In traditional societies, on the other hand, behavior and status are more heavily age-graded, so that the criteria by which excellence is regarded change with the nature of one's abilities and activities. As a result, the passage into old age is less a process of disengagement than of transition to a different but valued social role. Although old age precludes the elderly from certain activities, their status is determined by other factors: the political power they have accumulated, their knowledge and experience, their spiritual and moral resources.

Thus in many traditional societies elderly men enjoy continued or enhanced political power and prestige. Simmon's ethnographic study of seventy-one traditional peoples surveys the power they wield in political, religious and familial contexts, and while he acknowledges that prestige of the elderly is "practically universal in all known societies," such is especially the case in societies in which the aged perform important functions.[13] He notes the frequency with which chieftainship is a prerogative of old age and the influence the elderly wield as advisers to chieftains, as members of "great councils," as "authoritative dispensers of information," and as mediators in cultural disputes.[14] Anthropologists, particularly of East African cultures, note the prominence of gerontocratic social orders, in which a man's political power and prestige increase with the ascent from one age grade to the next and peak in old age.[15] The elderly often play crucial roles in religious and ritual life, controlling rites of initiation and acting as mediators between supernatural forces and the community.[16] Finally, almost all traditional cultures provide roles in which the elderly serve as "wise counselors" to the community, as judges, advisers, teachers and story-tellers. A recent quantitative study of twenty-six traditional societies establishes a connection between the esteem given the elderly and "the degree of control that the aged possess over utile information" — a kind of cost-benefit analysis of aged wise counsel.[17]

Where anthropological study of the elderly tends to measure their status in terms of their political control of a culture's traditions and to attribute this to extrinsic or social factors, recent psychological studies of traditional and preliterate cultures relate the social roles of the elderly to intrinsic or developmental factors as well. Cross-cultural field work by David Gutmann among the Druze, Navaho, and Maya suggests that younger men "reveal motives, attitudes and images characteristic of an active, production-centered, and competitive stance," where older men "give priority to community rather than agency, to receptivity rather than productivity, and to mildness and humility rather than competition."[18] This change, from what Gutmann calls "active mastery" to "passive mastery," is reflected in the frequency with which the elders of the community function as reconcilers, arbiters, and maintainers of the traditions, and particularly in their heightened religious and ritual activity. With the Druze, for instance, the "passive mastery" of elderly men finds expression in the role of the priests called *Aqil,* prestigious mediators between the divine and the mundane and bringers of life-sustaining forces into the community. In spite of — and in some sense because of — the physical diminution old age entails, the *Aqil* acquire new power and status, as "passive affiliation with supernatural power tends to replace the control and deployment of individual strength."[19]

The underlying ideology of traditional cultures serves to sustain or enhance the position and prestige of the elderly. As such groups identify themselves in terms of their past and the hallowed traditions that sustain them, the elderly, closer by birth to the sacred past and by death to divine and ancestral sources of power, are associated with the tribal history and participate in its sacred character: Max Weber describes the elders in gerontocratic communities as those "most familiar with the sacred traditions of the group."[20] In such cultures, the aging process as a whole will be perceived more in terms of enhancement and opportunity than of diminution and loss, and it is in this light that Meyer Fortes claims that where the modern world may regard the idea of aging with dread or disgust, "the idea that one might fear or resent growing up or growing old does not evidently occur in traditional preliterate, preindustrial societies." [21]

The literary configuration of old age in the Homeric poems is more complex and ambiguous than what we see in these social representations. In certain respects, Homeric society seems to correspond to traditional age-grade systems.[22] Warfare and athletic competition, along with the more practical aspects of ruling and management of the *oikos,* are primarily youthful occupations, while the elderly are distinguished for their speaking ability and wise counsel. The community in principle treats them with respect, and there is abundant evidence of a deference to age that Roussel, speaking in the historical context, calls "the principle of seniority." Nestor, who is introduced as the ἡδυεπὴς...λιγὺς Πυλίων ἀγορητής and whose antiquity is carefully documented (I.247-52; cf. 3.245, 15.196), offers the first response to the quarrel of Agamemnon and Achilles and enjoins them to heed his age and experience (259 ff.). Nestor recognizes Diomedes as the best speaker "among his peers," but claims preeminence by reason of his greater years (IX.53-62), and throughout the poem both gods and men lay claim to "know more" by reason of age.[23] Nowhere is the principle of seniority more explicit than at XI.783-89, where Nestor, as Patroclus' elder, counsels him to remember the advice of the elderly Menoetius and Peleus, and — as Achilles' elder — to give him good counsel. In Troy we see the δημογέροντες, kept by age from fighting but excellent speakers still (ἀγορηταὶ ἐσθλοί, III.150-51), discussing the war and the well-being of the city.

Likewise in the Assembly of *Odyssey* 2 it is Aegyptius, "who was bent over with age and had seen things without number" (ὃς δὴ γήραι κυφὸς ἔην καὶ μυρία ᾔδη, 2.16) who speaks first, just as among the Phaeacians old Echeneus (Φαιήκων ἀνδρῶν προγενέστερος , 7.156, 11.343) breaks the silence upon Odysseus' arrival and negotiates between his king and queen. Telemachus reflects a traditional deference to age in his reluctance to approach Nestor (αἰδὼς δ' αὖ νέον ἄνδρα γεραίτερον ἐξερέεσθαι, 3.24).

As a social group the elderly lay claim to such counsel as their special prerogative, and the γέρας or portion of honor derives etymologically from γήρας/γέρων and originally described the prerogatives of the elderly, a connection preserved in the formula τὸ γὰρ γέρας ἐστὶ γερόντων.[24] When Agamemnon reminds Nestor of the weakness of old age, Nestor uses the occasion to discuss the age-graded nature of excellence:

> Son of Atreus, so would I also wish to be that
> man I was, when I cut down brilliant Ereuthalion.
> But the gods give to mortals not everything at the same time;

if I was a young man then, now in turn is old age upon me.
Yet even so I shall be among the riders, and command them
with word and counsel; such is the privilege of the old men (τὸ γὰρ
γέρας ἐστὶ γερόντων).
The young spearmen shall do the spear-fighting, those who are born of a
generation later than mine, who trust in their own strength. (IV.318-23)

Nestor's skill in "word and counsel" (βουλῇ καὶ μύθοισι) wins him
visible privilege. Agamemnon honors him most of his advisors (II.21),
recognizing him for his speaking skill (ἀγορῇ) and wishing he had
ten more like him (II.370-72). He gives him place of honor at a feast
for the princes (II.405), and the Greeks award him the captive
Hecamede "because he was the best of all in counsel" (οὕνεκα βουλῇ
ἀριστεύεσκεν ἁπάντων, XI.627). Even an old servant may profit by
her age, as an angry Penelope tells Eurycleia (23.24).

As wise counselors, the elderly argue not for their own advantage
but for the common good, advising the leaders and charting a course
through the selfish interests of the other *basileis,* so that Segal speaks
of Nestor as "the voice of social expectation and approval" and of his
"commitment to the established order of things."[25] In Homer the
elderly are the visible link of the present generation with the past and
share in the reverence given the ancestral traditions: on the shield of
Achilles, the γέροντες of the city at peace sit as arbitrators on polished
stones in a sacred circle (ἱερῷ ἐνὶ κύκλῳ, XVIII.504). Such in
principle is the relation in Homer between the "passive mastery" of
the elderly and the "active mastery" of the youth, and the basis of the
privilege and prestige they are given in return.

To this extent, old age in Homer can be viewed as traditional, and
most scholarship has regarded old age and its exemplars in this spirit.
Yet alongside this respect and deference stands a second valuation
which is at tension with it, and which intimates a more critical and
ambiguous perception of old age. At odds with the heroic deference to
old age is an underlying disdain and even contempt for it reflected at a
number of levels. This perspective is underpinned by the poem's
diction and formulaic expression, and in the negative epithets old age
bears in both epics, where γῆρας is regularly qualified as χαλεπόν
(VIII.103, XXIII.623, 11.196), λυγρόν (V.153, X.79, XVIII.434,
XXIII.644, 24.249-50), στυγερόν (XIX.336), and ὀλοόν (XXIV.487).

These epithets and their associations locate old age within a conceptual nexus almost uniformly negative: death, disease, wrath, grief, Ares, the Erinys, and so on. That they are not unique to Homer (they are frequent in Hesiod, lyric and the Homeric *Hymns*) and are a part of the formulaic repertoire in no way compromises their force, and they are consistent with the negative verbs used elsewhere of γῆρας, which wears (τείρειν, IV.315, 24.233), seizes (μάρπτειν, 24.390), oppresses (ὀπάζειν, IV.321, VIII.103) and holds (ἔχειν, 11.497).

While it is sometimes suggested that these expressions are in contrast with the old age described as λιπαρόν,[26] the contexts reveal that the expressions are not antithetical. The λιπαρὸν γῆρας (which exists as a concept only in the *Odyssey*) represents a particular kind of old age spent in comfort, prosperity and security, sleek as though it glistened with oil.[27] Menelaus tells Pisistratus that his father is clearly blessed by the gods, who gave granted him excellent sons and "to grow old prosperously" (λιπαρῶς γηρασκέμεν, 4.210). The λιπαρὸν γῆρας represents an ideal completion of the heroic life, as Nestor possesses it and as it is promised to Odysseus in conjunction with a gentle death and a prosperous people (11.134-37).

The various negative epithets, however, are used differently. There it is old age itself which is dreadful, and not the particular circumstances in which the elderly find themselves. Nestor, for instance, is said not to yield to "sorrowful old age" (γήραι λυγρῷ, X.79), and Achilles fears that Peleus has died already or is still hanging on "in sorrow for the hatefulness of old age" (ἀκάχησθαι γήραι τε στυγερῷ, XIX.335-36). Nor do the elderly hesitate to apply these expressions to themselves: Nestor concedes that he can no longer compete in athletic contests and must give way to "gloomy old age" (γήραι λυγρῷ, XXIII.644). In this perspective, old age *is* simply wretched, so that these adjectives suggest an irreducible essence of old age.

This negative perception is reflected in the representation of the elderly, where old age is often presented as an object of pity, neglect or even scorn. Consider the precipitating event of the poem, Agamemnon's refusal to return Chryseis to her suppliant father:

> "Never let me find you again, γέρον, near our hollow
> ships, neither lingering now nor coming again hereafter,
> for fear your staff and the god's ribbons help you no longer.

> The girl I will not give back; sooner will old age come upon her (πρίν μιν
> καὶ γῆρας ἔπεισιν)
> in my own house, in Argos, far from her own land, going
> up and down by the loom and being in my bed as a companion.
> So go now, do not make me angry; so you will be safer."
> So he spoke, and the old man in terror obeyed him (ἔδεισεν δ' ὁ γέρων
> καὶ ἐπείθετο μύθῳ). (1.26-33)

It is no accident that the first two occurences of vocative γέρον in the poem come from Agamemnon: here (as often) with a contemptuous force; and at I.286 more respectfully to Nestor. Here Agamemnon ignores Chryses' status as ἱερεύς, seeing in him only a helpless old man he thinks he can abuse with impunity. He dishonors (ἠτίμασεν, I.11) him and does not respect (αἰδεῖσθαι, I.23) him. He flaunts the sexual service his daughter will be forced to render, and in such a way as to underscore his contempt for Chryses' age: Chryseis herself will be old before he will give her up. That Agamemnon's behavior is reprehensible is clear from the human and divine reactions it provokes, and at one level serves as an expression of his personal character.[28] But this aberration from the "normal" canons of behavior also serves to highlight the problematical position of the elderly in a community of warriors for whom old age may be a thing of little or no account.

Priam's supplication of Achilles in Book XXIV resumes the theme and frames the poem with confrontations between intractable heroes and suppliant elderly bearing ransom for their children. As with Chryses, it is Priam's status as γέρων rather than his kingship that is emphasized throughout, and commentators have observed the many verbal correspondences between the two episodes.[29] At one level, the scene functions as a reversal of the earlier scene. Not only does Achilles here yield to Priam, but young and old achieve a rapproachement signaled by a return to the norms of deference to the elderly: when the two have had their fill of lamenting, Achilles rises from his chair to offer his θρόνος to Priam (515), a simple gesture in honor of Priam's age, as the providing of food and sleep respects his status as guest.[30] The significance of these kindnesses is underscored by other moments when Achilles must struggle to control his anger at his enemy and the father of the slayer of Patroclus (560,582-86). There is a certain irony in the way the young hero even appropriates to himself the office of wise counselor, consoling Priam with the parables of the urns of Zeus and Niobe.

But unlike Chryses, Priam bases his appeal not only on his own tragic circumstances but on the pathos of age itself, and on his ability to summon up images of suffering which Achilles will assimilate to his own. In Book XXII Priam had sought to go and beseech Achilles immediately as an old man like his father (ἤν πως ἡλικίην αἰδέσσεται ἠδ' ἐλεήσῃ/ γῆρας· καὶ δέ νυ τῷ γε πατὴρ τοιόσδε τέτυκται,/ Πηλεύς, 419-21). He commences his supplication in just such terms, linking himself and Peleus as agemates (μνῆσαι πατρὸς σοῖο, θεοῖς ἐπιείκελ' Ἀχιλλεῦ,/ τηλίκου ὥς περ ἐγών, ὀλοῷ ἐπὶ γήραος οὐδῷ, 486-87), and reminding him how Peleus is surely harassed by those around him (488-89). But Priam also contrasts their situations: while both old men must sorrow without their sons, Peleus can at least hope to see his again (490-95). The poet suggests that Priam's portrayal of old age has had its desired effect. Achilles is moved to pity his "gray hair and beard" (515-16), and when Achilles compares Priam and his father it is for the suffering he has brought each after lives that had been prosperous: Peleus who grows old (γηράσκοντα, 541) without his care, and old Priam (γέρον, 543) whose children he has brought such sorrow. Priam succeeds by becoming for Achilles an instance of pathetic old age and of the plight of the elderly in war and in the death or absence of their sons.

Nestor, as we have seen, is as conspicuous a gerontocrat as is to be found among the Achaeans, but this portrait too can be read more ambiguously than is usually the case. That the superannuated hero should be present at Troy, much less participate in combat, is anomalous by Homeric standards,[31] but the incongruity is somewhat reduced by his remarkable physical and moral capacities. The cup Nestor uses easily would be difficult for any man to lift (XI.632-37). He sleeps with full armor at the ready (X.73-79), and when he awakens Diomedes the latter complains of his boundless energy, how he assumes tasks proper to the young and how impossible he is to deal with (X.164-67). Agamemnon commends his youthful fighting spirit (IV.313-16). Nestor's strength of course has its limits. When he is caught in the thick of battle before Hector's advance, Diomedes saves his life and reminds him that he is no match for the young with "hard old age" upon him (χαλεπὸν δέ σε γῆρας ὀπάζει, VIII.103), and

Achilles uses a similar expression in awarding him a consolation prize after the chariot race (ἤδη γὰρ χαλεπὸν κατὰ γῆρας ἐπείγει, XXIII.623). The poet characterizes Nestor's role as passive and advisory: he alone is distinguished as the οὖρος 'Αχαίων, "watcher" for the Greeks,[32] and Nestor himself defines such oversight as the γέρας of the old and recommends that combat be left to the young (IV.322-25, XXIII.643-45). But the incongruities in Nestor's representation serve to point up the ambiguities that attend old age in general. While his continuing military role is a tribute to his excellence and that of an earlier generation of heroes, it also suggests so restricted a concept of *aretē* that the dispensing of wise counsel is not sufficient in itself, and that in disengaging from the arena of youthful competition the elderly risk the loss of heroic status.

Nestor's rhetoric, perhaps the most clearly marked in the poem, is characterized by its lengthy digressions and emulation of a past of which he is the sole representative.[33] As has been shown, the epyllia of the *Iliad* are not senile garrulity.[34] They serve, on the one hand, to bolster morale and calm tempers among the younger warriors by putting the present in the light of history. But on the other hand, Nestor repeatedly grounds his authority in his youthful achievement and the respect he commanded rather than his age per se, implying that the latter in itself is no guarantee of his status.[35] Their self-justifying force is underscored by the transitional phrase by which they are introduced, "would that I were young again, as when. . ." (IV.318-19, VII.132-33, 157, XI.670-71, XXIII.629-30). Gutmann sees in the so-called nostalgia and reminiscing of the elderly an attempt to avoid being viewed as "other" and to secure their well-being by recalling to others their personal history.[36] Nestor's digressions provide such occasions for life review and explicit arguments for continued self-value, basing his present status not on his age but on his prior accomplishments.

Nestor's words are spoken κατὰ μοῖραν, and his counsel is often the best (cf. καὶ πρόσθεν ἀρίστη φαίνετο βουλή, VII.325, IX.94); his tactical advice, though generally uncontroversial, is sound and sensible.[37] However, Nestor's record as a wise counselor at critical moments is mixed, and his advice can be empty, ignored or tragically off-course. In *Iliad* I, his recommendations to Agamemnon and Achilles are disregarded. It is Nestor who suggests the failed embassy to Achilles, though the latter implies that a personal visit from Agamemnon is what is required (IX.372-73), and Nestor who suggests to Patroclus that he do battle in Achilles' armor. It is ironic that the "Evil Dream" which suggests the disastrous assembly of *Iliad* II takes his form and is seconded by him (II.79-83). Nestor's futile diplomacy in Book I is echoed in the comic parody of the quarrel on Olympus, with the officious and lame Hephaestus almost a burlesque of Nestor.

In Homer the whole type of the wise counselor is honored more in the breach than in the observance. Phoenix, like Nestor, serves in several capacities: as warrior (XVI.196), referee (XXIII.360) and ambassador to Achilles, and though in the latter capacity he makes more headway than the others his counsel falls short of its purpose. The δημογέροντες observe that the best course of action would be to return Helen and bring the war to a halt (III.159-60) and Antenor proposes this to the Trojan assembly, but Paris overrules him and Priam acquiesces (VII.347-64). When Hector announces at VI.114-15 that he is returning to Troy, it is not to consult with the elders (γέρουσιν βουλευτῆσι) but to ask them and the Trojan wives to pray; later he criticizes the κακότητι γερόντων (XV.721) for having prevented them from attacking the Greek ships. The ambiguous status of Homeric wise counselors, and the opposition between the beauty and the ineffectuality of their speech, is implicit twice early in the poem: in the contrast between the honeyed sweetness of Nestor's words (I.249-50) and his failed diplomacy, and in the "lily-thin voices" (ὄπα λειριόεσσαν) of the Trojan δημογέροντες, whose chirruping like cicadas (τεττίγεσσιν ἐοικότες) deep in the woods is a thing of delight but of no great moment (III.150-52).[38]

It is difficult to identify a distinctive role for the elderly in Homeric society. Old age is not a prerequisite for chieftainship, and may rather occasion the transference of domestic authority, as Laertes seems earlier to have given rule of the *oikos* to Odysseus (with Nestor again perhaps the exception that proves the rule).[39] Nor is religious authority a function of age per se: Nestor presides over sacrifices to Poseidon and Athena, and Priam over that before the duel in Book IV, but in Homer as in Greek culture generally the role of neither seer nor priest is age-specific.[40] The elderly clearly have no monopoly on wise counsel. Diomedes is conspicuous for the quality and frequency of his advice and often opposes Nestor, and in Book II it is Odysseus and not

Nestor who salvages the collapsing assembly. The Trojans find their wisest counselor in Polydamas, who declares wisdom a special gift of the gods (XIII.725-35), not a function of age, and Helenus tells Hector and Aeneas that they are the best both in fighting and in thought (μάχεσθαί τε φρονέειν τε, VI.79). It is telling that in the Greek Council the princes — regardless of their age — are regularly called γέροντες.[41] The varied fortunes of Homeric wise counselors are another indication of the ambiguity of old age, and are related to tensions within the heroic values that circumscribe the poem.

Homeric Heroism and the Threshold of Old Age

Few formulas from the Homeric epics are as well-known and yet as unclear as those which describe "the threshold of old age." In *Iliad* XXII, Priam pleads with Hector from the walls of Troy, describing the destruction Zeus will visit on him ἐπὶ γήραος οὐδῷ (60), and in Book XXIV uses the same formula (ὀλοῷ ἐπὶ γήραος οὐδῷ) when he begs Achilles to be mindful of his father who is, like him, old (487). In the *Odyssey,* Odysseus asks Eumaeus about Laertes, whom he left behind twenty years ago ἐπὶ γήραος οὐδῷ (15.348). Theoclymenus, who traces his genealogy for Telemachus, tells of Amphiareus, who never came to the threshold of old age (οὐδ' ἵκετο γήραος οὐδόν, 15.246), and Penelope uses a similar phrase, γήραος οὐδὸν ἱκέσθαι (23.212), in telling Odysseus how the gods begrudged that they should enjoy their ἥβη and arrive at old age together. The range of the formulas' use and the various contexts in which they appear suggest that they and the metaphor they employ were not original with Homer but were a ready resource in the formulary repertoire of heroic poetry.

The precise meaning of the formulas is less certain. As has often been observed, the usage in the *Iliad* might suggest a threshold from old age to Hades, that is, advanced old age—clearly how Plato understands the formula in the *Republic* when Socrates uses it of Cephalus (328e). The instances in the *Odyssey,* however, would better suit a threshold from the prime of life to old age, that is, early old age (as Herodotus uses it of Psammenitus at 3.14). But the formulas admit of another interpretation: that the threshold is neither to nor from old age but is old age itself, conceived as a threshold between life and death. That is, we should read the formulas as describing "the threshold (which is) old age," and understand γήραος in each case as a genitive of definition, by analogy with such expressions as μοῖρα θανάτοιο, ὀλέθρου πείρατα, and θανάτοιο τέλος.[42]

Such an interpretation has the virtue of providing a single meaning in all cases. With ἐπὶ γήραος οὐδῷ Priam can describe himself and Peleus as situated in the period between life and death, and Odysseus can note that Laertes was "already old" when the Trojan war began. γήραος οὐδόν with a form of ἱκέσθαι will mean to "make it to old age," and can be applied to the premature death of Amphiareus and to Penelope's complaint that she and Odysseus did not have a conventional married life: old age after a youth spent together. To view old age as a threshold is in keeping with the significance of thresholds cross-culturally and their prominence in Greek culture. To describe "the threshold of old age," far from being epic periphrasis, is to tap into its cultural significance, and that heroic poetry should describe old age as specifically liminal in character is to touch at a fundamental ambivalence in the poems. Where we might see old age as the final stage or even the culmination of a life, the heroic temper sees it as a passage away from real life and a diminution of its fullness. As a result old age is seen as a kind of transition, and is associated as much with death as with life: in the *Odyssey,* the hero wishes continued joy to Arete εἰς ὅ κε γῆρας/ ἔλθῃ καὶ θάνατος τά τ᾿ ἐπ᾿ ἀνθρώποισι πέλονται (13.59-60), pairing the gloomy realities that signal life's decline.

Nowhere is this perspective clearer than in the religious context of the poems, where deity is defined as ἀθάνατος καὶ ἀγήρως ἤματα πάντα. As has been observed, the formula is not a hendiadys: the gods are deathless and timelessly frozen in the radiance of youth or maturity, effected by a preservative diet of nectar and ambrosia.[43] In the *Odyssey,* the force of the formula is captured in the description of Odysseus' approach to the bronze threshold of Alcinous' house (7.84), where he admires its fine metalwork and the gold and silver watchdogs which Hephaestus wrought ἀθανάτους ὄντας καὶ ἀγήρως ἤματα πάντα (7.94). Like works of art, the gods are fixed in the fullness of their perfection, not subject to the laws of nature and corruption. Unlike the divine dogs of Alcinous, Odysseus' once-keen hunting dog Argus, whom he similarly sees as he approaches his own palace in Book 17, lies on a dungpile both aging *and* dying. As the divine and the aesthetic realms are assimilated in their immutable perfection, the human world in its perishability stands in opposition to both.

Death, of course, represents a negation of heroic values, of the pursuit of κῦδος and of delight in the physical and social world, as given quintessential expression in Achilles' rejoinder to Odysseus that he would rather be a hired laborer on earth than king of the dead (11.488-91). While the Homeric hero despises death, he recognizes it as the boundary that creates heroic possibilities. The hero chooses to make life not long but meaningful, and finds in his prowess in war and in κλέος ἄφθιτον a partial escape from death.[44] Old age becomes despised as marking the beginning of the process whereby the hero loses what he most values, and as the harbinger of death itself. In more traditional cultures the status of the elderly is enhanced precisely because of their proximity to death and reunion with sacred beings or ancestral shades: Gutmann suggests that "besides intersecting with the mythic past, the aged overlap the spirit world which they will soon enter; and as they blend with that world they acquire its essential physiognomy and powers."[45] But the grim afterlife that awaits the Achaean hero devalues, by association, the aging process.

Schadewaldt observes that nowhere in Homer do the young directly lament the fact of aging or speak of it as a terrible destiny, and this he attributes to a healthy and natural attitude to old age.[46] However, like the description of old age as χαλεπόν, λυγρόν, στυγερόν, and ὀλοόν, the association of age and death represents them as equally dread and unwelcome. Calypso's offer to make Odysseus ἀθάνατον καὶ ἀγήρων ἤματα πάντα (5.136) is predicated on her assumption that he will find agelessness as well as immortality enticing, and recalls the horrible destiny of Tithonus, who was granted one but not the other.[47] Sarpedon reminds Glaucus in *Iliad* XII that because they cannot live together ἀγήρω τ' ἀθανάτω τε (323), they should fight in the front ranks and go forth into battle "where men win honor" (κυδιάνειραν, 325). In the flush of martial success the hero can even experience himself as godlike and triumph over the doom of old age and death, as when Hector wishes only that he could be ἀθάνατος καὶ ἀγήρως ἤματα πάντα and honored like Athena and Apollo (VIII.538-40). The Homeric hero thus aspires to escape old age in two ways: as the ageless god he would (in Odysseus' case, could) be, or as the warrior who transcends age, permanently by his death or temporarily by his κῦδος.

As old age is demeaned by its association with death, so it is excluded from those opportunities whereby the hero transcends death. While the word ἥρως in Homer may not be age-specific, heroism clearly means youthful heroism, and as its mark is to be the speaker of words *and* the doer of deeds (IX.443) the elderly can aspire to distinction only in the first. The heroic ethos, to which the elderly themselves subscribe, identifies the fullness of life with heroic vitality and its public display, and confers meaning on individual life through the winning of φήμη and κῦδος. But the physical degeneration of old age disqualifies the elderly from the activities that mark one as a hero and redound to one's glory. The egotistical and competitive excellences, which are regarded more highly than the "quiet" ones,[48] and the identification of what is "good" with youth and its activities leave little room for the value old age places on community and continuity.

As a threshold between life and death, old age is like and unlike both. Because of the close association of old age and death, the elderly are at once both living and dead. On the other hand, because they stand between the fullness of heroic existence and its antithesis in Hades, the elderly are neither living nor dead.[49] Hence in the heroic and martial world of the *Iliad*, old age is *merely* a threshold, one that Priam describes as ὀλοῷ (XXIV.487). In this light are we to make sense of the διχθαδίας κῆρας that drive Achilles: the one to a κλέος ἄφθιτον that involves death, and the other to a νόστος and an αἰών...δηρόν (IX.413-15) without κλέος. To the degree that Achilles' destiny entails a choice, it implies not only an affirmation of deathless glory but a rejection of enfeebling old age.[50] Indeed, it is only with the dishonor Agamemnon does him that Achilles calls into question the value of his κλέος and imagines a long life, married to a local princess and delighting in the inheritance left by "aged Peleus" (IX.400). It is in the same vein that Phoenix, expressing the depth of his loyalty to Achilles, declares that he would not be left behind, "not were the god in person to promise/he would scale away my old age and make me a young man blossoming (γῆρας ἀποξύσας θήσειν νέον ἡβώοντα)/ as I was at that time when I first left Hellas, the land of fair women" (IX.445-47). Youth and age are antithetical values, the latter a growth to be "scraped away" from the smooth and perfect bloom of youth beneath. That Phoenix would elect an old age with Achilles to the fullness of young manhood without him is a kind of choice of Achilles in reverse, rendered more profound by the contrast between Phoenix's youthful sexuality and the sexual curse called upon him by his father, Amyntor, (IX.453-56), which has persisted into his own childless old age.

It is in war that the status of old age becomes most marginal. This is symbolized on the shield of Achilles: in the city in peace, the elderly sit in judgment over a murder trial (XVIII.503-8), but in the city at war the elders, with women and children, anxiously man battle stations on the wall, itself a kind of threshold between city and battlefield.[51] The image of the threshold applies with particular force to Priam. His authority is nebulous and his kingship largely honorific, with the real decision-making exercised by Hector and the younger heroes. His spatial orientation is similarly liminal: his vantage is from the city wall, and on other occasions he traverses the threshold between Greeks and Trojans, escorted by Hermes psychopompos, underscoring his location between life and death.

It is from the wall that Priam pleads with Hector, rehearsing the destruction Zeus will visit on him ἐπὶ γήραος οὐδῷ (XXII.60) and on his whole household. He concludes with a horrific vision of his own corpse, mutilated on the threshold of his palace by the dogs who should guard it.

> And myself last of all, my dogs in front of my doorway
> will rip me raw, after some man with stroke of the sharp bronze
> spear, or with spearcast, has torn the life out of my body;
> those dogs I raised in my halls to be at my table, to guard my
> gates, who will lap my blood in the savagery of their anger
> and then lie down in my courts. For a young man all is decorous
> when he is cut down in battle and torn with the sharp bronze, and lies
>   there
> dead, and though dead all that shows about him is beautiful;
> but when an old man is dead and down, and the dogs mutilate
> the grey head and the parts that are secret,
> this, for all sad mortality, is the sight most pitiful. (XXII.66-76)

Priam's speech has been criticized as incoherent and even hysterical,[52] but his desperate words give expression to the anxieties of the elderly in a community of warriors. Priam is described throughout not as king but γέρων (XXII.25, 33, 37, etc.), and his appeal suggests the impotence and degradation, the physical ills and loss of dignity, that come with age. He contrasts the "beauty" (cf. πάντα...καλά) of the slain youth, where all is becoming (νέῳ δέ τε πάντ᾽ ἐπέοικεν ἀρηικταμένῳ), with the "ugliness" of a dead old man, his gray hair and beard and genitals mutilated. Priam envisions his corpse in a kind of anti-funeral, savaged and consumed by the dogs he raised himself, an extension of the warrior's threat to make his foe "a feast of birds and dogs." So had Priam earlier imagined Achilles (42-43), as the use of ὠμησταί anticipates Hecuba's description of Achilles later (XXIV.207). The corpse, unburied and unmourned on the palace threshold, suggests not only the destiny of the defeated in war but the elderly's sense of themselves as peripheral.

Laertes and the Problematic of Old Age

In the postwar and domesticated world of the *Odyssey,* the prospect of old age is somewhat brigher—it is only here that the concept of a λιπαρὸν γῆρας is raised as a possibility—but the tensions between heroism and old age are very much present. The suitors behave with a youthful egotism that pays little deference to the elderly, and their hybris extends beyond the house of Odysseus to the community at large. In the assembly of Book 2 Aegyptius, Halitherses and Mentor all offer wise counsel: reminders of Odysseus' kingly virtues and warnings to the suitors about his return. The suitors ridicule and ignore them, and Eurymachus openly threatens Halitherses for taking up the part of Telemachus. Just as we saw in the *Iliad,* the suitors' attitude toward old age is marked by the overtones of vocative γέρον in its first appearances in the poem: in Telemachus' deferential response to Halitherses (2.40), and Eurymachus' contemptuous address to him (2.178, 192, 201).

Common practice is to see in the suitors the violation of "correct" behavior and an inversion of the "normal" order to be restored, as well a contrast with the more respectful attitude of Telemachus and his age-mate Pisistratus. But one can see in the suitors, whom Odysseus calls ἄριστοι κούρων εἰν ᾽Ιθάκῃ,[53] extensions of tendencies rooted in the nature of heroism itself. Preisshofen characterizes the suitors as a closed circle of youth, and draws attention to the youthfulness of even their servants (15.330) and their scornful abuse of Odysseus in his guise as aged beggar.[54] The suitors at any rate espouse heroic values, and their delight in feasting, song, and athletic competition are within the context of normal heroic practice.

Where the *Odyssey* differs from the *Iliad,* with regard to old age as with so much else, is in reformulating and even redefining the nature of heroism and heroic values. We see this in Nestor, where the ambiguities in his representation are marked more purposefully than in the *Iliad.* Nestor's rhetoric in the *Odyssey* becomes not just lengthy but long-winded, with the situation bordering at moments on the humorous. Nestor treats the newly arrived Telemachus to a pair of speeches, 98 and 74 lines respectively, and is self-conscious about his wordiness: were Telemachus to listen for years about the trials of the Greeks, he would sooner exhaust himself than the speaker (3.113-17). Athena-Mentor finally must cut short the conversation so they can all go to bed (3.331-36).[55] Although Telemachus' express purpose is to seek news of his father, Nestor's recollections are of inspirational value. But here in Nestor the normally complementary functions of memory and advice are separated, so that he comes to represent only the former and becomes almost a caricature of the wise counselor. His punctilious religiosity and smothering hospitality seem ostentatious, and his rhetoric of the heroic past more like garrulity and self-aggrandizement. His continued dominance of his *oikos* may suggest that, like his extended service on the battlefield, he is reluctant to transfer his authority.

The poet's representation of bourgeois Pylos, like that of Menelaus' and Helen's Sparta, seems increasingly obsolete and anachronistic, and functions in part as a disavowal of Iliadic concepts of the heroic: here are heroes incapable of sustaining heroic stature after Troy, and whose existence fairly wells ends with their *nostos.*[56] There is a decadent quality about the heroic opulence of both Pylos and Sparta, and while Telemachus is in awe of both palaces his journey to these centers of Mycenaean heroism is in a sense unproductive. It comes as no surprise when he indicates somewhat awkwardly to Pisistratus in Book 15 that he will pass up his father's effusiveness in favor of a speedier return to Ithaca.

The λιπαρὸν γῆρας embodied in Nestor is developed to be displaced by a different model. It is Ithaca that defines and exemplifies the post-heroic world, and it is in the γέροντ'...Λαέρτην ἥρωα, as he is introduced to us (1.188-89), that the problematic status of old age is most fully explored. Laertes functions in two related capacities. In the first, which we might call Iliadic, he provides an illustration of the devaluation of old age, though in terms that go beyond those of the *Iliad;* in the second, he suggests an alternate model of old age more appropriate to the post-heroic nature of the poem and its hero. Homer thus finds in him both a statement of the problematic of old age and a poetic resolution of it, though in terms that are admittedly compressed and suggestive rather than clear and detailed. That the *Odyssey,* like the *Iliad,* should conclude in the context of this theme is not accidental, and there are a number of regards in which the material evokes aspects of the Iliadic Nestor and Priam.

In Laertes the image of the threshold is fully developed. Physically he is near death, and events have moved him closer to his end. Anticleia's death, itself for grief for Odysseus (11.202-3, cf. 15.358), has aged Laertes beyond his years.[57] She tells Odysseus how he longs for his homecoming, with "harsh old age" (χαλεπόν...γῆρας) upon him (11.195-96), and Eumaeus says that with his grief now compounded Laertes hangs on but prays daily for his release (15.353-55). Telemachus' departure for the mainland has pushed the old man beyond the limit, so that he has ceased to eat, drink and work, and is literally wasting away (16.142-45). The situation is so urgent that Eumaeus wants to send news of Telemachus' return as soon as possible. Laertes' critical condition is symbolized in the shroud Penelope weaves and unweaves, which suggests the slender thread of his life.

Laertes' liminality is also spatial.[58] He lives on the fringes of Ithaca, and we hear repeatedly, from the initial descriptions of Athena-Mentes on, of his isolation: he no longer comes πόλινδε but suffers ἀπάνευθεν ἐπ' ἀγροῦ on the farm of Dolius, withdrawn from the affairs of house and city (1.188-93). Laertes' self-ostracism is in one respect an expression of the marginal nature of his social status. Politically he is a kind of rex emeritus, powerless to affect the situation in his son's absence and his grandson's immaturity, and his withdrawal suggests the impotence of the elderly before the younger and brash heroes. In the underworld Odysseus anxiously questions Anticleia about his father's status: do father and son still hold my γέρας, or does another man now hold it (11.174-76)? We get additional insight into the plight of such old kings in Achilles' interview with Odysseus, where he develops the anxieties implicit in *Iliad* XXIV.488-89. But here the issue is particularly urgent to Odysseus.[59]

and tell me anything you have heard about stately Peleus,
whether he still keeps his position among the Myrmidon
hordes, or whether in Hellas and Phthia they have diminished
his state, because old age constrains his hands and feet, and I
am not the man I used to be once, when in the wide Troad
I killed the best of their people, fighting for the Argives. If only
for a little while I could come like that to the house of my father,
my force and my invincible hands would terrify such men
as use force on him and keep him away from his rightful honor.
(11.494-503)

Achilles implies that without a youthful advocate the honor (cf. τιμήν,
495; ἀτιμάζουσιν, 496) of the elderly finds little protection
from the force (cf. βιόωνται, 503) of the young. Laertes' retirement
likewise suggests his helplessness and dishonor before the violence of
the suitors. When Penelope hears of the ambush for Telemachus, she
frantically suggests summoning Laertes to prevail upon the people of
Ithaca to stop them. But Eurycleia counsels against this: μηδὲ γέροντα
κάκου κεκακωμένον (4.754), a comment surely on not only his misery
but his ineffectuality.

In Laertes' physical condition we see another expression of the
pathos of age and of his inner despair. We learn from Anticleia of the
squalor of his clothes and living conditions, how he sleeps in winter
with the slaves in the ashes by the hearth and in summer on piles of
leaves throughout the orchard (11.187-96). When Odysseus
first catches sight of his father he is the image of abject old age: he is
filthy, with a patchwork cloak, stitched greaves, work gloves and a
goatskin cap. The poet indicates how Odysseus reads his appearance:
as expressions of oppressive old age and the grief he suffers for him
(γήραι τειρόμενον, μέγα δὲ φρεσὶ πένθος ἔχοντα, 24.233). Homer
implies that to some extent Laertes deliberately wallows in his grief:
we are told of the servant woman's kindly care for him (ἐνδυκέως
κομέεσκεν, 24.212), and how with his dress Laertes deliberately feeds
his own sorrow (πένθος ἀέξων, 24.231, cf. 11.195).

Odysseus declares to Telemachus his intention to "test"
(πειρήσομαι, 24.216) his father to see if he would recognize him in
spite of his long absence (πολὺν χρόνον ἀμφὶς ἐόντα, 217). As such,
the trial will involve not only his father's powers of perception but the
degree to which Odysseus himself has changed. As Penelope ironically

told the beggar, Odysseus had surely aged with time and hardship and come to look like him: αἶψα γὰρ ἐν κακότητι βροτοὶ καταγηράσκουσιν (19.360). Although Odysseus has heard repeatedly of his father's situation, he is so striken by his appearance that he first hides and weeps under a pear tree. But then (δ᾽ ἔπειτα, 235) he overcomes the urge to rush up and embrace his father and decides "first to question him and make trial of him in each thing" (πρῶτ᾽ ἐξερέοιτο ἕκαστά τε πειρήσαιτο, 238), testing Laertes' recognition by asking why he chooses to live as he does.[60]

Much ingenuity has been spent on this apparently purposeless decision to "test with teasing words" (κερτομίοις ἐπέεσσιν πειρηθῆναι, 240),[61] and on Odysseus' assuming one more time the ruse of disguise, fictitious name and biography, and cautious interview: that it derives from an earlier version in which disguise was necessary; that it dramatically builds suspense; that we have here the "Autolycan" Odysseus with his insuppressable instinct for deception; even that Odysseus' intent is therapeutic, to prevent the shock of too sudden a recognition.[62] Although none of these proposals is entirely convincing, we can usefully distinguish the need for a recognition scene in this particular situation from what is accomplished thematically by the form it takes,[63] and here I would emphasize in particular the symbolic value of the orchard and Laertes' work in it.

Odysseus first upbraids Laertes for his condition: he lavishes the finest care (κομιδή) upon the orchard but no such care upon himself.[64]

> But I will also tell you this: do not take it as cause for
> anger. You yourself are ill cared for; together with dismal
> old age (γῆρας λυγρόν), which is yours, you are squalid and wear four
> clothing upon you. (24.248-50)

Despite his kingly demeanor, Laertes dresses like a slave (252-53). Laertes' neglect is to be seen in its social aspects and in relation to heroic culture. Although the suitors make no mention of Laertes, whose substance they consume along with that of Odysseus, the ongoing contrast between their feasting and his deprivation serves to implicate them, and Laertes implies as much to Odysseus (ὑβρισταὶ δ᾽ αὐτὴν καὶ ἀτάσθαλοι ἄνδρες ἔχουσι, 24.282, cf. 352). Laertes' condition also illustrates the situation of those in old age who are bereft of their children and denied the θρέπτρα or parent-support on which their well-being depends.[65] In this light, the heroic ethic complicates the social situation, as is implicit in Odysseus' instructions to Penelope that she assume responsibility for his father, mother and son in the event that he does not return from Troy (18.266-70). As the hero risks his life in the pursuit of booty and κλέος, he also risks depriving his parents of the support he owes them; indeed, the two references to this institution in Homer describe slain warriors who could not properly repay their parents.[66] Homer focuses the problem by giving us a family with a single line of descent (cf. 16.117-21), making the situation of the elderly even more precarious. Laertes' self-imposed servility and premature assumption of this condition graphically suggest the destiny of those who lack what Hesiod calls a γηρόκομος (*Theog.* 605).

Odysseus understands the kind of life that is owed to his father: the δίκη...γερόντων is food and baths and gentle sleep (24.253-55). With his return, Odysseus assumes his responsibilities as Laertes' caretaker, arranging a feast and having the Sicilian servant woman bathe and clothe him. Their restorative powers are symbolized in the immediate change they work on his appearance and in Athena's enhancement of his stature (365-74). In assuming their proper roles as provider and recipient, father and son do more than reestablish order in the *oikos*. They also call into question the values which at once thrust the elderly into dependency and make demands of the young which undermine them.[67]

We see the same critical perspective in the way that the prolonged absence or death of the hero complicates patterns of inheritance. This situation is sketched in the *Iliad* in brief descriptions like that of Phaenops, who loses his sons to war and his estate to his kinsmen (V.152-58). In the *Odyssey,* the situation is intensified by the fragile line of descent and the limbo in which Telemachus finds himself. Odysseus' absence effectively freezes the status of the estates: Telemachus cannot protect them because he has not inherited them. But this crisis involves Laertes as well, whose concern in reflected in his preoccupation with the orchard, the outward sign of the inheritance and the continuity of the *oikos*.[68] He works and sleeps among its trees, labors to keep them healthy, and Odysseus identifies himself by rehearsing his childhood inheritance: thirteen pear trees, ten apple trees, forty fig trees and fifty vines. Odysseus established his sonship once in asking for the trees as a boy, and reaffirms it here in maintaining his claim to his patrimony.[69] The proper transfer of the estate is of crucial importance to the elderly, and Laertes' anxiety over its security is another dimension of the situation in which the fathers of heroes find themselves.

But particularly important is Laertes' response to the deprivations of old age in his return to the orchard, and the agricultural subtext beneath the pathos of the scene's exterior. Where the modern tendency is to see Laertes' cultivation of the orchard as servile or menial or a "puttering in the garden," the text makes it clear that the case is precisely the opposite, and is explicit in the distinction between Laertes' pathetic personal condition (which Odysseus criticizes) and the impressiveness of his labor, which his son commends. Of Laertes' farm we hear that it was beautiful, extensive, well-wrought, and that he had toiled much to found it (24.205-7; cf. 23.214, 221, 226); these are perhaps the same "far-off rich fields" (ἀπόπροθι πίονας ἀγρούς) Eurycleia speaks of at 4.757. It seems likely that not long after planting the orchard Laertes showed it to his young son and gave him various trees to call his own. Odysseus begins his "trial" of Laertes with a tribute:

> Old sir, there is in you no lack of expertness (ἀδαημονίη) in tending
> your orchard; everything is well cared for (εὖ τοι κομιδὴ ἔχει), and
>   there is never
> a plant, neither fig tree nor yet grapevine nor olive
> nor pear tree nor leek bed uncared for (ἄνευ κομιδῆς) in your garden.
> (24.244-47)

Odysseus recognizes the achievement that the orchard represents, and commends his father for the care he has lavished on it. The significance of the orchard as a σῆμα of recognition thus lies not only in its physical content but in Odysseus' reaffirmation of shared experience and interest. Odysseus appreciates the orchard for the labor it represents, and identifies himself by recalling not only his holdings but their quality, noting of the vines that "each of them bore regularly, for there were/ grapes at every stage upon them, whenever the seasons/ of Zeus came down from the sky upon them, to make them heavy" (342-44).

The orchard of Laertes resonates richly in comparison and contrast with the lush orchards of Alcinous (7.112-25). There too in four acres grow trees of pear, pomegranate, apple, fig, olive and vine, but without any reference to the toil it took to plant them or the labor that sustains them. The orchard of Alcinous is always in bloom, nourished throughout the year by the gentle west wind. Like the "immortal and ageless" dogs of precious metal which guard his palace (7.94), these trees escape the vicissitudes of human existence, with pear aging on pear, apple on apple (ὄγχνη ἐπ' ὄγχνῃ γηράσκει, μῆλον δ' ἐπὶ μήλῳ, 7.120). The trees Laertes tends produce seasonally, however, and he has assimilated his life to theirs, sleeping indoors in winter and among them in summer. Both orchards stand as images of perfection: Laertes' won by human labor and the other the gift of the gods.

There is within the heroic line of Laertes a rich agricultural tradition, one characterized specifically as an alternative to heroic warfare.[70] It is represented in the legend in which Odysseus, to avoid conscription for the Trojan war, feigns madness with a demonstration of agricultural ineptitude, plowing his fields with yoke of horse and ox, and Odysseus' behavior makes particular sense if it is prompted not by a prophecy of future hardships (as Hyginus suggests) but by a preference for farming over battle and booty.[71] In the *Odyssey* the theme is explicit in the hero's challenge to Eurymachus to match him in any of three contests: mowing hay, plowing with oxen, or combat with spear and shield.[72] It is reflected in the recognition scene with Penelope in Odysseus' reference to the olive tree, a symbol of agricultural stability and of the rootedness of the line of Odysseus in the earth itself. Throughout the poem Odysseus shows a keen eye for agricultural detail. He appraises the agricultural potential of the island of the Cyclopes (9.131-35), and stops to admire the orchards of Alcinous. He describes his relationship with his men with an agricultural metaphor (10.410-14) and is himself so described (5.488-91). It is no accident that when Odysseus likens Penelope's κλέος to that of a good king, he says that by his leadership "the black earth yields him/barley and wheat, his trees are heavy with fruit, his sheepflocks/-continue to bear young, the sea gives him fish" (19.111-13).[73] When Athena describes to him the virtues of Ithaca, she does so in terms of its agricultural abundance (13.244-47). Indeed, this entire *oikos* is characterized by usually close relations with its farmers and herders, and the *Odyssey* describes with uncommon detail the farms of Eumaeus, the extent of Odysseus' holdings (14.95-104), and even the volume of dung with which his servants manured his τέμενος (17.297-99). We shall see below the extension of this theme in Odysseus' inland journey.

Laertes' retreat to the agricultural interests in which he raised his son represents neither escapism nor self-abasement. Closer to the truth is the interpretation Cicero suggests in the *De Senectute,* where Cato describes the rewards to be found by the elderly in agriculture, declaring them superior to those of warfare and athletics (58). Clearly recalling the description of Laertes when Odysseus came upon him spading a plant (λιστρεύοντα φυτόν, 227; cf. φυτὸν ἀμφελάχαινε, 242), Cicero combines in Laertes an illustration of the *utilitate... stercorandi* and the therapeutic value of farming: at *Homerus... Laertem lenientem desiderium, quod capiebat e filio, colentem agrum et eum stercorantem facit* (54). Although Laertes is not specifically said to be manuring his farm when Odysseus finds him, Cicero suggests in the *stercus*/κόπρος idea the regenerative nature of the soil.[74] Cicero appreciates the cyclical nature of farming, and suggests that Laertes finds an outlet for his grief in the pattern of birth, growth and decay.

A comparison with the *Iliad* in this regard is instructive. There we read repeatedly of the κόπρος in which Priam grovels in his grief for Hector (XXII.414; XXIV.164, 640), and of the ὄνθος in which Aias slips during the footrace (XXIII.773-81). Where in the *Iliad* this material suggests filth, disgrace and failure, in the *Odyssey* it is mentioned in connection with its agricultural and regenerative uses. Odysseus notes the dung heaped up in the cave of the Cyclops (9.329-30), and his dog Argus lies on the mounds of dung (ἐν πολλῇ κόπρῳ, 17.297, 306) used to manure (κοπρήσοντες, 299) Odysseus' fields. Kirk aptly suggests a parallel between the neglect Argus suffers from the servant women and the neglect of Laertes, who lacks his protector.[75] But a difference is also established between the animal world, which must dumbly wait and accept such suffering, and the human consciousness which can transform its pain into knowledge and even life. Hence when Laertes receives the "news" of Odysseus death, pouring the dark soil over his gray hair (24.316-17), his disfigurement, unlike Priam's, is with the very earth that he tills.

The Laertes episode draws our attention to this alternative to heroic warfare which, while less public and competitive, is no less impressive and ennobling.[76] In his immersion in the orchard, Laertes finds an occupation which is, while in one sense passive, also productive and spiritual. In the primary rituals of planting and tending Laertes reasserts the connection between human life and the rhythms of nature. Work with the soil locates man closer to it and engenders a literal humility: when Odysseus comes upon Laertes he is working with face down (κατέχων κεφαλήν, 24.242). As cultivator, Laertes becomes a mediator between the divine and the human worlds, and the instrument by which the gods, the δοτῆρες ἑάων (8.325), express themselves in the fruitful and life sustaining earth. The "passive mastery" displayed by Laertes in his tending of the orchard suggests the virtues characteristic of many traditional cultures in which the elderly continue to contribute to the community: in the ethnographic survey noted above, Simmons concludes that it is in cultures of farmers and herders that opportunities for the elderly are greatest, and documents their enhanced condition in agricultural environments in virtually every category.[77]

Like his son, Laertes is experienced with both ploughshare and sword, is at once warrior and farmer, destroyer and nurturer, a distributor of wealth and a producer of it. Alongside the references to Laertes' agricultural achievements is that to his shield, a symbol of his youthful heroism, now hidden in the palace armory:

> ...the ancient shield (σάκος εὐρὺ γέρον), all fouled with mildew,
> of the hero Laertes, which he had carried when he was a young man.
> It had been lying there, and the stitches were gone on the handstraps
> (22.184-86).

The description of Laertes' sheild as γέρον, the only time the adjective is used of a thing rather than a person, associates it with its owner's former glories, and recalls perhaps the shield of Nestor, whose κλέος reaches the heavens (VII.192-93). Like the dusty shield, which does not get to participate in the slaughter of the suitors, Laertes' heroic abilities are hidden from sight.

Athena's beautification of Laertes after his bath suggests the heroic potential he retains: αὐτὰρ 'Αθήνη/ ἄγχι παρισταμένη μέλε' ἤλδανε ποιμένι λαῶν (368-69), an expression used of Odysseus

47

himself at 18.69-70, where ἀλδαίνω also suggests not literal rejuvenation but restoration and enhancement. His heroic aspirations are suggested in his wish that he had been present to help in the slaughter of the suitors, "as I was when I ruled the Cephallenians and took Nericus" (376-82), and then fulfilled in the skirmish with the fathers of the suitors, which is sketched throughout in terms of the conventional *aristeia*. Both sides of the battle arm themselves in an Iliadic formula: αὐτὰρ ἐπεί ῥ' ἔσσαντο περὶ χροΐ νώροπα χαλκόν (24.467=500=XV.383). Athena takes human form, stands by Laertes' side, and breathes μένος into him (516-20). He prays to Athena, brandishes his spear, drives it through Eupeithes' helmet (521-24). The enemy dies with the formula used six times in the *Iliad:* δούπησεν δὲ πεσών, ἀράβησε δὲ τεύχε' ἐπ' αὐτῷ (525). The scene is throughout in Iliadic terms, and the point of the passage is clear: in spite of his age Laertes retains heroic ability.

The episode as a whole serves to locate in Laertes a bridge between conventional heroism and the broader values of post-heroic Ithaca. By combining in Laertes both agricultural and heroic achievement, the poem effects a kind of reconciliation between differing sets of values, between the world that Odysseus leaves behind and that which he enters. In Laertes' hour of martial glory and his deep relationship with the earth and its fruits, heroism is redefined more broadly and the λιπαρὸν γῆρας is enhanced by a model more appropriate to the post-heroic world the poem ushers in.

Odysseus ὠμογέρων

The hero of the Odyssey represents not the youth of an Achilles but maturity, one of the heroes in what we would call "middle age" and closer in generation to Agamemnon. In *Iliad* XIX he counsels Achilles, impatient to return to battle after the death of Patroclus, reminding him that he is older and "knows more" (219). In Book XXIII Antilochus, after losing the foot-race to both Ajax and Odysseus, complains good-naturedly that the gods are now honoring the "older men" (παλαιοτέρους ἀνθρώπους, 788). Odysseus, he observes, is "of the earlier generation of older men" (προτέρης γενεῆς προτέρων ἀνθρώπων), in a "raw" or early old age (ὠμογέροντα),[78] but still a formidable runner, second only to Achilles (XXIII.790-92). Antilochus' comment is not without its edge. Odysseus' victory is credited to divine interference, yet even with such help he could not defeat Achilles, who now in the games—as earlier by his ships—sits above and beyond the struggles in time and space before him. The *Odyssey,* not surprisingly, characterizes Odysseus' vigor otherwise. In the Phaeacian games, when Laodamas wonders about the stranger's athletic abilities, he observes that Odysseus clearly does not lack "the strength of youth" (ἥβης, 8.137-38).

While age figures deeply in the dynamic between the two heroes, the difference is not so much of age per se as of their larger relationship to time. In applying the *hapax legomenon* of ὠμογέρων to Odysseus, the *Iliad* prefigures Odysseus as hero-in-process and suggests the particular nature of his temporality. Odysseus' goal is not only the winning of glory but the winning of home, and his heroism is revealed not in death but in survival and his polytropic ability to adapt himself to different worlds and changing circumstances. Where the Achillean hero reveals a disdain for old age and seems at times to transcend the temporality of existence, the *Odyssey* presents a hero embedded in the world of time for whom the prospect of old age, as we shall see, is an attractive one. In presenting a hero whose story transgresses the temporal boundaries of the poem, the poem's form suggests the fullness of the hero's temporality.

The *Odyssey* declares the superiority of its temporal perspective by arranging a concession speech from its rival. Nagy and others have observed how implicit in Odysseus' interview with Achilles in the first *nekuia* is his admission that he would in retrospect trade κλέος for νόστος (11.488-91) or, to put it differently, that he would be willing to trade the kind of κλέος he sought (which required death) for the kind that Odysseus has won by means of δόλοι (cf. 9.19-20).[79] In doing so Achilles, as one who had himself once forsaken δηρὸν...αἰών (IX.415), implicitly acknowledges the value of long life as it will ultimately be won by Odysseus. One cannot but wonder if the terms on which Achilles would now be willing to live (ἐπάρουρος ἐὼν θητευέμεν ἄλλῳ, 11.499) are significant not only as a statement of class—he would accept the quality of life Odysseus will assume in disguise—but as a recognition of agricultural as well as more conventional heroic values.

Odysseus' ultimate survival is prophesized by Tiresias, but compli- cated by the inland journey that is demanded of him. On the completion of this, the hero's future is secured: a "sleek old age," a prosperous people, a gentle death away from the sea.[80]

> θάνατος δέ τοι ἐξ ἁλὸς αὐτῷ
> ἀβληχρὸς μάλα τοῖος ἐλεύσεται, ὅς κέ σε πέφνῃ
> γήρᾳ ὕπο λιπαρῷ ἀρημένον ἀμφὶ δὲ λαοὶ
> ὄλβιοι ἔσσονται. (11.134-37; cf. 23.281-84)

The λιπαρὸν γῆρας which Tiresias foretells is the literal fulfillment of Odysseus' hopes and prayers. In Book 19, Eurycleia apostrophizes her ill-fated (though present) master, complaining that no one had ever sacrificed so abundantly to Zeus that he might reach a sleek old age (ἵκοιο γῆράς τε λιπαρόν) and raise his excellent son (19.365-68). The idea is foreshadowed ironically in Book 1, when Telemachus doubts his paternity and wishes instead he were the son of "some fortunate man, whom old age overtook among his possessions" (217-18). Odysseus' anticipation of long life is shared by his whole household—even Eumaeus imagines the happiness that would have been his if his master had grown old at home (εἰ αὐτόθ' ἐγήρα, 14.67)—and when the hero declines Calypso's offer to make him "deathless and ageless" he also accepts old age, setting him off from the Achillean hero for whom such a prospect is a matter of indifference.

The theme of the hero's old age comes into prominence at the end of the poem, only lines before its Alexandrian τέλος. At the moment of her recognition Penelope complains to Odysseus how the gods begrudged that they should enjoy their youth together and come to the threshold of old age (γήραος οὐδὸν ἱκέσθαι, 23.212). Odysseus and Penelope weep and embrace each other for hours, as Athena delays the dawn, and he finally mentions to her the ἀμέτρητος πόνος (23.249) Tiresias has revealed. The hero is clearly preoccupied with the suffering in store for him, as if only now appreciating the weight of the prophecy he had received without comment or complaint, and not wishing to dampen Penelope's joy only reluctantly tells her of the inland journey and the destiny revealed by Tiresias. In her last words in the poem, Penelope consoles Odysseus and helps him work through the prophecy by emphasizing its second half and the happiness it glimpses: if indeed the gods are bringing to pass a γῆρας...ἄρειον — an old age that will be better than the years of hardship that preceded (almost a gloss upon λιπαρὸν γῆρας) — then clearly there is hope (ἐλπωρή) for a κακῶν ὑπάλυξιν, an escape from the troubles that he still must face (23.286-87).

That Tiresias' words point beyond the poem to his old age and death is determined not by a history that exists for the hero outside the poem in cult or in the epic cycle, but by the kind of hero Homer constructs and the nature of his relationship to time. The *Odyssey* eschews the comfortable closure of its folktale prototype in favor of a narrative whose trajectory is outside the poem's time frame.[81] To the extent that the "real" closure of the narrative will coincide with the fulfillment of desire, such closure here is both secured and postponed. This hero will not only live into old age, but what happiness he is to have will be in old age.

While the λιπαρὸν γῆρας of Odysseus is outside the poem's narrative boundaries, we glimpse it in the suggestive treatment of Laertes, which effects a certain closure on the stories of both father and son. This reading is suggested by the fact that in his pathetic condition Laertes resembles only one other character in the poem—Odysseus himself—who as a beggar is humbled in class and age. Athena dresses him in rags, makes him bald and gives him the wrinkled skin of an aged old man (παλαιοῦ...γέροντος, 13.432), and in his disguise Odysseus is referred to frequently (and sometimes simply) as γέρων.[82] The condition of the aged resembles that of beggars in their neglect and helplessness (as in the formula πτωχῷ λευγαλέῳ ἐναλίγκιον ἠδὲ γέροντι, 16.273=17.202=24.157) and it is significant that as aged beggar Odysseus takes up his position on the threshold to the palace (17.339, 413, 466; 18.17, 33; 20.258). Odysseus experiences the twofold degradation of poverty and old age in heroic society, concepts Penelope links in her ironic remark to the beggar that one ages prematurely in misfortune (19.360).

The poet links Laertes and Odysseus in a number of ways. Laertes' bath by the Sicilian maidservant recalls the bath Eurynome gives Odysseus before his recognition by Penelope. Athena's enhancement of Laertes employs the same formula used when Odysseus is about to box with Irus and the bystanders marvel at his build (18.69-70=24.268-69), and the two share the title ποιμὴν λαῶν (18.70, 20.106, 24.368). In his brief *aristeia*, Laertes becomes the protege of Athena, who stands by him in human form as she has so often his son. The rout of their opponents is a reprise of the slaying of the suitors, with Laertes killing Eupeithes, the father of Antinous, with his first spear, as Odysseus had felled the son with his first arrow.

The settling of the quarrel with the families of the suitors marks the end of not only the present hostilities but in effect the Trojan cycle of legend. In the Laertes episode we have a fusion of the warrior and the farmer, which redefines the λιπαρὸν γῆρας and links the heroic and the post-heroic worlds. The agricultural tradition in the house of Laertes makes it particularly qualified to survive in such a world, and has produced in Odysseus a hero who can be rehabilitated for it: one whose experience has been with his orchards and his herdsmen, who is as ready to compete with the plow as the sword and who has experienced first-hand the vicissitudes of old age. The inland journey represents Odysseus' passage into such a world. His movement away from the sea represents an end to his wanderings and heroic adventures, just as the sacrifice he will render to Poseidon suggest the extension of his cult into new territory and the hero's appeasement of his heretofore implacable enemy. But Tiresias provides in the "clear sign" (σῆμα...ἀριφραδές, 11.126) that limits his journey another dimension of its transitional nature:

> When, as you walk, some other wayfarer happens to meet you,
> and says you carry a winnow-fan (ἀθηρηλοιγόν) on your bright shoulder,
> then you must plant your well-shaped oar in the ground, and render
> ceremonious sacrifice to the lord Poseidon (11.127-28).

Critics have observed that the motif of the mistaken oar is central to the prophecy, but have not appreciated its particular verbal content and unique application to Odysseus.[83] With this *hapax legomenon* from the agricultural world — ἀθηρηλοιγός, "destroyer of wheat chaff" — the chance passerby will signal not only that Odysseus has left the arena of his *nostos* but the character of what will take its place. The clarity of the sign resides both in its obscurity and its familiarity, not only in the coincidence that the traveler says it but that Odysseus should understand it, so that it is as much a clue about the hero as to him. That the oar, symbol of the hero's adventures, should be transformed into a winnowing fan and planted into the earth, like the olive tree of his bed or the trees of Laertes' orchard, symbolizes Odysseus' resumption of his agricultural interests. As in the earlier recognition scenes the σήματα of olive tree and orchard identified the hero to others, so here the prophecy of Tiresias presents a sequel in which the hero will recognize himself. The perception of his oar as a winnowing fan signals the role transition from hero to farmer and to the λιπαρὸν γῆρας he has been promised: an unheroic death away from the sea and amid the prosperity of his people. The inland journey thus becomes a final farewell to the heroic age and a passage to the peaceable kingdom.

The Laertes episode functions as the thematic and structural counterpart to the *Telemachia*.[84] Each develops a figure in transition: Telemachus in his passage into manhood and the heroic world, and Laertes—as exemplary of old age as a whole—in his passage away from conventional heroic norms. But in the *Laertia*, if we can call it that, the poet more insistently calls into question the heroic and martial perspective, by revealing the devaluation of old age it entails and by providing a model of old age both inside and outside the conventional heroic world. In this portrait of the hero as an old man, the poet provides a paradigm which applies to Odysseus as well, for whom the prospect of old age is of particular concern. If there is some unevenness in the sequence, we can appreciate the poet's difficulty in balancing his traditional materials and the untraditional ends to which he puts them. "Longinus" likened the poet of the *Odyssey* to the setting sun, which retains its grandeur without its intensity. But what he (and others since) ascribed to a decline in the poet's powers[85] is better understood as a change in the epic world itself: it is not Homer who has changed but the world he describes. Where "Longinus" was right was in recognizing that the genius shines through regardless. "I am speaking of old age," he tells us, "but nonetheless the old age of Homer."

Notes

The text throughout is that of T.W. Allen, *Homeri Opera*. Vols. I-V (Oxford 1902-12), with book numbers of the *Iliad* and *Odyssey* indicated by Roman and Arabic figures respectively. Translations are from R. Lattimore, *The Iliad of Homer* and *The Odyssey of Homer* (Chicago 1951 and 1965). The author wishes to express his deep thanks to Vivian Holliday, David Mankin, James Redfield and William Scott, who read the manuscript at different stages of its development and made a number of valuable suggestions.

1. Cf. Wade-Gery 1952.281: "The minstrels' tradition, centuries old in Greece, foundered beneath the *Iliad*"; Redfield 1973.145: "The composition of the *Iliad*, therefore, initiated the decline of epic poetry...the *Odyssey* looks less original, if only because it is clearly a sequel"; Clay 1983.26: "...in a sense, the *Iliad* is the canon against which the *Odyssey* measures itself."

   Other work speaks less in terms of sequence and sequel than of the overall complementarity and dynamic relation between the poems. Compare, for example, Nagy 1975.41, who regards the poems as "parallel products of parallel evolution," and Pucci 1987.18, for whom the poems "presume each other, border and limit each other, to such an extent that one, as it were, writes the other." The following analysis assumes the responsivity of the *Odyssey* to the *Iliad* in some form, whether as fixed text or more fluid tradition.

2. Redfield 1973.145.

3. On the concept of time in the poem, see esp. Whitman 1958.287 ff. and Bergren 1983.

4. As generally in traditional societies, the life stages or age grades in Homer are suggested not in terms of chronology but by a range of terms and implicitly in a character's physical maturity, social status, behavior or generational relationships. On age in general in Greek thought, see Nash 1978.

   Implicit in both poems is a distinction of four male age grades—that of the παῖς, the younger νέος or κοῦρος, the mature male at the prime of life (as Aristotle would say, ἀκμάζων; on the inconsistencies with regard to Greek concepts of and terms for maturity or middle-age, see Nash 1978.4-5), and the γέρων or πρέσβυς. In the *Iliad* these distinctions are articulated around the matrix of heroic warfare, embodied respectively in those not yet warriors (such as Astyanax); younger warriors at their physical peak such as Achilles and Diomedes; older, more mature warriors and leaders, such as Agamemnon and Odysseus, and elders like Phoenix, Priam and Nestor. In the *Odyssey* the older three grades are embodied by Telemachus, Odysseus and Laertes.

5. Cf. Whitman 1958.290: "even as the circular pattern was appropriate to the *Iliad*, as a poem of heroic being, the linear movement of the *Odyssey* is wholly inevitable for a poem of becoming."

6. where the temporality is enhanced by his belated and urgent assumption of the responsibilities of young manhood. On the *Telemachia* as "initiatory paradigm" and *rite de passage*, see Eckert 1963.

7. Little has been written on the Homeric representation of old age. For the most thorough treatments, see Schadewaldt 1960.44-50 and Preisshofen 1977.20-42. Also helpful are Kirk 1971.126-38, Querbach 1976, Stahmer 1978.31-34 and MacCary 1982.196-216 *passim*.

   I shall speak throughout of 'Homeric society' without implication to its historicity, although in general I would agree with Murray 1980.38 that "there is a historical basis to the society described in Homer, in the poet's retrojection of the institutions of his own day." For a similar conclusion and review of the problem, cf. Rose 1975.131-32. In any event, my working assumption is that of Finley 1965.43: that "essentially the picture of the background offered by the poems is a coherent one" and that it can sustain a cultural analysis.

8. 24.211, 225, 233, 249, 255, 387 (bis), 389 (bis), 390, 394, 406, 451.

9. Page 1955.101-36, followed e.g. by Kirk 1962.204-8 and 244-52.

10. See in particular the studies of Stanford 1965, Moulton 1974, J. Finley 1978 Appendices I and II, and Wender 1978.45-75.

11. See, for example, Gulliver 1968.157-62 and LaFontaine 1978.1-20. Gulliver's examples include cultures that have several categories for the aged.

12. First developed in Cumming and Henry 1961. Although disengagement was presented as a "universal" theory of aging, most gerontologists now see it as culturally determined and applicable only to certain aspects of modern urban and industrialized societies. See the valuable critique by Havighurst 1968.

13. Simmons 1945.79. The data is usefully analyzed in Slater 1964.231-34. Until relatively recently, Simmon's cross-cultural gerontology found few followers among anthropologists; see Clark 1968. For a survey of some of the work since, see Holmes 1976 and Kertzer and Keith 1984.19-61.

14. Simmons 1945.105-30.

15. See, e.g., Gulliver 1963.25-65, and Spencer 1965 chs. 4-7.

16. Simmons 1945.131-76.

17. Maxwell and Silverman 1970.

18. Gutmann 1976.89. Although I respect the empirical nature of Gutmann's findings, I have reservations about his claims to universality and to an inherent psychological basis for the patterns he discerns.

19. Gutmann 1977.308. In the Old Testament great old age was considered a sign of divine blessing and virtue, as evidenced by the abundance of aged

patriarchs, a view which still characterizes much of Middle Eastern culture (cf. Patai 1959.229-33).

20. Weber 1947.346.

21. Fortes 1984.119-120.

22. Cf. Redfield 1975.110-113.

23. The formula πρότερος γενόμην (γεγόνει) καὶ πλείονα οἶδα (ἤδη) is used to describe the superiority of Zeus over Poseidon (XIII.355), Odysseus over Achilles (XIX.219), and Poseidon over Apollo (XXI.440). Agamemnon similarly calls for Achilles to give up his anger "inasmuch as I can call myself the elder" (IX.161), and at XXIII.396 ff. Antilochus defers to Menelaus by reason of the latter's age and his own impetuous youth. Antenor praises the economy of Menelaus' speech, "even though he was only a young man" (III.215). Iris reminds Poseidon that the Furies "forever side with the elder" (πρεσβυτέροισιν 'Ερινύες αἰὲν ἕπονται, XV.204), and Zeus calls him πρεσβύτατον καὶ ἄριστον (presumably, after himself) at 13.142. But in none of these passages is the reference specifically to *old* age.

     The heroic practice of fighting in pairs is age-graded, with the younger warriors linked with older more experienced ones, on the premise that the impulsiveness of the youth (cf. III.108-10, XX.407-12, XXIII.589-90, 602-4) will be restrained by the company of someone older; cf. Nash 1978.7. But the older of the two need not, of course, be elderly, and Nestor plays this role only temporarily with Diomedes in Book VIII.

24. Cf. Chantraine 1968.I 216, s.v. γέρας. The formula occurs at IV.323 and IX.422, though in the latter γερόντων describes members of the Council generally; see note 41 below. Nestor not surprisingly intends it in its literal sense. Chantraine rejects the connection some (e.g., MacCary 1982.209) would make between γέρας/γέρων and Nestor's epithet Γερήνιος.

25. Segal 1971 discusses Nestor's astute perception of the quarrel and of the culpability of Agamemnon. Cf. also Donlan 1979, who distinguishes leadership based on "position-authority" from that based on "collective authority." While Donlan does not discuss the elderly as a special group, one can see in them the special spokesmen for the consensus of group values.

     Schadewaldt 1960.45 observes a symmetry "von Vörzügen und Mängeln auf beiden Seiten," and Preisshofen 1977.24 finds in young and old a reciprocity of word and deed: "so wie die Jugend auf den Rat der Älteren, so sind die Alten auf die Tatkraft der Jüngeren angewiesen."

26. E.g. Preisshofen 1977.35, and LSJ 348 s.v. γῆρας. On the metaphor in λιπαρόν, see Frisk 1970. II 126 f.

27. Cf. 4.210, 11.136, 19.365, 23.284.

28. On the character see Redfield 1975.92-98, and Donlan 1971. Agamemnon's abuse of Chryses is so explicit in its tone and language that I fail to understand the categorical claim at Preisshofen 1977.23: "An keiner Stelle in der Ilias äussert oder verhält sich ein Jüngerer abfällig gegenüber einem Älteren...und nirgends klingt in dem Wort γέρων —ob in einem Bericht oder als direkte Anrede gebraucht—eine abfällige Nuance mit."

29. Priam is described with γέρων, γεραιός, or γῆρας 44 times in Book XXIV; his only companion is the κῆρυξ...γεραίτερος (149, 178), and his age is set off against the ἥβη of Hermes (376) and the beauty of Achilles (630).

    Macleod 1982.33-34 notes the following similarities: XXIV.501-2, I.12-13; XXIV.555-57, I.18-20; XXIV.560, I.32; XXIV.569-70, I.26, 28; XXIV.571, I.33; XXIV.780-81, I.25. Whitman 1958.259 discusses the "geometric" relationship of the two books, but sees the restitution of Hector to Priam as corresponding mainly to the seizure of Briseis. On the symmetry between the two scenes, see most recently Minchin 1986.15 and n.23.

30. On the significance of the seating arrangements referred to at 515, 553, and 597 to Achilles' behavior throughout the scene, see Frazer 1976.

31. Cf. VIII.517 ff., where Hector takes the exceptional measure of assigning the young and πολιοκροτάφους...γέροντας temporary battle stations, and the similar scene on the shield of Achilles (XVIII.514-15). M. Finley 1965.89 says of Nestor: "his value to the army was only moral and psychological."

32. VIII.80, XI.840, XV.370, 659; 3.411.

33. For example, see I.254-74, II.337-38, IV.308-9, VII.124-60, XI.631-36. The principle is sometimes used by others (e.g. Agamemnon to Diomedes at IV.372 ff.), but only Nestor claims to embody the superiority of the past. Querbach 1976 points to the resentment such claims engender in the young, and how Diomedes in particular repeatedly points up the weaknesses in Nestor's counsel.

34. While I agree with Austin 1966 on their paradigmatic function, I also see their self-referentiality as psychologically and socially revealing.

35. Cf. Austin 1966.301-3 and Preisshofen 1977.26. Donlan 1979.53

observes that of necessity "the Homeric *basileus* is both leader and warrior/counselor," and that "position-authority" is "a complex of inheritance, remote divine sanction, age, personal wealth and numbers of followers."

36. Compare with Gutmann 1977.315-16: "societies that sponsor an egocentric, self-seeking spirit in the population will be lethal to young and old alike. But societies which sponsor altruism, and the formation of internalized objects, provide security to these vulnerable cohorts...By keeping his object status, the older person avoids becoming the *stranger,* and is thereby protected against the fear and revulsion aroused by the 'other.' There is a much noted tendency for the aged to reminisce, and even to relive their earlier life. Though taken as a sign of egocentricity, this may be an adaptive move to escape the lethal condition of 'otherness.' As they reminisce, the elders seem to be saying, 'See me not as I am, but as a total history, and as someone who was once like you.'"

37. Querbach 1976.55-56 observes that it is only Nestor's uncontroversial suggestions (e.g. II.337-68, VII.327-44, IX.52-78, X.191-93) that are heeded. Kirk 1971.129 calls his counsel obvious; cf. M. Finley 1981.163.

38. The simile suggests the myth of Tithonus *(Hom. Hymn. Aphr.* 218-38), whose advanced old age is frail and helpless, his speech childish prattle, and who (in other versions) is metamorphosed into a τέττιξ; see esp. King 1986. On the discrepancy between the titular authority and actual power of the elderly, cf. Schein 1984.171-72.

39. On the ambiguities surrounding age, kingship and Laertes' retirement, see M. Finley 1965.89-90 and Kirk 1971.131. On Athenian practice, see Lacey 1968.116-18.

40. On the misconception that there is an essential connection between prophecy and old age, see M. Finley 1981.163-64.

41. For γέροντες as counselors see II.21, 53, 404; IV.323, 344; IX.70, 89, 422, 574; XV.721; XVIII.448; XIX. 303, 338.

42. This understanding of the γήραος οὐδός was first suggested to me by Professor Martin Ostwald, whose insight I gratefully acknowledge. Hesiod uses the formula at *Op.* 331 where κακῷ ἐπὶ γήραος οὐδῷ seems to indicate old age in general.

   That the threshold is old age itself is recognized by Walter Leaf's commentary ad 22.60 and in Cunliffe's *Lexicon* though in a different sense, since they understand the threshold to be architecturally part of the μέγαρον itself, in which case the phrase becomes merely epic periphrasis.

43. See Clay 1983.141-48; on the formula, see Janko 1981. The meaning is developed most explicitly at 5.218, where Odysseus says to Calypso of Penelope: ἡ μὲν γὰρ βροτός ἐστι, σὺ δ' ἀθάνατος καὶ ἀγήρως.

44. On the relationship between heroism and death, see esp. Schein 1984 ch. 3.

45. Gutmann 1977.314.

46. Schadewaldt 1960.48: "die einfache naturgemässe Auffassung gesunder Völker."

47. The poet anticipates the formula in introducing the hero with the alternate formula for dawn, Ἠὼς δ' ἐκ λεχέων παρ' ἀγαυοῦ Τιθωνοῖο/ ὄρνυθ', ἵν' ἀθανάτοισι φόως φέροι ἠδὲ βροτοῖσιν (5.1-2), which suggests the complex relationship of old age, death and immortality. The idea is also implicit in Thetis' complaint to Hephaestus that she alone of the Nereids was married to a mortal who lies in his halls γήραι λυγρῷ...ἀρήμενος (XVIII.434-35), and in Zeus' lament that a team of horses ἀγήρω τ' ἀθανάτω τε (XVII.444) were given to Peleus.

48. See, for example, Adkins 1960.30 ff.

49. See Turner 1967.96-97 on the liminal status of initiates in traditional rites of passage: "The essential feature of these symbolizations is that the neophytes are neither living nor dead from one aspect, and both living and dead from another. Their condition is one of ambiguity and paradox, a confusion of all the customary categories."

50. See Edwards 1985.51-52 and MacCary 1982.196 ff.; MacCary suggests a connection between Phthia and φθίω/φθίνω as suggestive of "destructive old age."

51. See Arthur 1981 on the walls of Troy and the Scaean Gate as a kind of threshold between (female) city and (male) battle.

52. Cf. Kirk 1971.134, 137-38.

53. 23.121-22. Cf. also 2.96, 2.324, 331, 13.425, 16.248, 250, 18.6, 21.310, 22.30, 24.131; at 14.60-61 Eumaeus refers to the suitors as ἄνακτες...νέοι.

54. Preisshofen 1977.33-34: "das Bild eines...geschlossenen Kreises jünger Männer."

55. The later tradition develops Nestor's fits of rhetorical abandon: in the *Kypria*, when Menelaus invites him to join the expedition, Nestor apparently treats him to four separate epyllia.

56. Cf. Clay 1983.184: "Menelaus with his Helen lives on in embalmed splendor, no longer a *casus belli*, while the noble relic, Nestor, now

recounts incidents from the Trojan War rather than his youthful exploits. Neither is capable of heroic enterprise."

57. This is how I understand ἐν ὠμῷ γήραι θῆκεν at 15.357: that Anticleia's death "placed him in a raw (i.e., premature) old age." Cf. Hes. *Op.* 705.

   Preisshofen 1977.37-39 notes apropos of the Laertes episode that the *Odyssey* pays more attention to the physical details of aging than does the *Iliad*.

58. Austin 1975.102 finds in Laertes "the clearest example of orientation in space as an expression of psychological condition. . . In the autumn of his life he has moved both outward and downward."

59. Compare Edwards 1985.54-59 and J. Finley 1978.206-7.

60. Homer uses πρῶτ' ἐξερέοιτο ἕκαστά τε πειρήσαιτο in the same way in its only other occasion in the poem (4.119), when Menelaus, confounded by Telemachus' bursting into tears upon being welcomed, wonders if he should inquire into the reasons for it.

61. On this sense of κερτόμιος, cf. Macleod 1982 ad XXIV.649.

62. For interpretations of the scene, see Lord 1960.170 ff., Clarke 1967.25, Stanford 1968.60-61, Thornton 1976.116 ff., and Wender 1978.56-57.

63. Fenik 1974.47-50 suggests that "the criterion of functionalism has almost no value in interpreting scenes of identification in the Odyssey," and compares the pointlessness of Athena's deception of Odysseus in Book 13.

64. M. Finley 1965.90 (footnote) is troubled by what he sees as an inconsistency between the condition of Laertes here and as described earlier. But this is precisely Odysseus' objection: there seems to be no *reason* for his neglect. Cf. Kirk 1971.131-32 and Wender 1978.52-53.

65. On support of aged parents, see Richardson 1933.55-58 and Lacey 1968.116-18.

66. at IV.478 and XVII.302, as a motif to heighten pathos for a slain warrior.

67. The *Iliad* prefigures the situation in Achilles, who likewise complains of the single line of descent and how he cannot care for Peleus (XXIV.538-42). He provides Priam, as a kind of surrogate for the aged father to whom he cannot render the θρέπτρα, his first food and sleep since Hector's death.

68. Cf. Redfield 1975.111: "Because successful inheritance is the completion

of the householder's social task, each householder is (in effect) dependent on his heir."

69. Compare Whitman 1958.304-5 and Wender 1978.60-62.

70. Foley 1978.15-16 notes the active role Ithacan kings play in agriculture and sees in the recognition with Laertes Odysseus' revitalization of the process of economic reproduction. Walcot 1970.18-19 suggests that Homeric heroes generally were skillful in both warfare and farming. But most of his evidence comes from the line of Laertes, and there are no parallels elsewhere to the depth of Odysseus' agricultural interests or the unusual attention given them.

71. Hygin., *Fab.* 95; cf. also *Kypria* p. 103; Lykophron 815-18; Apollod. *Epit.* 3.7. There is no tradition of Odysseus as warrior before the Trojan war.

72. 18.368-86. Particularly striking is the competitive context of the references to farming, and the contrast between Odysseus' pride in such work and Eurymachus' derisive offer to hire him (18.356-64). Compare the ploughing scene on the shield of Achilles (XVIII.541-72), where the mood is peaceful and cooperative rather than competitive.

73. On the simile, cf. Foley 1978.11.

74. On Cicero's association of λιστρεύειν with fertilizing, see Boscherini 1969. On the association of κόπρος and rebirth, see esp. Schwartz 1975.

75. Kirk 1971.132-33.

76. Xenophon describes agriculture and warfare as complementary forms of *aretē* which involve the whole community (*Oecon.* 20.2.5). The tradition is also implicit in the *Contest of Homer and Hesiod* in opposing the poet of war and violence to the poet of farming and peace (cf. Walcot 1970.1-4)

77. Simmons 1945.47, 58, 85, 102, 105-6, 113, 175, 212. See also LeVine and LeVine 1985.30-32, who include among the essential characteristics of agrarian societies the "lifelong loyalty of children to their parents" and the hierarchical nature of their age-grading: "the later years—for those relatively few who reach them—bring more social power, public esteem, and personal choice."

78. The expression is related to ὠμῷ γήραι at 15.357; see above note 57.

79. Nagy 1975.35-36. On the *Odyssey*'s inversion of the terms of heroic κλέος, see Segal 1983; on κλέος in this scene, cf. Edwards 1985.51-52.

80. On the prophecy of Tiresias, see Hanson 1977, Nagler 1980 and

Peradotto 1986. On ἐξ ἁλός as "away from" rather than "out of" the sea with a review of the ancient and modern testimony, see Hanson 1977.42-48.

81. See Whitman 1958.290: "... in some sense, the *Odyssey*, overshadowed by the prophecy of Tiresias, never really ends." On the "proleptic perspective" of Tiresias and its relation to Odyssean narrative technique, see Bergren 1983. 50-54. On the prophecy of Tiresias as it relates to the conflicting demands of mythic narrative and *Märchen*, see Peradotto 1986.444-46 and 450-54.

82. 14.37, 45, 122, 131, 166, 386, 508; 16.199, 273, 456; 17.202, 337; 18.10, 21, 53, 74, 81; 24.157.

    Compare the many references to Odysseus' ragged clothes (e.g. ῥάκος ἄλλο κακὸν βάλεν ἠδὲ χιτῶνα, /ῥωγαλέα ῥυπόωντα, 13.434-35) and Laertes' κακὰ εἵματα (11.191), ῥυπόωντα...χιτῶνα ῥαπτὸν ἀεικέλιον (24.227-28).

83. Dornseiff 1937 sees in the ἀθηρηλοιγός the magic word (erlösende Wort) which breaks the power of the sea (as symbolized in the oar) over Odysseus. Gutenbrunner 1950 suggests ethnic humor at the expense of inland peoples for whom the stem *lopat*-indicated a winnowing shovel by seafarers for whom it signified an oar or rudder. Hanson 1977.34, 41-42 sees in the motif generally a dramatic way of marking the end of the journey, and notes that the planting of the oar need not be an aetiological reference to a Poseidon cult but simply a sign that Odysseus has no more use for it.

84. Cf. Bertman 1968.121-23.

85. See, for example, J.W. Mackail, "The Epilogue of the *Odyssey*," in *Greek Poetry and Life. Essays Presented to Gilbert Murray* (Oxford 1936) 8, who remarks that beginning with Book 21"...the handling weakens a little, as though from some ebbing force in a poet who has felt the touch of age."

References

Adkins, A.W.H. 1960. *Merit and Responsibility*. Oxford.

Arthur, M. 1981. "The Divided World of *Iliad*, VI," in *Reflections of Women in Antiquity*, ed. H.P. Foley, New York. 19-44.

Austin, N. 1966. "The Function of the Digressions in the *Iliad*," *GRBS* 7.295-312.

————. 1975. *Archery at the Dark of the Moon*. Berkeley.

Bergren, A. 1983. "Odyssean Temporality: Many (Re)Turns," in *Approaches to Homer*, eds. C. Rubino and C.W. Shelmerdine. Austin. 38-73.

Bertman, S. 1968. "Structural Symmetry at the End of the *Odyssey*," *GRBS* 9.115-23.

Boscherini, S. 1969. "Su di un 'errore' di Cicerone (*De Senectute*, 54). Nota di semantica," *QUCC* 7.36-41.

Chantraine, P. 1968-80. *Dictionnaire étymologique de la langue grecque*. Paris.

Clarke, H.W. 1967. *The Art of the Odyssey*. Englewood Cliffs, NJ.

Clark, M. 1968. "The Anthropology of Aging: A New Area for Studies of Culture and Personality," in *Middle Age and Aging*, ed. Bernice Neugarten. Chicago. 433-43.

Clay, J. Strauss. 1983. *The Wrath of Athena*. Princeton.

Cumming, E. and W. Henry. 1961. *Growing Old: The Process of Disengagement*. New York.

Donlan, W. 1971. "Homer's Agamemnon," *CW* 65. 109-15.

————. 1979. "The Structure of Authority in the *Iliad*," *Arethusa* 12.51-70.

Dornseiff, F. 1937. "Odysseus Letzte Fahrt," *Hermes* 72.351-55.

Eckert, C.W. 1963. "Initiatory Motifs in the Story of Telemachus," *CJ* 59.49-57.

Edwards, A.P. 1985. *Achilles in the Odyssey*, Königstein.

Fenik, B. 1974. *Studies in the Odyssey. Hermes Einzelschr.* 30. Wiesbaden.

Finley, Jr., J.H. 1978. *Homer's Odyssey*. Cambridge, MA.

Finley, M.I. 1965. *The World of Odysseus*. New York.

————. 1981. "The Elderly in Classical Antiquity," *G&R* 28. 156-71.

Foley, H. 1978. "'Reverse Similes' and Sex Roles in the *Odyssey*," *Arethusa* 11.7-26.

Fortes, M. 1984. "Age, Generation, and Social Structure," in Kertzer and Keith (below) 99-122.

Frazer, R.M. 1976. "The κλισμός of Achilles, *Iliad* 24.596-98," *Phoenix* 30.295-301.

Frisk, H. 1960-70. *Griechisches Etymologisches Wörterbuch*. Heidelberg.

Gulliver, P. 1963. *Social Control in an African Society*. Boston.

————. 1968. "Age Differentiation," in *International Encyclopedia of the Social Sciences*.

Gutenbrunner, S. 1950. "Eine nordeuropäische Stammesneckerei bei Homer?" *RhM* 93.382-83.

Gutmann, D. 1976. "Alternatives to Disengagement: The Old Men of the Highland Druze," in *Time, Roles, and Self in Old Age*, ed. J.F. Gubrium. New York.88-108.

————. 1977. "The Cross-Cultural Perspective: Notes Toward a Comparative Psychology of Aging," in *Handbook of the Psychology of Aging*," eds. J.E. Birren and K.W. Schaie. New York. 302-26.

Hanson, W.F. 1977. "Odysseus' Last Journey," *QUCC* 24.27-48.

Havighurst, R.J. et. al. 1968. "Disengagement and Patterns of Aging" in *Middle Age and Aging*, ed. Bernice Neugarten. Chicago. 161-72.

Holmes, L.D. 1976. "Trends in Anthropological Gerontology: From Simmons to the Seventies," *International Journal of Aging and Human Development* 7.3.211-20.

Janko, R. 1981. "'Αθάνατος καὶ ἀγήρως: The Genealogy of a Formula," *Mnemosyne* 34.382-85.

Kertzer, D.I. and J. Keith, eds. 1984. *Age and Anthropological Theory*. Ithaca, NY.

King, H. 1986. "Tithonus and the Tettix," *Arethusa* 19.15-35.

Kirk, G.S. 1962. *The Songs of Homer.* Cambridge.

————. 1971. "Old Age and Maturity in Ancient Greece," *Eranos-Jb,* 40.123-58.

Lacey, W.K. 1968. *The Family in Classical Greece.* Ithaca.

LaFontaine, J.S., ed. 1978. *Sex and Age as Principles of Social Organization.* New York.

LeVine, S. and R.A. LeVine. 1985. "Age, Gender, and the Demographic Transition: The Life Course in Agrarian Societies," in *Gender and the Life Course,* ed. A.S. Rossi. New York. 29-42.

Lord, A.B. 1960. *The Singer of Tales.* Cambridge, MA.

MacCary, T. 1982. *Childlike Achilles. Ontogeny and Phylogeny in the Iliad.* New York.

Macleod, C.W., ed. 1982. *Homer. Iliad XXIV.* Cambridge.

Maxwell R.J. and P. Silverman. 1970. "Information and Esteem: Cultural Considerations in the Treatment of the Aged," in *In the Country of the Old,* ed. J. Hendricks. Farmingdale, NY. 33-44.

Minchin, E. 1986. "The Interpretation of a Theme in Oral Epic: *Iliad* 24.559-70," *G&R* 33.11-19.

Moulton, C. 1974. "The End of the *Odyssey,*" *GRBS* 15.153-79.

Murray, O. 1980. *Early Greece.* London.

Nagler, M.N. 1980. *"Entretiens avec Tirésias,"* *CW* 74.89-106.

Nagy, G. 1975. *The Best of the Achaeans.* Baltimore and London.

Nash, L.L. 1978. "Concepts of Existence: Greek Origins of Generational Thought," *Daedalus* 107.1-21.

Page, D.L. 1955. *The Homeric Odyssey.* Oxford.

Patai, R. 1959. *Sex and Family in the Bible and the Middle East.* New York.

Peradotto, J. 1986. "Prophecy Degree Zero: Tiresias and the End of the

Odyssey," in *Oralita: Cultura, Letteratura, Discorso.* Rome. 429-59.

Preisshofen, F. 1977. *Untersuchungen zur Darstellung des Greisenalters in der frühgriechischen Dichtung, Hermes Einzelschr.* 34. Wiesbaden.

Pucci, P. 1987. *Odysseus Polutropos. Intertextual Readings in the* Odyssey *and the* Iliad. Ithaca, NY.

Querbach, C.A. 1976. "Conflicts between Young and Old in Homer's *Iliad,*" in *The Conflict of Generations in Ancient Greece and Rome,* ed. S. Bertman. Amsterdam. 55-64.

Redfield, J. 1973. "The Making of the Odyssey" in *Parnassus Revisited,* ed. A.C. Yu. Chicago. 141-54.

———. 1975. *Nature and Culture in the Iliad.* Chicago.

———. 1983. "The Economic Man," in *Approaches to Homer,* eds. C. Rubino and C.W. Shelmerdine. Austin. 218-47.

Richardson, B.E. 1933. *Old Age Among the Ancient Greeks.* Baltimore, MD.

Rose, P.W. 1975. "Class Ambivalence in the *Odyssey,*" *Historia* 24.129-49.

Roussel, P. 1951. "Étude sur le principe de l' ancienneté dans le monde hellénique de Ve siècle av. J.-C. à l' époque romaine," *Mémoires de l' Institut National de France, Académie des Inscriptions et Belles-Lettres* 43,2.123-227.

Schadewaldt, W. 1960. "Lebenszeit und Greisenalter im frühen Griechentum," *Hellas und Hesperien.* 41-59 (=*Antike* 9[1933] 285-302).

Schein, S. 1984. *The Mortal Hero.* Berkeley.

Schwartz, G.S. 1975. "The *Kopros* Motif: Variations of a Theme in the *Odyssey,*" *RSCI* 23. 177-95.

Segal, C. 1971. "Nestor and the Honor of Achilles," *SMEA* 13.90-115.

———. 1983. *"Kleos* and its Ironies in the *Odyssey,*" *AC* 52.22-47.

Simmons, L.W. 1945. *The Role of the Aged in Primitive Society.* New Haven, CT.

Slater, P.E. 1964. "Cross-cultural Views of the Aged," in *New Thoughts on Old Age,* ed. R. Kastenbaum. New York. 229-35.

Spencer, P. 1965. *The Samburu. A Study of Gerontocracy in a Nomadic Tribe.* London.

Stahmer, H.M. 1978. "The Aged in Two Ancient Oral Cultures: The Ancient Hebrews and Homeric Greece," in *Aging and the Elderly. Humanistic Pespectives in Gerontology,* eds. S. Spicker, K. Woodward, D. Van Tassel. Atlantic Highlands, NJ. 23-36.

Stanford, W.B. 1965. "The Ending of the Odyssey—An Ethical Approach," *Hermathena* 100.5-20.

————. 1968. *The Ulysses Theme.* Ann Arbor.

Thornton, A. 1976. *People and Themes in Homer's* Odyssey. London and Dunedin.

Turner, V. 1967. *The Forest of Symbols.* Ithaca, NY.

Wade-Gery, H.T. 1952. *The Poet of the Iliad.* Cambridge.

Walcot, P. 1970. *Greek Peasants, Ancient and Modern.* New York.

Weber, M. 1947. *The Theory of Social and Economic Organization.* New York.

Wender, D. 1978. *The Last Scenes of the Odyssey.* Leiden.

Whitman, C.H. 1958. *Homer and the Heroic Tradition.* New York.

2

Tithonos and the Tettix

Helen King

*I*n *Tragedy and Civilization* (1981) Charles Segal suggests that there is an important difference between Greek myth and its restatements in tragedy. Myth produces mediating figures which, although merging features of otherwise opposed terms, nevertheless serve to draw attention to their normal separation. The anomaly only shows where the lines of demarcation between gods and men, or between men and beasts, are usually placed. Tragedy, in contrast, "stresses less the unifying, synthesizing capacity of a mediator than the problematical and paradoxical status of the figure who stands at the point where opposites converge"; it "pushes back the structures and reopens the painful possibility of seeing life as chaos" (1981.21; 42). Myth both mediates and reaffirms opposition: tragedy breaks polarities apart and destroys the structure.

As part of his discussion of mythical narrative in early Greek poetry, Segal gives an extended analysis of the *Homeric Hymn to Aphrodite* (1981.22-4). In the course of this he states that "Just beneath the gods' full immortality stands Tithonos' eternity of old age" (1981.24). This siting of the aged but undying Tithonos "below" the immortal ageless gods, but "above" men who are subject to old age and death, allows Segal to outline a set of individuals and groups who are between gods and men: Ganymedes, Tithonos, Demophon, golden age peoples. They form part of a continuous scale from beast to god reminiscent of the Elizabethan Great Chain of Being, in which the classificatory space between God and men was filled with a hierarchy of different kinds of angels.[1]

This filling of the conceptual space between two otherwise opposed terms with beings that merge the features of both is given a methodological basis in structuralism. For Segal, "Structuralism, despite limitations which need to be frankly acknowledged, remains a powerful conceptual tool...Properly used, it can offer new insights and allow us to pose new questions to the text" (1981.14). What is most characteristic about Segal's form of structuralism, as applied to myth, is its emphasis on the mediation of opposed categories; for example, Tithonos as a mediator between the divine and human experiences of life, aging and death. The brief discussion of Tithonos' place in the *Homeric Hymn* which Segal gives in *Tragedy and Civilization* should be read as a restatement of the conclusions reached in his earlier article, "The Homeric Hymn to Aphrodite: a structuralist approach" (1973/4). Both concentrate on mediation; in the latter Segal looks at "the mediating power of eros" (1973/4.208) between gods and men, while in the former he says that, "Sex is here the mediating link between gods, men and beasts" (1981.22). The central place given to mediation is derived from the statement made by Levi-Strauss in his programmatic essay, "The Structural Study of Myth" (1955)—infamous for its treatment of Oedipus[2]—that "Two opposite and opposed terms with no intermediary always tend to be replaced by two equivalent terms which admit of a third one as mediator" (1955.224). Edmund Leach has interpreted this as, "In every myth system we will find a persistent sequence of binary discriminations...followed by a 'mediation' of the paired categories thus distinguished" (1962.4). This omits the gradual reduction of the polarity to manageable proportions, and implies not only that the binary oppositions are entirely fixed, but also that the direction of movement *from* opposition *to* mediation is the only way in which myth can function.

Such dogmatic and reductionist statements about the way in which myth operates are open to criticism from many directions. My own contribution however can claim some measure of originality in the position from which it comes; that is, from within symbolic structuralist methodology. Segal relegates to a position of relative obscurity the other main principle of Levi-Straussian structuralism, which is given equal weight to that of mediation in "The Structural Study of Myth." This is, "We define the myth as consisting of all its versions" (1955.217). Segal restricts his remarks on Tithonos to the version in the *Hymn*, a text which he uses as a paradigm of "myth." The "myths within the myth," of Ganymedes (202-217) and Tithonos (218-238), only act to "validate the original model (Anchises-Aphrodite) at still one more level. Repeating the initial pattern, the myth re-encodes it in dietary terms." Thus Tithonos eats both *sitos* and ambrosia (232) because he is between men and gods (1981.24): aging like men, deathless like the gods.[3] The circumstances in which one man shares both foods contrast with Odysseus' meal with Kalypso, in which man and divine being dine together, but each with a different diet (Homer *Od.* 4.190-9).[4]

Until other versions of myth of Tithonos are considered, only a very partial "structuralist approach" will be possible. When these are taken into account, it becomes clear that Segal has not yet discussed a very significant element in the wider myth of Tithonos; the transformation into a *tettix*. In what follows I will be proposing that Segal's "Just beneath the gods' full immortality stands Tithonos' eternity of old age" is an incomplete analysis of Tithonos because, depending on the way in which the story is told, eternal old age can be made to appear not just "beneath the gods" but even "beneath the beasts." In looking at the fuller myth of Tithonos I will be attempting to answer two related questions: firstly, why do some versions include Tithonos' transformation into a *tettix* and, secondly, why does the *Homeric Hymn* omit this element?

The Fate of Tithonos in the Homeric Hymn

The account of Tithonos in the *Homeric Hymn to Aphrodite* (218-38) is probably the earliest[5] and certainly the best-known version of the myth of the mortal loved by Eos, yet it ends in a way which is significantly different from the other surviving versions. It is told by Aphrodite herself, after she has slept with the mortal Anchises in a union planned by Zeus in retaliation for the numerous occasions on which he had himself been incited by the goddess of love to sleep with a mortal woman (45-55). Aphrodite is firstly worried that the gods will laugh at her (198-9; cf. 247 ff.), and so she tries to convince herself that the *genos* of Anchises is particularly godlike in *eidos* and *phyē* (200-1). She does this by recalling the stories of Ganymedes and Tithonos, two earlier members of the *genos* who were loved by gods. Secondly, however, she is telling Anchises that he must not expect any further favors from her; Ganymedes may have been made immortal, but Anchises will not receive this gift. The first point is made most clearly in the story of Ganymedes, the second in that of Tithonos; both are

70

"experiments in a kind of mythical logic" (P. Smith 1981 b.6).

According to this double reading, the discussion of old age, into which the myth of Tithonos leads, should be seen as far more than a simple example of composition by the association of ideas. Van Eck (1978.78) presents the single theme of both myths as the beauty of the *genos* of Anchises, but then suggests that the story of Tithonos leads the poet on to consider another subject, old age; aging would then appear incidental to the theme of the poem. Other writers go further, and suggest that the stories of Ganymedes and Tithonos are themselves "only loosely attached digressions" (discussion in P. Smith 1981 b.4).

In contrast, I follow Segal in regarding the relationship between men and gods as the central theme of the poem. It concerns their sexual union, arising from Aphrodite who causes *glykys himeros,* sweet desire, in gods, men and beasts (2-5; Segal 1981.22). Only three goddesses escape this force to which all other beings are subject: Artemis, Athena and Hestia (7-32). The poem then concentrates on gods and men. With the three stated exceptions, none can escape Aphrodite *oute theōn makarōn oute thnētōn anthrōpōn (35)*. The *Hymn* returns to its subject, Aphrodite, since there was a time when she herself had not slept with a mortal man (45-8), although she had joined the gods to women and the other goddesses to men (50-2; see Hesiod *Th.* 963-1020 for examples). The *Hymn* celebrates her power, which is also the means of her humiliation (Kamerbeek 1967.394).

Having demonstrated that gods and men are in some ways so similar that they can unite sexually and even have children by each other (for Aphrodite will bear a mortal yet anomalous child, Aeneas[6]), the poet then tries to re-establish the distance between the two terms. The experience of old age is chosen because it is unknown to the gods yet an inevitable part of being human. The gods alone are immune from old age and death (Soph. *Oed. Col.* 607-8); with the exception of the Graiai, none of the gods is aged (Griffin 1980.187), and even they were grey-haired from birth (Hesiod *Th.* 271) and thus lack that previous experience of youth and maturity which, for mankind, makes extreme old age so terrifying. The "underlying concern" of the *Hymn* is therefore "the limitation in time of mortal life" (P. Smith 1981 b.5); beneath this there is however a still deeper concern, the separation of gods from mortal men.

The story of Ganymedes introduces the idea of the dual nature of the gods' immortality. His disappearance without warning, to be cupbearer to the gods, was a source of grief to his father Tros, but Zeus compensated with a gift of horses, and Tros was comforted with the knowledge that his son was "deathless and ageless like the gods" *(athanatos kai agērōs isa theoisin,* 214; cf. Janko 1981.382-5).

The story of Tithonos, however, separates these two components of true immortality (Clay 1983.141). Eos asks Zeus that Tithonos may be deathless and live forever (221) but forgets to ask for agelessness and its specific corollary, eternal youth. In this she is foolish *(nēpiē,* 223). It is important here to distinguish between two senses of "youth." As the gods experience it, this is a positively-valued feature, meaning the absence of old age and the power to stay adult, or younger, forever. The other sense of "youth" refers to the period before maturity, in which case it is negatively valued. In forgetting to ask for "youth" for Tithonos, in the first sense, Eos acts like someone "young" in the second sense. This is emphasized by *nēpiē.* Semonides addresses as *nēpioi* young men who do not expect to grow old or die (—Sim. 8, West), and in Hesiod (*Erga* 131) it is the silver race, who experience an extended childhood, who are *nēpioi.* By describing her as *nēpiē* the impression is thus given that Eos, eternally young in the positive sense of never going through old age, also lacks the wisdom of age and thinks like a foolish child. The eternally "young" thus brings to her lover eternal age,[7] both are used to show the negative features of the extreme poles of human aging. At the poles of life is foolishness: only between them is it possible to possess wisdom.

The eventual fate of the aged Tithonos can also be used to show that human life ends in much the same way as it began. In the *Homeric Hymn* Tithonos, when very old and unable to move, is at last shut in an inner room where he remains forever, totally alone, weak and babbling (236-8). This is not followed by all versions of the myth, one of which omits altogether this stage of his life. Propertius emphasizes Eos' kindness to Tithonos: despite his age, she loves him (*Elegies* 2.18A). In the *Hymn* Eos keeps away from his bed, but otherwise cherishes him (230-2), until he is so old that he is shut away. Propertius stops before this point, and imagines the goddess continuing even to sleep with her aging lover. The point of the elegy may be, "I am still young, yet you spurn me; even when Tithonos became very old his lover did not reject him in the way you reject me." P. Smith suggests that Propertius is here "self-consciously straining the traditional story" (1981 b.86). The scholiast to Lykophron *Alexandra* 18, like the writer of the *Homeric Hymn,* regards the goddess (here, Hemera) as being responsible for the wrong request, but he describes Tithonos' age in the terms of extreme youth, in the negative sense, thus emphasizing the equation of the poles of human aging: Tithonos is placed in a wicker cradle *(liknon)* as if he were a little baby *(brephyllion;* cf. Tzetzes *Chil.* 8.166.76-8).

The use of *atitallen* in line 231 of the *Homeric Hymn* should also be considered here. Van Eck (1978.81) notes that, "In Homer this word also refers to the nursing of children" but "here the sense is broader." This need not necessarily be the case. The verb derives from *atalos,* most commonly used of the young but also capable of extension to other age groups.[8] By feeding the aged Tithonos as *atalos* Eos suggests that in mental weakness, in physical weakness and in diet the very old approach the very young. This evokes Aristotle's discussion of whiteness; all things are white at birth, and children at first have white heads, eyelids and eyebrows, just like someone nearing old age, because the very young and very old are weak and cold so that not enough nourishment reaches their extremities *(On Colors* 798a 30-5; 22-3). Tithonos could therefore be said to receive the "eternal youth" for which he asked, but only in a negative sense.

Tithonos, the Sibyl and the Tettix

Other versions of the myth take it further than does the *Homeric Hymn*. In a scholion to *Iliad* 11.1 (Hieronymus fr. 15 We=Erbse III p. 123) it is Tithonos himself who requests immortality but forgets to mention agelessness. On realizing his mistake he begs for death; unable to grant him this, Eos instead turns him into a cicada *(tettix)* so that she will still be able to hear his voice. The transformation into a *tettix* also occurs in the scholion to Lykophron *Alexandra* 18, and the song of this insect, given as the reason for its choice, is as proverbial as Tithonos' old age itself.[9]

A version in which it is Tithonos himself who makes the foolish request combines youthful folly and the incoherent babbling of old age in one person. It also frees Eos to take on a wiser role, to which I will return below. Finally, it aligns the myth with those of the Cumaean Sibyl. In Ovid's version, which is the fullest, the Sibyl tells Aeneas that,

73

when the god Apollo was trying to persuade her to sleep with him, he offered her gifts. She pointed to a pile of sand, and asked for one year of life for every grain; she forgot to ask for eternal youth. He gave her this gift and offered youth as well if she would yield, but she was foolish— *vana* (138), recalling *nēpiē* in the *Homeric Hymn* (223)—and so she refused. She says that she has now lived for seven hundred years and will not die for another three hundred, but will shrink with age until her body is unrecognizable. Even then, she goes on, *vocem mihi fata relinquent* (153): the Fates will leave her her voice, by which she will be known (*Met.* 14.101-53).[10]

The Cumaean Sibyl shares many features with Tithonos. The story she tells Aeneas recalls the story his mother told his father, although the circumstances are different. Like Tithonos, she receives a long life from a god (although not full immortality) but lacks eternal youth. She shrinks as she ages, and it is even possible for Trimalchio to claim that he has seen her hanging in a flask at Cumae (Petronius *Satyr.* 48.8). Tithonos is put into a basket as though he were a tiny baby (above).[11] Like Tithonos in the scholion to *Iliad* 11.1, the Sibyl begs for the death which is denied her (*Satyr.* 48.8). In both cases, all that remains of the old self is the voice, for when Tithonos becomes a *tettix* it is supposed to be so that his immortal lover can still hear his voice. In the *Homeric Hymn* version, the survival of the voice is included in a different form, since when Tithonos is shut away his voice *rheei aspetos* (237). This is sometimes translated as "flows endlessly," but Van Eck suggests that *aspetos* here means "unspeakably great"; hence, "powerful" (1978, on line 237). The old men of Troy are compared to the *tettix* because they are still good speakers,[12] according to Eustathius (*ad Od.* 1527.64 ff.), very old men are mocked as "Tithonoi." Like them, Tithonos and the Sibyl are left with weak bodies, but powerful voices.[13]

Two folk-tales given by James (1892.74) and Frazer (1929.114) introduce the feature of diet to these myths. The correlation between diet and status has been noted above; Tithonos' diet of human *sitos* and divine ambrosia reflects his position in the *Homeric Hymn* between men and gods, but he is eventually fed as a baby when he receives the negative side of the "youth" he wanted. Both stories concern women who wanted to live forever but forgot to ask for eternal youth. Each shrinks and is eventually hung up in a church (in a bottle/basket). In Frazer's versions, one was fed as though she were a child (cf. *atalos* of

Tithonos in the *Homeric Hymn*), but after that seems to have eaten nothing; the other survives on one roll of bread each year.

Taken together, the myths of Tithonos and the Sibyl suggest that the very old are perceived to be like the very young, in that they are weak, lacking reason, fed in a similar way, and small in size but with a disproportionately powerful voice. The woman who had lived on no food at all, however, recalls once more the insect into which Tithonos was transformed: the *tettix,* which was believed to exist without food or drink, or only on dew, or on dew and air.[14] Aristotle believed that, of all animals, the *tettix* ate the least (*PA* 682a 18-29).

For the Greeks, diet is very significant in distinguishing gods, men and beasts from each other. What then is the significance of the diets proposed for the *tettix,* and why does Tithonos become one? There are other grounds, apart from its powers of song, which may account for the choice of this insect; an understanding of the place of the *tettix* in the gods/men/beasts matrix can suggest the reason for its omission from the *Homeric Hymn.*

The earliest reference to the metamorphosis of Tithonos into a *tettix* occurs in a fragment of the fifth-century Hellanikos of Lesbos.[15] The fullest version is late; it is found in Eustathius, writing on *Iliad* 11.1. In this Tithonos asks Eos for death. As she cannot grant this, he begs to become an animal, presumably as an indirect means of reaching the death that he desires. The word which he uses is *aloga* (825.60); literally, without speech/reason. The animal that he becomes is the *tettix,* and Eustathius makes much of the parallels between the two: the "cold" *tettix* and the aged, hence "cold," man;[16] the talkative *tettix* and Tithonos' many prayers to Eos. It could therefore be supposed that Tithonos wants to become a dumb beast, but is frustrated in this and becomes an insect famed for its vocal powers and as cold as the old man he was. This would make the *tettix* appear as a restatement of Tithonos himself, but situated in the world of the beasts.

The coldness of the *tettix*—a negatively-valued attribute—may be found in other sources. It accounts for its ability to sing at the height of the summer, in conditions of the most extreme heat (Hesiod *Erga* 582-4; Alkaios fr. 347.3 [LP]). Aristotle calls it the coldest of all insects—and he classes insects as the coldest of all animals—adding that it only lives for a few days (*PA* 682a 18-29), the logical result, for a beast, of eating nothing but dew (*HA* 532b 13).

There is however a contrasting set of values associated with the *tettix* which suggests an entirely different view of this insect. Far from making it the most short-lived of short-lived beasts, its freedom from the need for food[17] can place it nearer to the immortals than to other animals. Other features of descriptions of the *tettix* support this position. For example, it is addressed as "of bloodless flesh" *(anaimosarke)* in the *Anacreontea* (32.17). In Aristotle's hierarchy of living things, the bloodless are at the bottom and man at the top (Said 1982.3; e.g., Ar. *HA* 523a-b); the bloodless are cold (*PA* 679a 25) and the *tettix* is the coldest of all animals (*PA* 682a 18-29).[18] However, Aristotle's theories of blood can point towards a more positively-valued sense of "bloodless." Just as the man who is outside the structures of the *polis* is either more or less than an *anthrōpos* (*Politics* 1253a 3-4), like a beast or a god (1253a 26-9), so the absence of another possible defining characteristic of humanity, blood, can lead in either direction. Blood is the final form taken by food *(trophē, PA* 651a 14-15): food becomes blood, and blood is the food of the body *(PA* 650a 34-5; Byl 1980.41). The *tettix* eats the least of all animals. No food means no blood, and no blood means a weak body and a short life (Ar. *On longevity* 466a 6-7; 10-11). Or, of course, no blood is a sign of having transcended that dependence on food which characterizes "men who eat *sitos*" (e.g., Vegetti 1979.99-101; Vernant 1979a.61), and will therefore be found with other "godlike" features. In *Iliad* 5.341-2 Homer says that the gods, since they neither eat *sitos* nor drink wine, are bloodless *(anaimones)* and are called *athanatoi.* When a god's flesh is cut, it is *ichōr,* described only as *ambroton haima,* "immortal blood," which flows (*Il.* 5.339-40; on medical uses of *ichōr*—which term is never used for human blood—see Duminil 1983. 164-84). The connections made in Homer are therefore:

eat *sitos*	blood in the body	mortality
eat no *sitos*	bloodless body	immortality

Clay suggests that Homer plays with the terms *brótos,* blood, and *brotós,* mortal: "Untroubled by scientific etymology, the Epic joins these apparent homonyms to suggest a conception of what it means to be mortal" (1983.143-5). The *tettix* eats no *sitos,* hence imitating the diet which produces immortality, but does not eat nectar and ambrosia, the positive components of the divine diet. Its flesh is bloodless, but it cannot be fully divine.

A further element of the stories of the *tettix,* showing the particular form of immortality which its diet enables it to achieve, is the belief that it sheds its skin/age. The Greek *gēras,* old age, is also used of the cast skin of a snake (LSJ),[19] and it was thought that creatures which cast off their skins possessed a degree of immortality because they were never trapped in old age. Lucretius says that *tettiges* drop their *tunicae* in summer (4.58). Kallimachos asks to become a *tettix* so that *gēras* . . . [*authi t*]*o d'* [*ek*]*duoim*[*i*] "I may cast off my skin"/"I may divest myself of old age" *(Aitia* fr. 1.33-5). Tzetzes *(Chil.* 8.166.79) says "*tettiges* renew themselves as snakes do"; elsewhere, "*tettiges,* just like snakes, renew their *gēras* when old" (ad Lyk. *Al.* 18; see also Ar. *HA* 601a 6). The *tettix* is told, "old age does not distress you. . .you are almost divine" *(Anacreontea* 32.15; 18).[20] The first part of this expresses perfectly the identity of the *tettix* as a godlike beast. On the one hand it sheds its skin and recovers its youth, resembling the gods who are not distressed by old age because they are both immortal and ageless; while on the other it has a diet so sparse that it cannot survive for more than a few days, and so never reaches any reasonable age. It thus avoids old age from both directions.

This dual picture of the *tettix*—short-lived, less than man, a particularly lowly beast: able to renew itself, more than man, almost like a god—would suggest that, in making Tithonos into one, Eos is partly fulfilling his request that he should be transformed into a beast, but is also simultaneously conferring on him a lesser version of the ageless immortality which had been the original intention.[21] Where the first Tithonos possessed only immortality, the *tettix*-Tithonos has agelessness. The division of the two components of the gods' ageless immortality is caused in the *Homeric Hymn* by Eos' foolishness; in later versions it is through the action of the same goddess that Tithonos receives the second part, the ability to stay young. This is however achieved only by the loss of the first part; by being made into a beast.

The diagram on page 79 maps out the progress of Tithonos: wanting to be immortal and ageless, he finds immortality as the weak and child-like old man of the *Homeric Hymn,* while as the *tettix* of other versions he may be presented as ageless.

The Absence of the Tettix from the Homeric Hymn

There remains one further problem to consider: why does the *Homeric Hymn* omit the transformation of Tithonos into a *tettix*? One obvious possibility is that this only entered the myth after the composition of the *Hymn;* even the eternal old age of Tithonos is not described in Homer or Hesiod, although it is known to the elegiac and lyric poets. Mimnermos says that he was given "old age, which is more wretched than painful death" (fr. 4 West). Sappho, too, wrote on Tithonos; although fr. 58 (LP) does not mention his name, it refers to Eos, to "fine gifts" (11, cf. *H.H. Aphr.* 232), "hair which was black" (14, cf. *H.H. Aphr.* 228) and "knees which will not hold" (15, cf. *H.H. Aphr.* 234); on the basis of these verbal echoes, Stiebitz restored Tithonos' name in line 20, to read "(old age) seized Tithonos" although he was the immortal spouse of Eos.[22]

The story of Tithonos' old age may have existed before that of the transformation to a *tettix*; the author of the *Homeric Hymn* may have composed before the transformation entered the myth. Kakridis and Borthwick appear to be alone in suggesting that the transformation to a *tettix* is in fact implicit in the *Homeric Hymn* (1930.32; 1966.109). Borthwick says that, in the *Hymn,* Tithonos becomes "a loquacious and ageless cicada kept in a closed *thalamos* and nurtured on ambrosia." An examination of lines 236.8 does not support this view; Tithonos is still a man when he is shut away.

There are however good contextual reasons for the absence of the transformation from the *Hymn.* If, as I have concluded from the traditions surrounding this insect, Tithonos' life as a *tettix* could be represented as an ambiguous form of ageless immortality, then Aphrodite would not wish to bring it to the attention of Anchises; not because Anchises would wish to become a *tettix,* but because even that ambiguous immortality evokes the true, divine immortality. In the wider structure of the poem, Aphrodite is pregnant because she has slept with a mortal. This poses a classificatory problem as well as a personal one; if sexual union between god and human is not only possible but fruitful, then the god/man opposition is threatened. One way of resolving this problem is suggested by Apollo's promises to the Sibyl: the human partner may be made divine.

Aphrodite raises Anchises' hopes of such immortality by mentioning

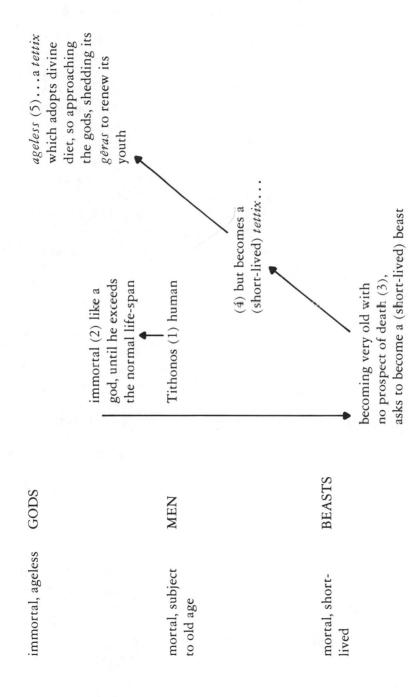

immortal, ageless GODS

ageless (5)...a *tettix* which adopts divine diet, so approaching the gods, shedding its *gēras* to renew its youth

immortal (2) like a god, until he exceeds the normal life-span

Tithonos (1) human

(4) but becomes a (short-lived) *tettix*...

mortal, subject to old age MEN

mortal, short-lived BEASTS

becoming very old with no prospect of death (3), asks to become a (short-lived) beast

Ganymedes. As Podbielski points out (1971.71), by telling the stories of Ganymedes and Tithonos the goddess can form an attitude to her own mortal lover. She tries to make comprehensible to herself her desire for Anchises by describing the beauty of others of his *genos* but, in order to balance the effect on her listener of hearing of Ganymedes' reward she must tell the cautionary tale of Tithonos, as a warning of how a goddess' requests on behalf of a mortal lover may lead to a terrible fate. The theme of Tithonos' story is that feature of life entirely outside the gods' experience, but unavoidable for humans: old age. It is described here in terms designed to horrify (see especially 233-8; 244-6) and Aphrodite emphasizes that it is common to all *anthrōpoi* (245, and possibly 244). The story has been cut short at a point which must terrify the listening Anchises, and Aphrodite has immediately gone on to reassure him that she does not plan such a fate for him (239-40). She thus makes human aging appear almost as the mediating term between Ganymedes and Tithonos; unlike Ganymedes, Anchises will remain mortal, but unlike Tithonos he will age in a way which is *oulomenon,* fatal (246).[23]

To be fully mortal, to experience the aging which destroys, is better than to be like the aging but undying Tithonos (cf. P. Smith 1981a.56; 1981 b.7). By stopping at point (3) in the above diagram, Aphrodite creates a model in which the normal condition of mankind, between the eternally young Ganymedes and the eternally old Tithonos, seems something to be desired. The god/man opposition is strengthened but, instead of being the negative pole, "man" for a moment becomes the middle term of a new opposition.

Conclusions

This discussion, both of the myth of Tithonos in the *Homeric Hymn* and elsewhere, and of some relevant beliefs about the *tettix,* does not in any way claim to be exhaustive. As Segal notes in his most recent discussion of myth and tragedy (1983), where he again uses Tithonos in the *Homeric Hymn* as an example of how myth operates, a full treatment of the *Hymn* would go beyond structuralist analysis to cover in addition those aspects specific to this type of literary production, as well as those setting the *Hymn* apart from others, such as the double role of deception.

I would only add to this that such a treatment would need to range widely outside the *Hymn,* examining other versions of the myths told there in order to appreciate the way in which the *Hymn* uses them. It would also have to include the *tettix,* and would ideally go on to relate the stories of transformation to their own literary and historical contexts of production.[24]

Segal's comments on myth and tragedy should now be recalled. The movement out from the *Homeric Hymn* to the wider myth of Tithonos shows that Tithonos is only in a very limited sense a "mediator" between gods and men. In the *Hymn* he combines divine immortality with human aging. As Aphrodite tells his story, it ends with the reminder to Anchises that, despite their sexual union, there *is* a god/man dichotomy, based here on old age, and that he is on the "man" side of it. But because Aphrodite is manipulating myth,[25] this position of "man" seems not a loss, but a gain, for it is destructive old age, not endless old age, which man experiences. As Aphrodite presents it, Tithonos' "eternity of old age" does not stand "Just beneath the gods' full immortality," but far lower. It is made to appear not desirable, but terrifying.

In other versions the "mediation" is even more limited, since Tithonos becomes a *tettix.* To call the *tettix* a mediator is to disguise the peculiar quality of its mode of operation. It is both short-lived, and ageless: both beast and god. Hence to make Tithonos a *tettix* is to fulfil his second request (to become a beast) and his first (to become a god), although they should be mutually incompatible. Any definitive statement on the place of the *tettix* would be impossible, as it has no "absolute meaning."[26] Sources which subdivide the *tettiges* do not say that some are divine, others sub-bestial, but instead use only criteria of size, seasonal appearance, singing ability and so on (Ar. *HA* 532b 15 ff.; Pliny *NH* 11.92; Aelian *NA* 1.20; 10.44 and 11.26; Xenarchos *Hypnos* fr. 14 Kock). It is to some extent possible to "push" the *tettix,* like "men" in the gods/men/beasts matrix, one way or the other, by emphasizing one of its aspects at the expense of the other. Thus *Anacreontea* 32 addresses the *tettix* as a god, but the initial chaos of its identity returns with "old age does not distress you," an idea suggesting both beast and god.

The wider myth of Tithonos shows many other ways in which myth can operate. The *tettix* is both a restatement of the aged Tithonos (cold, garrulous) and a reversal (ageless but short-lived/aging but immortal). Similarly, the Sibyl both repeats and reverses features of Tithonos. The suggestion that Tithonos' old age is like a return to childhood—that the poles of human aging are equally weak, foolish and cold, sharing a similar diet, small in size but powerful in voice— produces a type of opposition in which the poles are equivalent, and the central term is positively valued. As Aphrodite tells the stories of the *genos* of Anchises, Tithonos is not a mediator between gods and men, but men are mediators between the gods and Tithonos.

It is striking that Tithonos, Segal's exemplar of myth, can so easily stand on the other side of the opposition that he draws between myth and tragedy. Tithonos and the *tettix* are figures "at the point where opposites converge." Tithonos separates the components of ageless immortality, by experiencing one after the other, but only through the symbol of the *tettix*, a divine beast which calls into question the whole gods/men/beasts structure. In Segal's definition of tragedy, that it "simultaneously validates and disintegrates the mythic system" (1983.174), I would see both as tragic figures, making present "the painful possibility of seeing life as chaos" (1981.42).

Notes

1. Lovejoy 1936.ch.3; Tillyard 1943.ch.5. In the fifth century A.D. model of Dionysius there were nine orders between God and man; Seraphim, Cherubim, Thrones, Dominations, Virtues, Powers, Principalities, Archangels and Angels. At certain periods the precise arrangement of these angelic orders was more fluid.

2. For a discussion of classicists' responses to Lévi-Strauss on Oedipus, see Detienne 1975.3-24.

3. Borthwick 1966.109 misrepresents this diet, making ambrosia the diet of the *tettix*-Tithonos and ignoring the mixed diet of the immortal and ageless Tithonos. Segal 1981.24 contrasts the diet of Tithonos with that provided by Ganymedes, who serves nectar to the gods (206); in the latter case the mention of nectar evokes Ganymedes' own immortality. P. Smith 1981 b.79 calls Tithonos' diet "a unique combination."

4. For W. Smith 1966.552 the division between the diets of Odysseus and Kalypso, and the Homeric idea that diet is related to the liquid flowing in

the veins, forms an early version of the idea that "you are what you eat"—influential in Greek medicine.

5. Probably late seventh century (e.g., Pellizer 1978, although Freed and Bentman 1955 date it to the fourth). Janko 1982.169 suggests "within Hesiod's own lifetime, in the interval between *Th.* and *Erga.*" The myth is only mentioned briefly by Hesiod *(Th.* 984-5) and Homer (e.g., *Il.* 11.1). The story of Eos and Tithonos was a common theme of lyric poetry; e.g., Ibykos *(PMG* 289), and see below for Mimnermos and Sappho.

6. On Aeneas, see Segal 1981.24 and 1973/4.208. In other versions of the myth of Tithonos, Eos bears him another anomalous child, Memnon, king of the "long-lived" Ethiopians. On the Ethiopians: Hdt. 3.114; 3.16-26; Last 1923; Lesky 1959; Vernant 1979b. On Memnon: Hesiod *Th.* 984-5; Ovid *Met.* 13.578-622; Paus. 10.31; *Kypria,* in Proclus *Chrestomathia* 189-90. The nymphs who care for Aeneas provide another kind of anomalous aging experience; noted by Porter 1949.259 note 25.

7. "Immortal age beside immortal youth," in Tennyson's *Tithonos.* Tennyson concentrates on the error of the mortal who "seem'd/To his great heart none other than a God!" and therefore begged his immortal lover for immortality; but he comes to regret this, asking to be returned to "happy men that have the power to die." The *Homeric Hymn* describes not only the tragic hero but also the foolish divinity, as part of a general concern with the gods/men separation. This of course raises the question of scope; if a myth consists of all its versions, then should the analysis stop at Eustathius?

8. LSJ s.v. *atalos* cites Aesch. *Pers.* 537 *atalais chersi* or perhaps *apalais chersi,* "with trembling hand," and says that this shows *atalos* could be used of the aged. This is in fact far from clear. Reading *pollai d'atalais chersi* (and not *poliai),* all that is certain is that this is not a reference to small children, but to adult women, probably mothers. On *atalos* and *atitallein* see Laser 1983.71 (in the *Hymn* this means "looked after like a child"); Leumann 1950.139-41, with criticisms in Kamerbeek 1967.386.

9. On the song of the *tettix,* below; on *Tithōnou gēras,* CPG 1. 166.16-19; 449.9-10=II.87.3. Aristo, a pupil of Zeno, wrote a work on old age in which the speaker was Tithonos (Cic. *De senect.* 1.3). The pre-Socratic Akysilaos also knew of Tithonos' immortal old age (DK 9 B 8).

10. Bouché-Leclerq 1880.vol.2. 186-7 explains this as a crude interpretation of the idea that her *prophetic* voice could cross a thousand years (e.g.,

Herakleitos DK 22 B 92). The emphasis on the voice in the myths of Tithonos does, however, suggest another approach.

11. The eventual destination of Tithonos is a basket or wicker cage *(talaros, kartallos)* in Eust. *ad Od.* 1528.1; *ad Il.* 1330.15); Tzetzes in Lyk. *Al.* 18. This is "hung up" in Athenaeus 548c and in Eustathius. In the scholion to Lyk. *Al.* 18 the *talaros* is a *liknon,* a cradle. The Sibyl is instead placed in a type of flask—*phakos* (ps-Justin, *Cohort. ad Graecos* 37, p. 35 E); *hydria* (Paus. 10.12.8) or *ampulla* (Petronius). For Bonner 1937, this makes the Sibyl the origin of legends about imps and genii in bottles. According to Cook 1940.vol. 3.1, 246-8, the basket links Tithonos to stories of the infant Erichthonios (on whom see Loraux 1981.ch.I), and being placed in a basket and fed on honey/dew/ambrosia confers immortality. This could perhaps be supported by Ovid *Met.* 7.317, where it is suggested that shrinking is a necessary preliminary to rejuvenation because the young are small (taken with *H.H. Aphr.* as evidence that the *Hymn* contains a reference to the transformation to a *tettix*—shrinking is an aspect of this—by Kakridis 1930.32). Although an implicit reference to Erichthonios is possible in the story of Tithonos, I think that Tithonos is fed ambrosia not to make him immortal, but because he has already become immortal (even if not ageless), while he is later placed in a basket/cradle because he is shrunken through extreme old age. In *H.H. Hermes* 240-1, Hermes in his cradle tries to make himself appear even smaller, like a new-born child.

12. Homer *Il.* 3.150-3; Kirk 1971.126.

13. Maxwell-Stuart 1977.159-62 suggests that *rheei aspetos* means a voice which flows on and on, but inarticulately. While I see little point in trying to decide whether or not Tithonos is a description of "acute polyneuritis" (see other "diagnoses" in Laser 1983.71), I would see this interpretation as suggesting the *tettix* of later versions; it is famed for its song yet, because it is a beast, that song must remain incomprehensible to men (and to Eos). If the *tettix*-Tithonos is inarticulate, this would imply that, beneath the similarity to the Sibyl, there is a contrast between oracular and inarticulate utterance. P. Smith 1981 b.81 emphasizes the present sense of *rheei:* Tithonos' voice is still flowing on, even *now.* See also Kakridis 1930.28-30.

14. Nothing: Aristoph. *Clouds* 1360; Plato *Phaedrus* 259c. Dew: *Anth. Pal* 6.120; *Anacreont.* 32.3; Ar. *HA* 532b 13; Hesiod *Aspis* 393. Dew and air: Plut. *Mor.* 660 f.; Kallim. *Aitia* fr. 1.34.

15. FGH 4.140: *contra* Keller 1920(II).406. Jacoby thought that only the

genealogical part of this fragment could be attributed to Hellanikos: see P. Smith 1981b.131-2 n. 101 and, *contra,* Kakridis 1930.26 and n.4. Kakridis argues for an early date for the transformation to a *tettix;* Dornsieff 1931 suggests that the *Homeric Hymn* is the first text in which it occurs.

16. The old have cold bodies, e.g. Hipp. *Aph.* 1.14/L 4.466; *Reg.* 2/L 6.76.

17. The life of the beasts is concentrated on reproduction and eating. Ar. *HA* 589a 3-5, and men can sink to this level (*Pol.* 1253a 35-7). On the *gastēr* as the most bestial part of man, see Homer *Od.* 6.133-4; 7.219-20; 17.228 with Vernant 1979a.95 and Xen. *Mem.* 1.6.8 and 1.2.1; Ar. *Pol.* 1253a 35-7; *HA* 589a 3-5.

18. I am grateful to Andrew Palmer for drawing to my attention the problem of the diet of John the Baptist; locusts *(akrides)* and wild honey. In the middle ages and earlier it was thought that locusts were not sufficiently vegetarian for an ascetic's diet, and attempts were made to read *enkrides* (cakes of oil and honey) or *agrodrya* (wild fruits), or to take *akrides* as "tips of plants" (from *akris*). Allegorical interpretations were also used; the locust sloughs off its wings as the Baptist rids people of their sins (Brock 1970). My argument from the *tettix* would suggest that insects of this kind do not count as "meat": this would make them both "above" the more normal human diets and hence appropriate to a holy man, and also "below," as in the case of the Locust-eaters of Diodorus Siculus, who are very short-lived; possibly, he goes on, because of their strange diet (3.29.4-7).

19. McCartney 1929 says that the belief that *people* can renew their youth by shedding their skins is the origin of this dual usage.

20. In place of *to de gēras ou se teirei*—old age does not weary you— Giangrande 1975.195-6 instead reads *to de geras eu se tērei,* "the gift which he (Apollo) gives you (your voice) preserves you well": that is, you need no food because you feed on your song. Even if this is correct, Stephanus and later editors accepted the first reading for good reasons; firstly the parallel with *se gēras teirei* in *Il.* 4.315, and secondly the established connection of the *tettix* with immortality in the texts already cited. Another positively-valued aspect of the *tettix* is its habit of laying its eggs in the earth, as a result of which it becomes a symbol of autochthony (see Cook 1940.vol.3.1, 250 nn.7-8; Keller 1920 (II). 401-2; Borthwick 1966.107).

21. Indeed, Tzetzes *Chil.* 8.166.80-4 explains the transformation as follows;

to say that Eos turned Tithonos into a *tettix* is simply a way of saying that Tithonos had the power to renew himself, as snakes and *tettiges* do.

22. The verbal echoes are noted also by Heitsch 1965.38 n. 1, and in Van Eck 1978.77. See P. Smith 1981 b.82-6. Sappho fr. 21 (LP), which repeats the words *chroa gēras ēdē* from fr. 58.13, may also concern Tithonos; if this is the case, then *petatai diōkōn* "flies in pursuit," may refer to the flight of the *tettix* and would thus constitute a very early reference to the transformation.

23. See also Pindar *Pyth.* 10.41 on the Hyperboreans' exemption from this. *Contra* Van Eck 1978.77, who translates "cursed."

24. See e.g., Dihle 1966.110 for an attempt to link the image of the *tettix* in the *Anacreontea* poem with Stoic doctrine.

25. Segal 1983.184. Segal is surely correct to emphasize the complexity of the *Homeric Hymn* here, since it tells the myth through the persona of Aphrodite, who herself has specific motives for deceiving Anchises. My own arguments on the deliberate omission of the *tettix* from the *Hymn* could indeed act as an illustration of Segal's point. P. Smith 1981 b.83 similarly proposes that the *Hymn* omits any reference to Tithonos' son, Memnon, in order to show him "utterly without human connections" and thus even more pitiful.

26. A phrase used by Segal 1981.14 to characterize an approach which, unlike structuralism, concentrates on a particular element rather than on the system of elements within which it operates and from which it gains its "meaning."

References

Bonner, C. 1937. "The Sibyl and bottle imps," in *Quantulacumque: Studies presented to Kirsopp Lake,* 1-8. London.

Borthwick, E. 1966. "A grasshopper's diet—notes on an epigram of Meleager and a fragment of Eubulus," *CQ* 16.103-12.

Bouché-Leclerq, A. 1880. *Histoire de la Divination dans l'Antiquité* 2. Paris.

Brock, S.P. 1970. "The Baptist's diet in Syriac sources," *Oriens Christianus* 54.113-24.

Byl, S. 1980. *Recherches sur les grands traités biologiques d'Aristote: sources écrites et préjugés.* Brussels.

Clay, J.S. 1983. *The Wrath of Athena: Gods and Men in the Odyssey.* Princeton.

Cook, A.B. 1914-40. *Zeus.* Cambridge.

Detienne, M. 1975. "Les Grecs ne sont pas comme les autres," *Critique* 31.3-24.

Dihle, A. 1966. "The poem on the cicada," *HSCPh* 71.107-13.

Dornsieff, F. 1931. "Der homerische Aphroditehymnos," *ARW* 29.203-4.

Duminil, M.-P. 1983. *Le sang, les vaisseaux, le coeur dans la collection hippocratique.* Paris.

Frazer, J.G. 1929. *Ovid: Fasti* (vol. 3). London.

Freed, G. and Bentman, R. 1955. "The Homeric Hymn to Aphrodite," *CJ* 50.153-9.

Giangrande, G. 1975. "On the text of the Anacreontea," *QUCC* 19.177-210.

Griffin, J. 1980. *Homer on Life and Death.* Oxford.

Heitsch, E. 1965. *Aphroditehymnos, Aeneas und Homer.* Göttingen.

James, M.R. 1892. "The Sibyl in Petronius," *CR* 6.74.

Janko, R. 1981. "Athanatos kai agēros: the genealogy of a formula," *Mnemosyne* 34.382-5.

———. 1982. *Homer, Hesiod and the Hymns: diachronic development in epic diction.* Cambridge.

Kakridis, J.T. 1930. "Tithonos," *Wiener Stud.* 48.25-38.

Kamerbeek, J.C. 1967. "Remarques sur *L'Hymne à Aphrodite,*" *Mnemosyne* 20.385-95.

Keller, O. 1909-20. *Der antike Tierwelt.* Leipzig.

Kirk, G.S. 1971. "Old age and maturity in ancient Greece," *Eranos -Jb* 40.123-58.

Laser, S. 1983. *Medizin und Körperpflege*. Göttingen.

Last, H. 1923. "Aithiopes makrobioi," *CQ* 17.35-6.

Leach, E. 1962. "Genesis as myth," in *Myth and Cosmos* (ed. J. Middleton), 1-13. Austin.

Lesky, A. 1959. "Aithiopika," *Hermes* 87.27-38.

Leumann, M. 1950. *Homerische Wörter*. Basel.

Lévi-Strauss, C. 1955. "The structural study of myth," in *Structural Anthropology* I (1963), 206-31. New York.

Loraux, N. 1981. *Les enfants d'Athéna: idées athéniennes sur la citoyenneté et la division des sexes*. Paris.

Lovejoy, A.O. 1936. *The Great Chain of Being: a study of the history of an idea*. Cambridge, Mass.

McCartney, E.S. 1929. "On the shedding of skins by human beings," *CW* 22.176.

Maxwell-Stuart, P.G. 1977. "Tithonos, a medical note," *LCM* 2.159-62.

Pellizer, E. 1978. "Tecnica compositiva e struttura genealogica nell'Inno omerico ad Afrodite," *QUCC* 27.115-44.

Podbielski, H. 1971. *La structure de l'hymne homérique à Aphrodite à la lumière de la tradition littéraire*. Wroclaw.

Porter, H.N. 1949. "Repetition in the Homeric Hymn to Aphrodite," *AJPh* 70.249-72.

Saïd, S. 1982. *Woman and Female in the Biological Treatises of Aristotle*. Odense.

Segal, C. 1973/4. "The Homeric Hymn to Aphrodite: a structuralist approach," *CW* 67.205-12.

————. 1981. *Tragedy and Civilization*. Cambridge, MA.

————. 1983. "Greek myth as a semiotic system and the problem of tragedy," *Arethusa* 16.173-98.

Smith, P. 1981a. "Aineidai as patrons of *Iliad* XX and the Homeric *Hymn to Aphrodite*," *HSCPh* 85.17-58.

————. 1981b. *Nursling of mortality: a study of the Homeric Hymn to Aphrodite*. Frankfurt.

Smith, W.D. 1966. "Physiology in the Homeric poems," *TAPhA* 97.547-56.

Stiebitz, F. 1926. "Zu Sappho 65 Diehl," *Philol. Woch.* 46.1259-62.

Tillyard, E.M.W. 1943. *The Elizabethan World Picture*. London.

Van Eck, J. 1978. *The Homeric Hymn to Aphrodite*. Utrecht.

Vegetti, M. 1979. *Il coltello e lo stilo*. Milan.

Vernant, J.-P. 1979a. "A la table des hommes," in *La cuisine du sacrifice en pays grec* (eds. M. Detienne and J.-P. Vernant), 37-132. Paris.

————. 1979b. "Manger aux pays du soleil," in *La cuisine du sacrifice*, 239-49. Paris.

3

Old Men in the Youthful Plays of Aristophanes

Thomas K. Hubbard

We are fortunate in possessing five extant plays of Aristophanes firmly dated to successive years (425-421 BC) during the earliest phase of the comic poet's career. This is useful in discerning the young poet's development and concerns during a most critical period both in his own work and in Athenian society as a whole.[1] One of the most noticeable features of Aristophanes' youthful plays is their use of old men as main characters and choruses, and their focus on intergenerational relationships as a primary theme: Dicaeopolis, Demos, Strepsiades, Philocleon, and Trygaeus are all socially emblematic figures, as are the old Archarnians and Wasps. Some critics have seen the origins of comedy in a ritual conflict of Old and New,[2] but the results of this conflict in Aristophanes are far from one-sided or univocal. Old Comedy by its nature relies on the inversion of social structures and the exaltation of marginal social groups, but it is in Aristophanes' earliest plays (*Acharnians* through *Peace*) that old men are brought to the foreground as the poet's favorite outcast group,[3] as opposed to the emergence of women (*Lysistrata, Thesmophoriazusae, Ecclesiazusae*) and other groups in Aristophanes' later plays.[4]

Aristophanes' old men are complex and ambivalent.[5] They can appear aggressive and violent, like the Acharnians and Wasps (and as Strepsiades and Philocleon in fact are), but can at the same time be revealed as feeble and in need of guidance by those who are physically and mentally more capable. Many critics have seen the Marathon-veterans as symbols of the superior virtue and valor of the "good old days,"[6] but in the modern context the old warriors often ally themselves with new political and intellectual leaders whose values are contrary to traditional concepts of virtue and excellence. Genuine patriotic sentiment is manipulated, misguided and perverted, and members of the older generation become political pawns rather than the moral paradigms and counselors that they should be.[7] The old men of Aristophanic comedy are not figures of wisdom or authority,[8] and do not (at least initially) occupy a position of honor within the social structure framed by each comedy. Even as they may exemplify social or political orthodoxy of one sort or another, they are oppressed by the very social system that they uphold and defend. They rejuvenate themselves (and thus by definition cease to be old men) precisely when they abandon the prevailing orthodoxies, as all of them eventually do. This transformation from passive conformity to vigorous and youthful self-assertion seems basic to the intentions of Aristophanic comedy, and paradigmatic for its intended effect in renewing and revitalizing Athenian society. In this sense, Aristophanes' old men represent the mature, settled, and somewhat self-satisfied Athenian audience that the reform-minded young poet confronts and addresses.

The ambivalence of the young poet's attitude toward the older generation is well illustrated by his remarks about his aging competitor Cratinus, in the parabasis of the *Knights* (424 BC). The coryphaeus here explains the poet's reasons for not previously producing plays under his own name, and cites the poet's reluctance to submit himself to the same vicissitudes of popular favor and taste which his older rivals have experienced:

He long ago saw that you are seasonal in your nature,
And betrayed former poets along with old age.
He knew what Magnes suffered along with falling gray hair,   520
Magnes, who raised the most victory-trophies of all competing choruses,
Sending out to you all manner of voices—twanging, flapping,
Lydianizing, gall-fly buzzing, coloring himself frog-green,
He did not suffice, but finishing in old age, no longer young,
He was thrown out by you, an old man, because he lost his jest.   525
Then he remembered Cratinus, who once overflowing with praise
Streamed through the flat plains; sweeping from their station
Oaks and plane-trees and uprooted enemies, he carried them off.
One could not sing anything at a symposium save "Fig-slippered Doro"
And "Builders of Handy Songs." Thus did he flourish.   530
But now you have no pity, as you see him muttering,
With the amber-studs falling out of his lyre and the tune undone,
The strings gaping loose. But though an old man, he runs around

91

Like Connas, wearing a dry crown and sorely thirsting for drink.
For his past victories, he ought to drink in the Prytaneum.   535
And not mutter, but be a spectator, sitting in splendor beside Dionysus.
What spite and maltreatment Crates has endured from you,
Crates, who sent you off after feasting you at small expense,
Kneading most urbane insights from his most cabbage-dry mouth.
This man only sufficed, sometimes failing, sometimes not.   540
Fearing these things has our poet delayed, biding his time.
(*Knights* 518-41).

Although on one level commiserating with his comic precursors, Aristophanes is on another level commenting on the decline of ability which seems to be an inevitable adjunct of old age. Magnes won more victories than any rival and introduced many theatrical innovations, possibly including the use of animal choruses, but as soon as old age approached, he lost his ability to "jest" (σκώπτειν) and was "thrown out" (*Eq.* 520-5).[9] At the opposite extreme from Magnes' rather coarse and primitive antics are the "urbane ideas" (ἀστειοτάτας ἐπινοίας) of Crates, who at best received only a mediocre response from the public, "sometimes failing, sometimes not" (*Eq.* 537-40). But the high point of Aristophanes' description of his predecessors is the vivid portrait of the senescent Cratinus (*Eq.* 526-36), who—although still living—is enumerated between the dead Magnes and Crates, with the implication that he is just as much a has-been.[10] Cratinus is generally credited as the seminal figure who turned Old Comedy in the direction of personal attacks and *ad hominem* invective against contemporaries;[11] as the preeminent "blame poet" in the comic tradition, he is appropriately described as at one time flattening everything in his path, like a flooding river. But Cratinus, once so caustic and pitiless in his treatment of others, is now a helpless old man in need of his audience's pity (and manifestly without it). His lyre is in disrepair, and Cratinus himself is given over to drink. The picture of Cratinus (and the two other poets) is not unlike Pindar's famous description of "reproachful Archilochus in his poverty fattening himself on nothing but heavy-worded hate" (*P.*2.54-6), or the familiar stories of *Vita*-tradition concerning the violent and disgusting deaths of other literary misanthropes, often at the hands of a vengeful public or victim (e.g., Thersites beaten to death by Achilles; Aesop thrown off a cliff by the Delphians after being falsely accused; Heraclitus packing himself in dung as a cure for dropsy, only to be eaten by dogs; Euripides torn apart by Macedonian hunting dogs, Orpheus by Thracian Bacchants).[12]

Although Aristophanes complains of the treatment accorded his predecessors, we should not make the mistake of thinking that his sympathy was sincere. The portrait of Cratinus as a drooling and incompetent old man in the grip of advanced senility was hardly flattering, or true. If Cratinus was turning toward alcoholism[13] and allowing his lyre to fall apart[14] (i.e., declining in musical/poetic ability), this was hardly the fault of the theatrical public. Even when Aristophanes presumes to commiserate and wish for better treatment (*Eq.* 535f.), he only calls attention further to Cratinus' descent into drink (*Eq.* 535 "to drink in the Prytaneum," *Eq.* 536 "beside Dionysus"); by wishing that Cratinus have a prosperous retirement, Aristophanes is also implying that the not-yet-retired Cratinus (who was competing against this play) ought to be retired, himself a member of the audience (*Eq.* 536 θεᾶσθαι) rather than a competitor. Cratinus himself certainly did not feel that Aristophanes was paying him a compliment: the *Pytinē,* presented in the following year, not only defended the poet against the charge of alcoholism, but attacked Aristophanes in turn.[15] Aristophanes attempts to establish that it is time for a new generation of comic poets—such as himself—to emerge, but Cratinus' response shows that there is still considerable life left even in the elders.

Balancing the poet's youthful self-assertion and ridicule of the older generation are the reflections of the youthful Knights-chorus in the parabasis-epirrheme concerning their fathers:

We wish to eulogize our fathers, because	565
They were men worthy of this land and of Athena's robe,	
Who in battles both on land and sea	
Always glorified this city, winning everywhere.	
Never did anyone of them count the enemy whom he saw,	
But his spirit was straight on guard like Amynias.	570
If they should anywhere fall on their shoulder in some battle,	
They would have wiped it off and denied having fallen	
And would wrestle again. And no general of those before today	
Would have ever asked Cleainetus for free meals;	
But now, if they don't get honored seating and free meals,	575
They say they won't fight. But we think it right	

Nobly to defend our city and native gods for free.
In addition, we ask nothing more than only this:
If peace ever comes and we cease from our travails,
Do not begrudge us our long hair and bath-scrapers.   580
(*Knights* 565-80)

The knights praise their fathers for military self-sacrifice, both on land (*Eq.* 567 πεζαῖς μάχαισιν) and on sea (ναυφάρκτῳ στρατῷ), and find in this heritage a model for their own selfless dedication to the defense of the state (*Eq.* 576-80). The young knights' respect for their elders shows a traditionalism and reverence quite antithetical to the popular *Zeitgeist* described in the parabasis proper, always in quest of new leaders, new models, and new entertainments (and despising the old guides of the past).[16] Indeed, the selflessness of the knights and their fathers is contrasted quite explicitly with the venality and greed of the present leadership (including the demagogue Cleon, evoked by the allusion to his father Cleainetus in *Eq.* 574).[17] Whereas the elders were viewed as senile and incapable in the parabasis-anapests, they are here praised for their strength and vigor in the prime of life, and exalted as positive paradigms; the knights' praise of their fathers is not just aristocratic pride in the supremacy of birth, but constitutes a praise of the entire Marathon/Salamis-generation and its values.[18] By aligning themselves with their hardy and non-aristocratic forebears, the knights attempt to ward off popular resentment of their putative softness and effeminacy (represented by the long hair and hot baths of *Eq.* 580).

The ambivalence between specific contempt and generic respect is also seen in the treatment of the old Demos—the nominal master of the household, whose apparent mental infirmity, however, seems to put him at the mercy of his manipulative slaves. The Paphlagonian slave (=Cleon) is responsible for his nurture and care (cf. *Eq.* 715, 799, 1164-1204), but keeps most of the food for himself: Paphlagon is depicted as a wet-nurse chewing bits of food for the toothless infant/old man, and swallowing three-fourths of it (*Eq.* 716-8). Despite his senility in political situations (as on the Pnyx—*Eq.* 754f.), Demos is by nature mentally acute (*Eq.* 753 ἀνδρῶν δεξιώτατος). Indeed, it is revealed near the end of the play (*Eq.* 1111-50) that his helpless dependence on the politicians was merely a pose adopted for the purpose of better exploiting them himself, and that Demos has really been in control of the situation all along. Once liberated of political hacks like Cleon, the old Demos undergoes a miraculous rejuvenation, and is an old man no longer. Like the poet transforming his audience through the cathartic effects of comedy, the Sausage-seller makes Demos young and handsome by boiling him in a cauldron. (*Eq.* 1321).[19] But his youth does not consist of the adoption of modern ways so much as of a return to the ancient customs and habits:

Such a man as he was back when he took his meals with Aristides and
    Miltiades.
But you will see him, for already I hear the noise of the Propylaea being
    opened.
Now raise a shout for the old Athens as it is displayed,
Wondrous and much-sung, the place where the famous Demos lives.
(*Knights* 1325-8)

This is the man to see, wearing the grasshopper-brooch, brilliant in his
    ancient dress,
Smelling not of voting shells but of peace-libations, anointed with myrrh.
(*Knights* 1331-2)

As in the case of the young knights who imitate their fathers, youth manifests itself in traditionalism—the way Athens used to be at the time of the Persian Wars, when its Demos was younger. Even so, the young Aristophanes uses the allegory of the Demos as an old man brought back to youthful vigor to suggest that Athens can look to the values of the older generation for a renascence of national spirit.

Demos' rejuvenation and return to his former prosperity were modelled in no small part on that of Dicaeopolis,[20] the old farmer-hero of the *Acharnians* (425 BC), who gives up on the ineffective and corrupt machinations of the politicians to return to his farm with his own private peace treaty. Again, we see the idea that the elderly are ill served by the processes of a democratic society. It is only when liberated that Dicaeopolis is free to barter with all Greece, and is restored to the pleasures of flesh and food, as provided respectively by the Megarian and Boeotian traders. In an appealing inversion of roles, we see Dicaeopolis at the end of the play drinking voraciously and enjoying whores like a young man,[21] while the young general Lamachus complains of physical pain and debility (*Ach.* 1190-1234).

The chorus of old Acharnians do not share in Dicaeopolis' rejuvena-

95

tion and renewal; if anything, their development within the play is from vigorous activity to a state of weak and helpless passivity. In the parodos, the old farmers appear menacing and implacable, militant supporters of Athens' current war policy, eager to avenge the damage done to their deme by the Spartans. But Dicaeopolis' arguments gradually convince them that they are not well served by Athens' present leadership and policies. Indeed, in the parabasis, the chorus shows itself well aware of its victimization by the system:

We old men blame the city,
For not in a way worthy of those naval victories which we won
Are we fed by you in our old age, but we suffer terribly from you,
Who throw us old men into indictments
And allow us to be laughed at by young orators,   680
We, who are nothing, but dumb and exhausted,
For whom our staff is now our un-stumbling Poseidon.
Muttering with old age we stood at the voting table,
Seeing nothing but the fog of the trial.
The young man, hastening to speak against him,   685
Taking ahold of him with smooth round phrases, strikes him quickly,
And then dragging him up, questions him, setting up word-traps,
Tearing apart, mixing up, and stirring around the Old Tithonus.
He mumbles in his old age, and then goes off owing a fine,
Then whines and cries and says to his friends,   690
"I go off owing as a fine this money with which I should have bought my
   coffin."

   How is this right,
      To destroy at the water-clock
      A gray old man,
   Who has performed many tasks   695
      And wiped off much warm and manly sweat,
   A man good for the city at Marathon?
   When we were at Marathon, we pursued,
   But now we *are* pursued
      By evil men,   700
      And taken too.
      What will some Marpsias answer to this?

How is it right that a stooped old man of Thucydides' age
Be destroyed by being tangled up with the "Scythian desert,"
The son of Cephisodemus, the blathering accuser?   705

Such that I pitied him and wiped away a tear, seeing
An elerly man pushed around by a bowman.
By Demeter, when that man was really Thucydides,
He would not easily have endured Achaea herself,
But would first have wrestled down ten Euathluses,   710
And yelling, would have shouted down 3,000 bowmen,
And would have outbowed the kinsmen of the accuser's father.
But since you don't allow old men to have any sleep,
Decree that lawsuits should be separate, so that
To an old man should be an old and toothless accuser,   715
And to young men a wide-assed and blathering son of Cleinias.
And for the future, you should banish, and if guilty, fine
An old man through an old man, a young man through a young man.
(*Acharnians* 676-718)

In the antode, the Acharnians complain that even as they "pursued"
the enemy at Marathon (*Ach.* 698 ἐδιώκομεν), so now they "are
pursued" in their old age (*Ach.* 699 διωκόμεθα). This parallels the
progression in the character of the chorus which takes place within the
play: reminiscent of their valorous past, they enter the drama in hot
pursuit of anyone associated with the city's foreign enemies, but they
are eventually brought around by Dicaeopolis into recognizing that
they, like him, are victims exploited by the current Athenian power
structure. The antithesis both embodies the contrast between the
Acharnians' past vigor and present decrepitude[22] and expresses, more
broadly, a contrast between Athens' glorious past of united sacrifice
against the external enemy (symbolized by the victory at Marathon)
and the city's present degeneration into self-destructive domestic
infighting and litigiousness. In an inversion of the usual epic
dichotomy between young warriors and old counselors, contemporary
Athens contrasts the old warriors with young orators:[23] *erga* are
abandoned in favor of *logoi.*

Dicaeopolis' conversion of the chorus helps them better comprehend
their own situation. They now understand that the present war (of
which they were once enthusiastic supporters) is nothing like the
noble war for freedom they fought many years ago, and that the
present generation of political leaders cannot compare with once
towering figures such as Thucydides the son of Melesias. (*Ach.* 708-
12), who have now been shoved aside. In a way, the old rustic
Dicaeopolis enacts the wish fulfillment of the chorus' desires. In his

agon with the younger Lamachus (*Ach.* 572-625), we have seen the old
man triumph rhetorically. Then, in his private marketplace, we see
him set up an ideal state completely free of sycophants and their
litigation (*Ach.* 725f., 836-59, 904ff.).

Short of realizing such a fantasy, the best hope the chorus can have is
that young men will sue only other young men, and old men will be
sued only by their peers (*Ach.* 714-6). The litigation motif has been
central throughout the *Acharnians,* whether in Dicaeopolis' statements about being prosecuted by Cleon (*Ach.* 377-82, 501-7) or the
coryphaeus' remarks in the parabasis-anapests about the poet's
experience with Cleon (*Ach.* 630-2, 659-64).[24] Cleon is doubtless the
paradigm for the "young orators" criticized throughout the syzygy.[25]
And at the time of this play, Aristophanes was indisputably a very
young man: his implication may be that not only can he defend himself
against Cleon, but he is in fact just the man to deal with Cleon and thus
protect the public as a whole.

Many of the *Acharnians'* themes are also taken up three years later in
the *Wasps.* Here too we find the motif of excessive litigation, the
poet's self-presentation as a would-be reformer, the rejuvenation of a
senescent hero, and a chorus of elders who complain that they have not
been sufficiently valued. As in the *Acharnians* and *Knights*, the
epirrhematic syzygy of the parabasis is constructed around a central
contrast between the industrious public service of the older generation
(here, wasp-tempered jurors) and the self-serving greed of the
younger:

> We were once long ago valiant in the chorus,   1060
> Valiant in battle,
> And the most valiant men especially in this thing here.
> These things were before, before, and now
>   Are gone, and whiter than a swan
>   Do these hairs bloom.   1065
> But even from these remains we must
> Hold onto youthful strength, as I think
> That my old age is stronger than the curls
>   And fashion and wide-assedness of many young men.   1070

If someone of you, O spectators, looks at my nature
And, seeing me wasped-through around the middle, then wonders
What the point of our sting is,

I shall easily teach him, "even if he be museless before."
We, who possess this rump, 1075
Are the only truly native earth-born Attic men,
A most manly race and the race helping this city most
In battle, when the barbarian came,
Filling the whole city with smoke and setting it ablaze,
Wishing by force to drive us out of our hives. 1080
Immediately running out "with spear and shield"
We did battle with them, having taken a swig of acrid spirit(s),
Standing man to man, biting our lip in anger.
One couldn't see the sky for all the arrows.
But all the same, with the gods, we pushed forward till evening, 1085
For an owl flew through our host before doing battle.
And then we pursued them, harpooning them in the trousers,
And they fled, stung in their jaws and brows,
So that everywhere among the barbarians, even now,
Nothing is called more manly than an Attic wasp. 1090

    I was terrible then, such as not to fear anything,
    And I threw down
    The enemy, sailing there in the triremes.
    We did not then have any thought
     Of how we should deliver a good speech 1095
      Or denounce someone,
    But of who would be the best oarsman.
    Thus, having taken many cities of the Medes,
    We are most responsible for the receipt of the tribute, 1100
     Which the younger men steal.

Examining us from many places and in every way, you will find us
Most like wasps in our habits and life.
First, no animal, when angered, is more
Sharp-tempered or difficult than us. 1105
And then, we devise all other things most like wasps.
For gathering together in swarms just as into hives,
Some of us judge where the archon is, others in the court of the Eleven,
And some in the Odeon, so thickly packed against the walls,
Bending to the ground, hardly moving, 1110
Just like grub-worms in their cells.
In the rest of our life we are most inventive,
For we sting every man and provide a livelihood.
But there are drones sitting among us

Not having a sting, who wait for the offspring of our tribute   1115
And eat it up, not going through any of the toil.
This is most painful to us, if someone who was never a soldier,
Slurps down our pay, never in service of this country
Taking ahold of an oar, a spear, or a blister.
But in short, it seems to me that from now, those of the citizens   1120
Who don't have a sting shouldn't take three obols.
(*Wasps* 1060-1121)

The ode begins by parallelling the wasps' vigor as a chorus (*Vesp.* 1060 ἄλκιμοι μὲν ἐν χοροῖς) with their erstwhile military valor (*Vesp.* 1061 ἄλκιμοι δ' ἐν μάχαις): they view dramatic activity as a means of defending the city, not unlike their courageous self-sacrifice in war (elaborated in *Vesp.* 1077-90). But they were "the most valiant men especially in this thing here" (*Vesp.* 1062 καὶ κατ' αὐτὸ τοῦτο μόνον ἄνδρες ἀλκιμώτατοι), by which they refer to their phallus, now a thing of the past (*Vesp.* 1063f.). The place of their once vigorous phallus is now taken by their wasp-sting, which is described at length in the epirrheme as the essence of their manliness (*Vesp.* 1077 ἀνδρικώτατον γένος, *Vesp.* 1090 μηδὲν 'Αττικοῦ καλεῖσθαι σφηκὸς ἀνδρικώτερον).[26] Similarly, Philocleon's juridical resolve is expressed in terms of phallic potency, which he loses at the moment that he begins to doubt the system (*Vesp.* 713f.).[27] Although old, the wasps are hearty and fearless souls who defended Athens even against the overwhelming might of the Persians (*Vesp.* 1077-90), again like Philocleon, who fought at Marathon (*Vesp.* 711). Whereas the jurors' waspish irascibility and hard-spirited nature has been censured throughout the play, it is here made a matter of self-praise (*Vesp.* 1082f., 1104f.), even as the "anger of Heracles" is praiseworthy.[28] The wasps' sturdy masculinity, accented by the final word of the epirrheme (*Vesp.* 1090 ἀνδρικώτερον), even in old age overshadows the frail effeminacy of modern youth, with their curls, postures, and sodomy, vividly portrayed at the end of the ode (*Vesp.* 1067-70).

The antode and antepirrheme, as is customary, become more specific in their application of the contrast. Here, the young men are not just silly, but a positive threat to the political order and stability created through the sacrifices and labor of the Marathon and Salamis generations.[29] While the old wasps were concerned with defeating the Persians by hard rowing at sea (*Vesp.* 1091-7), the younger generation

100

practices oratory (*Vesp.* 1095), sycophancy (*Vesp.* 1096), and theft of the tribute made possible by their fathers (*Vesp.* 1098-1101). The latter charge—that the allies' tribute is being embezzled by Athens' present political leadership, rather than given to the public—is of course the very heart of Bdelycleon's argument in his debate with his father (*Vesp.* 655-718). The wasps take their jury duty just as seriously as their long past military accomplishments (*Vesp.* 1106-11), but complain of drones among them who earn the money without ever having served in the military and suffered hardship (*Vesp.* 1114-21). These unworthy jurors resemble the unwarlike and larcenous young demagogues attacked in both the ode and antode, and thus exemplify on one more level the idea that rewards are not going to those who have truly deserved them. It is significant that the old wasps' attitude toward the young is primarily characterized by resentment and animosity, based on the perception that their life has been easier due to the wasps' own ill-rewarded toil: the wasps' last remaining resource is their jury service, which gives them power to vent their resentments, although in a purely negative and condemnatory way.

The wasps' resentment in many ways reminds us of the old Acharnians, who also claimed to be valiant Marathon-veterans (*Ach.* 692-700) now suffering maltreatment by the young orators and sycophants (*Ach.* 676-91). However, the wasps are themselves a part of the legal system responsible for the Acharnians' problems; although they have been persuaded by Bdelycleon of their leaders' corruption, even as the Acharnians were persuaded by Dicaeopolis, the wasps do not abandon their identity as jurymen. Whereas the Acharnians, so fearsome at the moment of their entrance, are progressively softened by Dicaeopolis' rhetoric and ultimately revealed to be helpless old men in the parabasis-syzygy, the wasps, if anything, gain in resiliency: they enter in the parodos as slow old men, dependent on young boys for guidance (*Vesp.* 230-72)[30] and unable to rescue their imprisoned companion, but in the parabasis appear spirited, vigorous, and defiant. The wasps' development is thus not unlike the hero Philocleon's. Although on a rational level defeated by Bdelycleon's arguments, the wasps' "nature" (*Vesp.* 1071 φύσιν) is intractable and emerges proudly triumphant.

The role of the old jurymen in the play parallels and reinforces that of their chief compatriot—Philocleon. The relations between the old

Philocleon and his socially ambitious son dramatize what appears to have been a fairly common tension in Greek family life, that between a retired father and newly married son who has come to be the head of the household.[31] The once-powerful father becomes marginal and insignificant in the running of the house, and seeks compensation by acquiring a sense of power in serving on juries and convicting prominent defendants.[32] Through a combination of forcible detention, rational persuasion, and metatheatrical legerdemain, Bdelycleon succeeds in separating his father from the juries, but is not as successful in acculturating him to the modern tastes and conventions of polite society. Dressed in new clothing, and taught how to drink at symposia and sing witty skolia, Philocleon undergoes a rejuvenation not unlike Dicaeopolis'.[33] But the rejuvenated Philocleon does not become a respectable member of society, as his son had hoped; instead, he feels himself released from all legal constraints, drinking, whoring, singing, dancing, insulting, and assaulting without inhibition. Rejuvenation of the old in Aristophanes never integrates them with modernity, instead causing them to reassert their past with renewed strength and vigor.

Indeed, we may be meant to see in the figures of the young Bdelycleon (Cleon-hater) and his father Philocleon (Cleon-lover) the confrontation between the crusading young comic poet Aristophanes and the obstinate, incorrigible Athenian public he attempts, with only limited success, to reform.[34] He achieves his objective with political comedies like the *Acharnians* and *Knights* (both of which win first prizes), just as Bdelycleon does in weaning his father away from Cleon and the juries. But Aristophanes fails to win public favor with his more subtle intellectual and cultural criticism, as seen in the *Clouds* (which had been defeated the previous year, ending in third place).[35] Similarly, Bdelycleon cannot educate his father into cultural sophistication or even into a significantly new pattern of social behavior. We thus see that the young Aristophanes again uses the figure of the old man as an archetype for his public, as he also did with Dicaeopolis and Demos; and in each case, the old man's spiritual rejuvenation is paradigmatic for the effect of Aristophanic comedy.

The *Wasps* differs from the *Acharnians* and *Knights* in viewing the relation between generations through the framework of family relations. Bdelycleon's concern for his father is the conventional (and legally mandated) care of a son for his aged parents,[36] and despite his failure to reform his father completely, the chorus at the end of the play praises him for his filial piety and devotion (*Vesp.* 1462-73).[37] Cleon had transformed the Athenian juries into a sort of pension for the elderly, by means of which he could command and manipulate their political loyalty.[38] But by bringing his father home to sit in comfort as a judge over domestic disputes, Bdelycleon reasserts the primacy of familial support for the elderly over any statist solution, necessarily replete with fraud and manipulation. As with Dicaeopolis' private peace, purchased for the enjoyment of himself and his family, Aristophanes insists on the fundamental importance of the family unit as an economic and social entity, whose demands ultimately transcend obligations to an increasingly corrupt and intrusive political system.

Generational conflict and family relations are also a primary theme of the *Clouds.*[39] This play is Aristophanes' most cynical and negative statement concerning the older generation in its relationship to modern times. Whereas the old men of Aristophanes' other plays in this period are all essentially sympathetic characters, despite their flaws and obsessions, Strepsiades is a malign parody of the usual comic hero—stupid rather than clever, socially destructive rather than constructive, and totally unsuccessful in achieving any transcedent vision. His is a mock rejuvenation, in which he is educated like a child but learns nothing except his own ineducability.[40]

Our initial impression of Strepsiades in the prologue does evoke some sympathy: we see him as an old rustic who married above his social station and has a spendthrift son, whose debts he must find some way of evading. But the alienated old man addresses his problem by seeking help from the most discreditable and inappropriate source, whose true nature and consequences he scarcely comprehends. The old man's grotesque misunderstanding of Socrates' doctrines and his inability to be taught even the most rudimentary elements of educated discourse show the seemingly unbridgeable gulf between the traditional values of the average Athenian and the modern intellectual world of science, rhetoric, and sophistic relativism: even as Strepsiades presumes to embrace the powers of the Lesser Discourse, he cannot tolerate its ultimate consequences, which justify not only the defrauding of creditors but also Strepsiades' thrashing at the hands of his own son—a violation of one of the most fundamental legal and moral obligations in Athenian society.[41] Strepsiades attempts to use modernity to achieve selfish ends, but himself winds up becoming a victim of modernity. Again, we see the theme of the old maltreated by the young, as in the *Acharnians* and *Knights*; but here, the old are revealed to be themselves culpable for their predicament. That Strepsiades' humiliation represents the hypocrisy and failure of his entire generation is indicated by the parallel defeat of the Greater Discourse, who embodies allegorically the traditional values and spirit of old Athens[42] but allows selfish motives to corrupt his moral vision.

In summary, we can see that old men play a prominent role in each of Aristophanes' extant plays in the period from the production of *Acharnians* through that of the *Peace* (425-21 BC), as does the theme of a rejuvenation which liberates the hero from social and political constraints.[43] In the *Acharnians* and *Knights*, old men are viewed as victims manipulated by the system: in the first play, the aged hero rescues himself through his own enterprise and efforts, while in the second, the old men are defended by younger allies (the knights, the Sausage-seller, the poet). However, with the *Clouds,* Aristophanes takes a more pessimistic view of the prospects that the old can survive in the contemporary intellectual milieu. We find a similar, though more compassionate educational pessimism in the *Wasps.* But the *Peace* takes a more positive view: there is not so much emphasis on old age itself as on rejuvenation as a symbol for the renewal and reinvigoration of the Athenian spirit after years of war.[44]

It is difficult to extract from Aristophanes' dramatic characterization of old men any precise sociological information about their status in Athenian society, or even a firm and coherent view of old age on Aristophanes' part.[45] What we can see from his repeated use of elderly heroes and choruses is the perception that the old constitute an alienated and resentful class at the margins of society and thus appropriate material for comedy. But in Aristophanes' Athens, the marginal has become normal, and the normal marginal. Paradoxically, Aristophanes' old heroes are also an idealized version of Everyman, projecting the common citizen's resentments, fantasies and desires. Relative to the precocious young comic iconoclast, most of the citizens in his audience in some sense *were* old men, and were certainly made to feel old and irrelevant (like Dicaeopolis) by their political leadership. The young Aristophanes avoids the potential *phthonos* of his older audience[46] by expressing his ideas from the standpoint of old characters or choruses who have been alienated and victimized by the system in one way or another. The apparent evolution of the poet's attitude toward the older generation in his early plays may thus express his evolving attitude toward his audience as a whole and his own relationship to it—whether as a successful savior (like the Sausage-seller and the knights) or as a frustrated educator (like Socrates and Bdelycleon). Although all of Aristophanes' old men are resentful of their treatment by the young, we progressively come to see that they are in many ways responsible for their own situation, as is the Athenian audience generally, which the young Aristophanes both loves and reproves.

Aristophanes' old men are thus not to be interpreted exclusively as old men. There were very few Marathon-veterans like the Acharnians or Salamis-veterans like the wasps still living in the 420s; there were surely no veterans of Leipsydrium like the old men of the *Lysistrata*, produced in 411. These choruses rather embody the hardy spirit that belongs to the common soldiers and sailors of all ages who fought (or are now fighting) on Athens' behalf. The elderly provide the comic poet with a potent symbol for traditional values and the primary importance of family obligations in a society that increasingly neglected them, as Thucydides (2.52.3-2.53.4) tells us in his portrait of Athens' moral and spiritual disintegration after the plague. Aristophanes avoids the simple idea that the past is necessarily better than the present, but he is clearly aware that not all the answers lie with the present; the modernism of the clever young poet whom the aged Cratinus derided as εὐριπιδαριστοφανίζων (fr. 342 PCG) is tempered by a reverence (albeit an amused reverence) for past greatness and inherited memory. Through his elderly characters, the youthful Aristophanes expresses his hope for rejuvenation of the human spirit, although he perceives that it can sometimes be achieved only very imperfectly.

Notes

1. In regard to Aristophanes' youth, Σ*Ran.* 504 informs us that he was σχεδὸν μειρακίσκος at the time that the *Banqueters* was produced (427 BC). This also seems to be the implication of *Nub.* 530f. For a review of

the available information on Aristophanes' date of birth, see Kent 1905.153-5.

2. See Cornford 1968.9-13, 30-3, and more recently, Reckford 1987.41.

3. If commentators are right in supposing that *Vesp.* 1038-42 refers to a lost play produced either at the Dionysia of 424 or the Lenaea of 423 (cf. Meineke 1839.II, 1113-8, Zelle 1892.24f., Starkie 1897.316f., Platnauer 1949.7, MacDowell 1971.267, Sommerstein 1977.271f.), this play would also have dealt with the generational conflict, as implied by the image of the young men "who by night strangled their fathers and grandfathers" (*Vesp.* 1039).

4. In one way or another, old age or old characters figure in all the plays of Aristophanes: Peisthetaerus and Euelpides are old (*Av.* 320, 337), as is Euripides' kinsman (*Thesm.* 63, 585) and the chorus of *Lysistrata.* But generational conflict is not a primary dramatic tension in any of these plays, although old age must have been a dominant theme in the lost *Gēras* (*"Old Age"*), which can be dated to 410 (cf. Gelzer 1970.1410). It should be noted that the plays of Aristophanes' old age (*Ecclesiazusae* and *Wealth*) are precisely the ones which display old characters in the ugliest and least sympathetic light: see especially *Eccl.* 877-1111 and *Plut.* 959-1096, and the comments of Byl 1977.67-72.

5. There is no extended treatment of Aristophanes' reflections on old age: Richardson 1933.20f., 28, and Byl 1977.52-73, see his attitude as essentially negative, while Ehrenberg 1951.207-11 regards him as more sympathetic, as does Henderson 1987.105, 108-10, 127f., in a recent treatment of old women in Aristophanes. On the general ambivalence of the Greek attitude toward old age, see Lacey 1968.116f., Finley 1981.164f.

6. Cf. Süvern 1836.165, Ehrenberg 1951.207, Whitman 1964.148 and Kirk 1971.152f. But as Gomme 1975.79-82 notes, the Marathonomachai are usually on the wrong side.

7. On the archetype of old men as counselors, see Richardson 1933.31-3.

8. See Auger 1979.76-8. Some recent critics have challenged the assumption that old age was ever particularly associated with wisdom in ancient thought: cf. Kirk 1971.127f., 145, and Finley 1981.163f., as against the more conventional view of Richardson 1933.16-20.

9. The passive expression τοῦ σκώπτειν ἀπελείφθη in *Eq.* 525 (parallel to the passive ἐξεβλήθη at the beginning of the line) creates an impression of helplessness on Magnes' part. In a comic poet, though, such helplessness can only come from a decline in imagination.

10. On the order of presentation, see the remarks of Sommerstein 1981.171, and Harriott 1986.23.

11. For Thersites: *Aethiopis,* fr. 1 (= Proclus, *Chrest.*). Aesop: *Vitae* G, W (Perry), and the discussion of Nagy 1979.279-88. Heraclitus: 22A1a D.-K. (=Suidas). Euripides: *Vita Eur.* 122f., and the discussion of Lefkowitz 1981.76-8. Orpheus: Ovid, *Met.* 11.1-66.

12. See Athenaeus 268d; Platonius, *Diff. Char.* (=*Test.* 17 PCG); Poppelreuter 1893.28-32; Norwood 1931.141-4; Pieters 1946.51-131; Schwarze 1971.5-90; Mattingly 1977.239-45; Rosen 1983.145-60.

13. On indulgence in wine as a stock characteristic of old men, see Richardson 1933.40. In reference to old women, see Henderson 1987. 119f.

14. For the interpretation of the image, see Perusino 1982.151-8. I do not believe, however, that we are to understand Cratinus himself as a lyre (as she and most other commentators do), but as the owner of such a lyre (which mirrors his own dissolution).

15. Cratinus charged Aristophanes with plagiarizing from Eupolis (fr. 213 PCG) and with imitating Euripides at the same time that he criticized him (fr. 342 PCG, plausibly assigned to the *Pytinē* by Runkel; compare Aristophanes' response in fr. 488 PCG). Pieters 1946.151f. even thinks that Aristophanes and Eupolis may have been presented as dramatic characters in the *Pytinē*. The last laugh was indeed Cratinus', inasmuch as the *Pytinē* won the first prize in the Dionysia, as opposed to the *Clouds'* humiliating third place.

16. On the basis of a cross-cultural study, Slater 1964.232f. notes that the status of the elderly is lowest in democratic cultures (i.e., those that value change and freedom while being suspicious of authority and tradition). It therefore should not surprise us that the aristocratic knights appear in this play as the defenders of the elderly, while the older generation is disparaged in the more democratic arenas of the theatre and politics (where the old man Demos is neglected and clad in rags).

17. The allusion to *proedria* in *Eq.* 575 also points to Cleon/Paphlagon, who brags of his *proedria* in *Eq.* 702.

18. Edmunds 1987.253-6, has acutely emphasized the role of the entire syzygy in reconciling the interests of the upper-class knights with those of the general public (who formed Athens' naval force): *Eq.* 565-8 in fact claim the knights' descent from common soldiers and sailors, not cavalry.

19. As commentators have noted, the motif is derived from the familiar myth about Medea convincing the daughters of Pelias to boil their father for the sake of rejuvenation (cf. Pindar, *P.*4.250; Apollodorus, *Bibl.* 1.9.27; Diod. Sic. 4.51f.; Pausanias 8.11.2f.; Plautus, *Pseud.* 869-71; Hyginus, *Fab.* 24). Here, of course, the results are happier. For a cross-cultural study of the motif of rejuvenation through boiling in a cauldron, cf. Frazer 1921.II,359-62.

20. Demos, like Dicaeopolis, is a displaced farmer who will be reinvigorated once he is returned to the land; cf. *Eq.* 805-8.

21. Renewed sexual interest is a hallmark of rejuvenation in Aristophanes, as we see in Philocleon's dalliance with the flute-girl *(Vesp.* 1342-81) or Trygaeus' marriage to Opora *(Pax* 856-67); compare also fr. 144, 148 PCG, from the *Gēras,* and the remarks of Süvern 1836. 156-63. Even the old Acharnians are affected with erotic desire for Peace and rejuvenated by the thought of its consummation *(Ach.* 989-99).

22. That the Acharnians are represented as old and infirm may reflect the diminished importance and vitality of the agrarian elements in Attic society of the late fifth century; on which see Ehrenberg 1951.73-94. Dicaeopolis, of course, embodies a reinvigoration and reassertion of the agrarian party, which could be brought by peace.

23. Cf. Pucci 1960.27.

24. For the identification between Dicaeopolis here and the poet's experience (as revealed in the parabasis), cf. Landfester 1977.43f., Bowie 1982.30, Harriott 1986.33f, and Reckford 1987.188-90. Some critics have even gone so far as to argue that Dicaeopolis' role must have been played by the poet or producer: cf. Müller-Strübing 1873.607, Schrader 1877.396, Briel 1887.26, Bailey 1936.231-40, Lever 1956.112.

25. The phrase ταράττων καὶ κυκῶν *(Ach.* 688) is explicitly used of Cleon in *Eq.* 692 and *Pax* 654; on the metaphorical significance of these terms, see Newiger 1957.27-30. Note also that Cleon has just been called λακαταπύγων *(Ach.* 664), in reference to his litigation against the poet, even as the litigious son of Cleinias is εὐρύπρωκτος *(Ach.* 716).

26. For the equation of the wasps' stings with surrogate phalluses and the general idea that their aggressive nature compensates for erotic frustration, see Reckford 1987.236-8. It should also be noted that φύσιν in *Vesp.* 1071, referring on the primary level to the wasps' form and appearance, is also a term used with specific application to the genitals (cf. Nicander, fr. 107.3 [Schneider], and Henderson 1975.5).

27. For "sword" (ξίφος)-jokes as double entendres, see *Lys.* 155f., 632, and Henderson 1975.122.

28. On the theme of anger (*orgē*), see the discussions of Whitman 1964.147, Konstan 1985.32f.

29. The wasps' hostility to the younger generation reflects the conventional conflict between νεώτεροι and πρεσβύτεροι attested so often in Greek politics and political theory; on which, see Roussel 1951.204-14 and Reinhold 1976.29-38, with particular reference to the late fifth century.

30. On the ways that this dependence foreshadows the relationship of Philocleon and Bdelycleon, see Paduano 1974.207f., Long 1976.19.

31. On paternal retirement and the resulting relationship, see Lacey 1968.106f., 117f.

32. Philocleon's defense of the juror's life in his debate with his son (*Vesp.* 548-630) emphasizes the feeling of power and self-importance which he obtains from jury-service, and ends by asserting his renewed importance within his own household (*Vesp.* 605-14). On the family relationship and the sociological/psychological basis for Philocleon's behavior, see Paduano 1974.167-239.

33. Philocleon treats his son as an older and more responsible relative in *Vesp.* 1352-65; this is particularly true if we assign the verses on an "imminent coffin" (*Vesp.* 134f.) to Philocleon as speaker, as proposed by Rusten 1977.157-59.

34. Bdelycleon's identification with the comic poet is made explicit by *Vesp.* 650f., which serves as an apologetic preamble to his debate with Philocleon: "Curing an ancient disease inbred in the city is difficult and the mark of a clever judgment greater than one finds among comic poets." This statement recalls the similar remarks made about comedy by Dicaeopolis (*Ach.* 377-84, 496-508). On the identification, see also Russo 1962.194, Paduano 1974.71, and Reckford 1987.254f., 273-5.

35. Aristophanes' disappointment over the reception of the *Clouds* is clear from *Vesp.* 1043-50 and from his remarks in the revised parabasis of the *Clouds* itself (*Nub.* 518-62, on which see my comments in Hubbard 1986.185-96).

36. On which, see *Ath. Pol.* 56.6, Aeschines 1.28, 1.99, and Richardson 1933.55f., Lacey 1968.116f., Reinhold 1976.25-7, Finley 1981.167f., Henderson 1987.111.

37. On the applicability of this praise also to the poet, with regard to his concern for the public, see Russo 1962.194.

38. Many, including Finley 1981.167f., have noted the lack of any organized state support for the elderly in antiquity. But it is rather clear that the jury-system of this period amounted to the same thing; few able-bodied men would volunteer for the modest salary of three obols a day, and the juries were thus composed mostly of retired citizens (cf. *Ach.* 375f., *Eq.* 255f., 977-9, 1332, *Pax* 349-52); see MacDowell 1971.3f.

39. For a more detailed treatment of the problem, see the remarks of Reckford 1976.89-118, and Byl 1977.57-61. On the close relation of the *Clouds* and *Wasps* in this regard, see Whitman 1964.119.

40. On the old man's forgetfulness and inability to learn anything new, compare *Nub.* 492f., 628f., 646, 655, 790.

41. See note 36 above. Mistreating one's father seems to have been a common topos of moral dissolution in Aristophanes: cf. *Vesp.* 1039, *Av.* 757-9, 1337-71, fr. 445 PCG. On the general decline of respect for parental authority in this period, under the influence of sophistic ideas, see Roussel 1951.215-27 and Reinhold 1976.33f., 37f.

42. Also central to the Greater Discourse's system of *paideia (Nub.* 961-83) is the concept of respect for elders, which comes to be discredited along with the Greater Discourse himself.

43. In addition to these plays, rejuvenation also plays an important role in *Wealth, Frogs* (especially *Ran.* 345-50), and of course *Gēras* (note fr. 129 PCG, and the remarks of Süvern 1836.141-5). On the importance of rejuvenation as part of comedy's overall ritual pattern of death and rebirth, see Cornford 1968.42-5 and Paduano 1974.226f.

44. The rejuvenation encompasses both Trygaeus, who becomes younger as a bridegroom to Opora (*Pax* 856-67), and the chorus, who cast off their role as severe old jurors (inherited from the last play) to become younger and milder (*Pax* 349-52).

45. On the difficulty of extracting any consistent political views from Aristophanes, see the important essay of Gomme 1975.75-98.

46. On the characteristic Greek distrust of literary or artistic precocity, particularly after the widespread diffusion of literacy, see Kirk 1971.123, 148-51.

References

Auger, D. 1979. "Le Théâtre d' Aristophane: le mythe, l' utopie et les femmes," in *Aristophane: Les femmes et la cité*, 71-101. Fontenay-aux-Roses

Bailey, C. 1936. "Who Played Dicaeopolis?," in *Greek Poetry and Life: Essays Presented to Gilbert Murray*, 231-40. Oxford.

Bowie, A. M. 1982. "The Parabasis in Aristophanes: Prolegomena, *Acharnians*," *CQ* 32.27-40.

Briel, A. 1887. *De Callistrato et Philonide*. Berlin.

Byl, S. 1977. "Le Vieillard dans les comédies d' Aristophane," *AC* 46.52-73.

Cornford, F. M. 1968. *The Origin of Attic Comedy*, 2nd ed. Gloucester.

Edmunds, L. 1987. "The Aristophanic Cleon's 'Disturbance' of Athens," *AJPh* 108.233-63.

Ehrenberg, V. 1951. *The People of Aristophanes*, 2nd ed. Oxford.

Finley, M. I. 1981. "The Elderly in Classical Antiquity," *G&R* 28.156-71.

Frazer, J. G. 1921. *Apollodorus: The Library*. London.

Gelzer, T. 1970. "Aristophanes," *RE Suppl.* 12.1392-1569.

Gomme, A. W. 1975. "Aristophanes and Politics," in H.-J. Newiger (ed.), *Aristophanes und die alte Komödie*, 75-98. Darmstadt.

Harriott, R. M. 1986. *Aristophanes: Poet and Dramatist*. Baltimore.

Henderson, J. 1975. *The Maculate Muse: Obscene Language in Attic Comedy*. New Haven.

————, 1987. "Older Women in Attic Old Comedy," *TAPhA* 117.105-29.

Hubbard, T. K. 1986. "Parabatic Self-Criticism and the Two Versions of Aristophanes' *Clouds*," *ClAnt* 5.182-97.

Kent, R. G. 1905. "The Date of Aristophanes' Birth," *CR* 19.153-5.

Kirk, G. S. 1971. "Old Age and Maturity in Ancient Greece," *Eranos-Jb* 40.123-58.

Konstan, D. 1985. "The Politics of Aristophanes' *Wasps*," *TAPhA* 115.27-46.

Lacey, W. K. 1968. *The Family in Classical Greece*. Ithaca, NY.

Landfester, M. 1977. *Handlungsverlauf und Komik in den frühen Komödien des Aristophanes*. Berlin.

Lefkowitz, M. R. 1981. *The Lives of the Greek Poets*. Baltimore.

Lever, K. 1956. *The Art of Greek Comedy*. London.

Long, T. 1976. "The Parodos of Aristophanes' *Wasps*," *ICS* 1.15-21.

MacDowell, D. M. 1971. *Aristophanes: Wasps*. Oxford.

Mattingly, H. B. 1977. "Poets and Politicians in Fifth-century Greece," in K. H. Kinzl (ed.), *Greece and the Eastern Mediterranean in Ancient History and Prehistory*, 231-45. Berlin.

Meineke, A. 1839. *Fragmenta Poetarum Comoediae Antiquae*. Berlin.

Müller-Strübing, H. 1873. *Aristophanes und die historische Kritik*. Leipzig.

Nagy, G. 1979. *The Best of the Achaeans: Concepts of the Hero in Archaic Greek Poetry*. Baltimore.

Newiger, H.-J. 1957. *Metapher und Allegorie: Studien zu Aristophanes*. München.

Norwood, G. 1931. *Greek Comedy*. London.

Paduano, G. 1974. *Il giudice giudicato: Le funzioni del comico nelle "Vespe" di Aristofane*. Bologna.

Perusino, F. 1982. "Cratino, la *Kline* e la Lira: Una Metafora ambivalente nei *Cavalieri* di Aristofane," *Corolla Londinensis* 2.147-59.

Pieters, J. T. M. F. 1946. *Cratinus: Bijdrage tot de Geschiedenis der vroeg-Attische Comedie*. Leiden.

Platnauer, M. 1949. "Three Notes on Aristophanes, *Wasps*," *CR* 63.6-7.

Poppelreuter, J. 1893. *De comoediae atticae primordiis*. Berlin.

Pucci, P. 1960. "Saggio sulle Nuvole," *Maia* 12.3-42, 106-29.

Reckford, K. J. 1976. "Father-Beating in Aristophanes' *Clouds*," in S. Bertram (ed.), *The Conflict of Generations in Ancient Greece and Rome*, 89-118. Amsterdam.

———, 1987. *Aristophanes' Old-and-New Comedy*, Vol. I: *Six Essays in Perspective*. Chapel Hill, NC.

Reinhold, M. 1976. "The Generation Gap in Antiquity," in S. Bertram (ed.), *The Conflict of Generations in Ancient Greece and Rome*, 15-54. Amsterdam.

Richardson, B. E. 1933. *Old Age Among the Ancient Greeks*. Baltimore.

Rosen, R. M. 1983. *Old Comedy and the Iambographic Tradition*. Ph.D. thesis, Harvard University.

Roussel, P. 1951. "Étude sur le principe de l' ancienneté dans le monde hellénique de Ve siècle av. J.-C. à l' époque romaine," *Mémoires de l'Institut National de France, Académie des Inscriptions et Belles-Lettres* 43,2.123-227.

Russo, C. F. 1962. *Aristofane, autore di teatro*. Firenze.

Rusten, J. S. 1977. "*Wasps* 1360-1369: Philokleon's τωθασμός," *HSCPh* 81.157-61.

Schrader, H. 1877. "Kleon und Aristophanes' Babylonier," *Philologus* 36.385-414.

Schwarze, J. 1971. *Die Beurteilung des Perikles durch die attische Komödie und ihre historische und historiographische Bedeutung*. München.

Slater, P. 1964. "Cross-cultural views of the aged," in R. Kastenbaum (ed.), *New Thoughts on Old Age*, 229-35. New York.

Sommerstein, A. H. 1977. "Notes on Aristophanes' *Wasps*," *CQ* 27.261-77.

_____, 1981. *The Comedies of Aristophanes: Vol. 2, Knights*. Warminster.

Starkie, W. J. M. 1897. *The Wasps of Aristophanes*. London.

Süvern, J. W. 1836. *Two Essays on "The Clouds" and on "The ΓΗΡΑΣ" of Aristophanes* (trans. W. R. Hamilton). London.

Whitman, C. H. 1964. *Aristophanes and the Comic Hero*. Cambridge, MA.

Zelle, H. A. W. 1892. *De Comoediarum graecarum saeculo quinto ante Christum natum actarum temporibus definiendis*. Halle.

4

The Wrath of Alcmene: Gender, Authority and Old Age in Euripides' *Children of Heracles*

Thomas M. Falkner

*P*erhaps more than any other of the early plays of Euripides, the *Children of Hercules* is characterized by abrupt and even shocking changes of mood and tone.[1] Nowhere are these more striking than in the closing scene of the play. When Eurystheus is brought before Alcmene, she bitterly catalogues the abuse she and her family have suffered, wishing only she could kill him more than once (959-60). When his rights as prisoner of war suddenly threaten to deprive her of the vengeance she savors, she confronts her Athenian protectors angrily, winning a concession shameful to both parties: she will kill him first, and they will have the body to do with as they please (1021-24). In her final words in the play, as if she had forgotten her own agreement, she orders her attendents to "kill him and throw him to the dogs" (1050-51). Alcmene's stark and brutal behavior effectively subverts the values and sympathies the play had worked to establish, throwing into darkness and disorder what might have seemed to that point a conventional suppliant play and a simple exercise in patriotism.[2]

Earlier scholarship saw the scene as an instance of the play's generally shoddy and episodic construction, like the melodramatic sacrifice of Macaria or the fantastic metamorphosis of Iolaus, its artistic shortcomings matched by the condition of a text Murray judged a *fabula misere mutila*. Grube reflects both points of view in maintaining that "no amount of additions or alterations can make this into a good play."[3] More recent criticism has tended to regard the play's discontinuties as characteristically Euripidean, and to appreciate the scene

114

for the meanings and insights it generates rather than for the readerly (and Aristotelian) conventions it disappoints. While this approach has prompted readings of the play's historical, political and social significance,[4] relatively less attention has been paid to its ethical dimension, in particular the implications of making Alcmene the vehicle for the dénouement. While it is true that neither she nor any of the play's personae are developed as fully individualized characters, neither is it necessary to regard them, as one critic does, as simply "masked abstractions."[5] The poet finds in Iolaus and Alcmene, who are identified insistently and repeatedly as γέρων and γραῖα, an occasion to characterize old age more generally, and the play's dramatic form draws extensively on their elderly status.[6] To the extent that the poet develops Alcmene as in some sense a *typical* figure, her characteriza-tion takes on a significance that might seem obvious had it not gone virtually unremarked: that as Iolaus is emblematic of old age, it is more specifically of *male* old age, and the representation of Alcmene correspondingly involves a representation of elderly *women* in general. Although discussion of Iolaus regularly focuses on his age, critics have not appreciated Alcmene in her capacity as an old woman, nor have they illuminated the relationship we are left to draw between her age and her vengeance at the play's end.

Euripides develops Alcmene's character throughout in largely nega-tive terms, in relation to other characters, and reveals her as increasingly aggressive, authoritative and almost "masculine" in nature. Ironically, this potential is latent in her very name, "strong in wrath," the elements of which are heavily gendered. In ἀλκ- is suggested male strength, defense, and battle, which Iolaus explicitly tells Alcmene is "men's work," just as childcare is women's: ἀνδρῶν γὰρ ἀλκή· σοὶ δὲ χρῆν τούτων μέλειν 711).[7] In μην- is implied the epic and unforgiving wrath which, no less than the μῆνις of Achilles or the gods, propels her: hers is, the chorus says, a frightening hatred (δεινόν...νεῖκος, 981-82) for Eurystheus, as earlier they had called it δεινόν that Argos should harbor such a μῆνιν for Athens (759-62). Like Medea, Hippolytus, and other Euripidean characters who realize the tragic potential of their names, Alcmene comes to be defined by this strength and wrath, and her conduct provides a focus for the play's reflections on the problematical relationship of gender, authority and old age.

These themes are established in the prologue. Iolaus, Heracles' nephew and helpmate during his labors and a younger man elsewhere in the tradition, is here conspicuously superannuated.[8] The poet makes him of the generation not of Heracles' children but of his aged mother, and takes pains to establish the two elders as a pair. Iolaus introduces Alcmene with a military metaphor: δυοῖν γερόντοιν δὲ στρατηγεῖται φυγή (39), and the duals present the two as a pair of generals in charge of the Heraclids' retreat.[9] He explains the division of their strategic labors (40-44): he (ἐγὼ μέν) outside the temple with the boys; she (ἣ δ' αὖ) inside, sheltering (σῴζει; cf. σῴζω, 11) the girls (τὸ θῆλυ...γενός, νέας...παρθένους), lest they immodestly be exposed to public scrutiny. The poet provides in Iolaus and Alcmene parallel expressions of senectitude and cohorts of the same generation and experience, whose common history of suffering Iolaus rehearses in the prologue.

Alcmene is thus located in two frames of reference, as age-mate to Iolaus and as grandmother to the Heraclids. These relationships (noted at 445-46, 584, 630-31) are developed in her dramatic entrance at 646:

> What's all the ruckus out here, Iolaus? Not another herald from Argos to push us around, is it? I may be weak, but you'd better get this, stranger: you won't touch these kids as long as I'm alive, or I'm not the mother of Heracles the great. If you so much as lay a hand on them, you'll have a glorious battle with this pair of oldsters! (646-53)

With this scene the play divides roughly in two, and Alcmene's appearance sustains a number of earlier motifs.[10] As the play begins with the arrival of Copreus, Alcmene rushes out afraid that another herald (τις...κῆρυξ, 647-48) has come, and takes up her position over the children as had Iolaus. Her words recall those of her cohort. Her reference to her ἀσθενὴς...ῥώμη (648-49) picks up Iolaus' ἐρρώμεθα at 636 and the references to weakness at 23 and 274, as βιάζεται (647) further develops the theme of Argive βία.[11] She repeats several of Iolaus' expressions verbatim, describing herself and him as δυοῖν γερόντοιν (653; cf. 39) and vowing that the children won't be taken "as long as I'm alive" (ἐμοῦ ζῶντός/ζώσης ποτε, 66, 650). The verbal echoes underscore the basic similarities in their situations, since each of them has the opportunity to speak, negotiate, and decide for the group. Each is served a restriction upon the field of action which brings about an aporia and threatens the group's safety: Demophon reports the oracles' demands, and the chorus declares Eurystheus' inviolate status. The poet thus effects a strong symmetry in the play, giving it an almost diptych structure and establishing its second part as something of a reprise of the first.

To this point, Macaria alone has appeared from inside the temple to represent the feminine world within. She enters with apologies for her boldness (θράσος, 474) and words that echo those of Sophocles' Ajax to his captive wife Tecmessa (293): "I know what is best for a woman: silence, and modesty, and to stay indoors quietly" (γυναικὶ γὰρ σιγή τε καὶ τὸ σωφρονεῖν/ κάλλιστον, εἴσω θ' ἥσυχον μένειν δόμων, 476-77). Macaria's demeanor toward Alcmene and Iolaus is tender and reverent. Her appearance is prompted by the weeping of Iolaus, whom she addresses politely as γέρον (501, 548) and πρέσβυ (560, 574), and in her farewell she admonishes her brothers to honor καὶ τὸν γέροντα τήν τ' ἔσω γραῖαν δόμων (584).

Alcmene's appearance is striking for its contrast with Macaria's demure manner, heroic self-sacrifice and dignified exit. As Macaria embodies the αἰδώς that Iolaus and Alcmene seek to protect (cf. αἰδούμεθα, 43), Alcmene's boisterous entrance suggests her disregard for the canons of womanly deference and prefigures her protests later in the play. At precisely the moment when she refuses to abide by the Athenian *nomos* that protects Eurystheus, she rejects the constraints of her womanhood in terms that explicitly recall those of Macaria: "You can talk about my boldness (τὴν θρασεῖαν), and say I'm not behaving as a woman should (τὴν φρονοῦσαν μεῖζον ἢ γυναῖκα χρή), but I will kill him all the same!" (978-80). Both the chorus and Eurystheus respond by addressing her here, as nowhere else in the play, as γύναι (981, 983). Like Macaria, Alcmene recognizes that the crisis requires the suppliants to take responsibility upon themselves and actively affect the situation rather than passively accept it. But where Macaria's self-sacrifice wins her testimonies for her εὐγένεια and εὐψυχία, Alcmene's personal initiative toward the Argive king's death brings her "great blame" (πολλὴν...μέμψιν, 974).

The scene also strikes a contrast between Alcmene and Iolaus, who minutes earlier was crouched on the ground with eyes downcast, unable even to recognize the servant of Hyllus. Iolaus tells him that old age is a thing of weakness — γέροντές ἐσμεν κοὐδαμῶς ἐρρώμεθα (636) — and looks to him to be a savior from their ills (σωτήρ... βλάβης, 640). Although Iolaus has been successful in winning protection for the group, his old age has been characterized primarily by his physical weakness and utter dependence on the goodwill of others: as the chorus says (702-3), his will may be young (λῆμα μὲν...ἡβᾷ) but his body is "gone" (σῶμα δὲ φροῦδον). For him old age brings insult (Copreus calls him "an old man, a grave, a nothing," γέροντος..., τύμβου, τὸ μηδὲν ὄντος, 166-67) and even physical abuse: his manhandling by the herald brings tears to the eyes of the elderly chorus (127-29). When the oracles are reported, Iolaus founders as the play's action grinds to a halt. When Macaria saves the day, he applauds her noble sentiments but counters with the bathetic suggestion that they select the victim by lottery. Equal neither to the crisis nor its remedy, Iolaus balks at Macaria's request to stand beside her in death (464), collapses in a faint and is propped against the altar and covered up.[12] His helplessness, at first pathetic, becomes outright comical when, in a parody of the traditional scene of arming, he exchanges his suppliant paraphernalia for spear and sheild: Iolaus is unable to carry his own armor, and the servant, putting a spear in his one hand and supporting the other, "nursemaids" (παιδαγωγεῖν, 729) him off to war.[13] As Iolaus totters offstage he apostrophizes his own right arm, recalling its youthful (ἡβήσαντα, 740) glory in service to Heracles. Our expectations are reversed, of course, when Iolaus proves to be the hero of the battle and Eurystheus' captor, but this is achieved by virtue not of his old age but of its abeyance, in his miraculous metamorphosis as a νέος...ἐκ γέροντος αὖθις αὖ (796) and through the intervention of the gods themselves.[14]

Alcmene's spirited entrance begins her gradual appropriation of the dramatic situation, giving us theatrically as well as linguistically "dual protagonists" and defining each as the antithesis of the other. Male old age, as exemplified in Iolaus, is weak and infirm, and his relation to the events around him, for all his good intentions, is passive, ineffectual and at times slightly irrelevant.[15] Female old age, as embodied in Alcmene, is energetic and aggressive, and she wields such power and authority as she has purposefully and resolutely. Appropriately, while the theme of helplessness (ἀμηχανία) was a primary one earlier in the play (cf. 148, 329, 464, 472, 487, 492, 495), it does not recur while Alcmene holds center stage. Where Iolaus' development moves broadly speaking from "tragic" to "comic," Alcmene's is the inverse, and what begins as feisty high spirits is transformed into fearsome depths of self-will and anger.

Alcmene's confused and frightened state at first throws all into near-comic confusion.[16] She snaps at Iolaus for alarming her, pesters the herald for news of Hyllus, and abruptly disclaims interest as he describes the military situation (654-65). She is silent while Iolaus receives the report and suddenly insists on joining the battle. But with the herald offstage she minces no words: he is out of his mind (σῶν φρενῶν οὐκ ἔνδον) to leave her alone with the children (709-10). Alcmene's earlier fears (cf. φόβου, 656) now find a new object, and for a second time Iolaus must calm them (cf. μὴ τρέσῃς, 654, 715).

> Al. And what if you die? What will happen to *me?*
> Io. Your grandchildren will survive to take care of you.
> Al. And if—god forbid—they are not so lucky?
> Io. Don't worry, our friends here won't abandon you.
> Al. Well, I'm glad you can be so confident, *I'm* certainly not.
> Io. And I'm sure that Zeus too is concerned for your plight.
> Al. *Well,* I'm certainly not going to badmouth Zeus, but *he* knows if he's done right by me or not. (712-19)

Alcmene's anxieties clearly center less on the group than on herself (cf. ἐγώ 712; ἐμοῦ 718; ἐμέ 719), and her earlier self-assertiveness begins to look more like sheer self-interest.

From his opening lines in the play, Iolaus espouses a set of values whose terms are consistently reiterated: family and kinship, friendship and loyalty even in adversity, gratitude for kindness, the individual's obligations to the group. He pledges his undying thanks to Athens, and gives the idea visual expression in the handclasp that joins Athens and the Heraclids. He is ready to die for the group, and commends Macaria's spirit of self-sacrifice. These values are reflected in his life of service as Heracles' πιστὸς...παραστάτης (125; cf. 88) and are emphasized linguistically in his extensive use of σύν and μετά and its compounds. He has shared Heracles' labors (μέτεσχον, 8) as his σύμπλους (216) and σύμμαχος (457). In the prologue he distinguishes the man who is δίκαιος from the self-centered man who is πόλει τ' ἄχρηστος καὶ <u>συν</u>αλλάσσειν βαρύς (4) and says of his loyalty to the Heraclids: ἐγὼ δὲ <u>σὺν</u> φεύγουσι <u>συμ</u>φεύγω τέκνοις/ καὶ <u>σὺν</u> κακῶς πράσσουσι <u>συμ</u>πράσσω κακῶς (26-27). His words reach a climax in his declaration that he will join the battle (κἄγωγε <u>σὺν</u> σοί ταὐτὰ γὰρ φροντίζομεν, φίλοις παρόντες, ὡς ἔοιγμεν, ὠφελεῖν...<u>μετασχεῖν</u> γ' ἀλκίμου μάχης φίλοις, 681-83).

Where Iolaus defines himself in terms of his ties to others, Alcmene acts as an individual responsible only to herself, and her responses correspondingly reflect her personal fears and desires. The poet reflects Alcmene's capacity for self-assertion in her speech, which abounds in singular references to "I/me/mine" (cf. 712-19 above) and culminates in a string of angry assertions of her right to execute her prisoner based only on herself. When the chorus objects that no one may kill Eurystheus she counters "but *I* will, and I remind you that *I* am someone too" (<u>ἔγωγε</u> καίτοι φημὶ <u>κἄμ</u>' εἶναι τινα, 973)..."and now that he has fallen into *my* hands (ἐπείπερ χεῖρας ἦλθεν εἰς <u>ἐμάς</u>, 976)..."the deed will be done and *I* shall do it" (τὸ δ' ἔργον τοῦτ' <u>ἐμοὶ</u> πεπράξεται, 980). Her last two exchanges in the play similarly end in blatant appeals to her own interests: "By his death, he will pay me *my* punishment" (οὗτος δὲ δώσει τὴν δίκην θανὼν <u>ἐμοί</u>, 1025); and "don't expect that you'll live to drive *me* from *my* fatherland again" (μὴ γὰρ ἐλπίσης ὅπως/ αὖθις πατρῴας ζῶν <u>ἔμ</u>' ἐκβαλεῖς χθονός, 1051-52).

This contrast is sustained in their religious attitudes. Where Iolaus counsels trust in Zeus, Alcmene is convinced of his indifference (718-19).[17] Only in the hour of victory, and after dramatic evidence of the gods' concern, does she begrudgingly acknowledge them.

> Cho. O Zeus, giver of victory, now our terrible fear is gone and our freedom is restored.
> Alc. O Zeus, I guess you took some time to notice my suffering (τἄμα...κακά). But just the same I'm grateful for what you've done. For my part (ἐγώ), I never really believed my boy was with the gods, but now I know it well enough. (867-72)

Alcmene's skepticism has its foil in Iolaus' profound and prosaic piety, which is echoed in the sincere if occasionally platitudinous wisdom of the chorus. For Iolaus the βωμὸς...θεοῦ (61) is a true sanctuary he hesitates to leave even when his situation is secure (344-47); he regards its violation as an affront (ἀτιμία, 72; ἀτιμάζων, 78) to the gods. These he imagines with unabashed anthropomorphism as potent presences. He rallies Demophon by reminding him that "our gods are every bit as strong as theirs" (347-52). When the oracle is delivered he accepts it as god's will (θεοῖσι...δοκεῖ τάδε, 437) and repeats it uncritically to Macaria (488-91), and is careful even in her exit not to offend (δυσφημεῖν, 600) the deity. His defense is quite literally in Zeus, whose temple provides the armor he borrows for battle. When he opposes the chorus' advice to act his age (706) and their insistence he can never be young again (οὐκ ἔστιν ὅπως ἥβην κτήσῃ πάλιν αὖθις, 707-8), his strength of will is ultimately upheld by the gods themselves. His rejuvenation is clearly presented as a reward for his piety and loyalty, with the scene's religious setting (beyond "godly Athene's holy hill of Pallene," 849-50), his prayer to Zeus and Hebe, and the astral epiphany of Heracles and Youth herself to make him a fine specimen of youth (cf. ἡβητὴν τύπον, 857-58). His story finds a fitting epilogue in the trophy he erects to Zeus (936-37).

With the exit of Iolaus the dramatic focus moves fully to Alcmene. At the messenger's arrival she is again fearful (φόβος, 791) for the news of who has lived and died. But where the chorus afterwards celebrates the end of their fear (φόβου, 867), the news of Eurystheus' survival gives her new (and justified) reason to be apprehensive:

> But what in the world was Iolaus' intent in sparing Eurystheus, and not killing him on the spot? Tell me. In *my* book this is none too smart — to capture your enemy and then not take your punishment. (879-82)

What Alcmene sees as οὐ σοφόν, Iolaus ironically had done in deference to her (τὸ σὸν προτιμῶν, 883), affording her the opportunity to see her enemy in defeat and to delight (τέρψαι θέλοντες σὴν φρέν', 939) in the reversal of fortune that has befallen him.

This reversal is described in terms of power and authority. The herald had earlier characterized Eurystheus and the Argives as masters and rulers (τοῖς σοῖς δεσπόταις, 99; σοῦ κρατοῦντες, 100), making the suppliants like runaway slaves finally apprehended.[18] The peripety reverses the metaphor: Eurystheus is described as σῇ δεσποτούμενον χερί (884) and Alcmene taunts him imperiously: "so now you no longer rule but *are* ruled" (κρατῇ γὰρ νῦν γε κοὐ κρατεῖς ἔτι, 944).[19] The inversion of the metaphor of master and slave, however, is mediated in Alcmene's *domestic* authority over her servants, who address her as δέσποινα at 784 and 928 (cf. 678) and whose freedom, we are twice reminded, lies in her hands: Alcmene promises the messenger his freedom for the good news he bears, and he later recalls her promise as a matter of noblesse oblige (788-89, 889-91). However, Alcmene, in offering the servant his freedom, ironically asks him to free *her (*ἐλευθερῶσαι...ἐλευθεροῖς, 789-90) from the fears which enslave her. Through these metaphors the poet suggests the totality of her power over Eurystheus as well as its lack of public or institutional sanction. She extends such power as she has by sheer force of her character and personality, and — important to remember — in the absence of Iolaus and Demophon: it is hard to imagine her debating and negotiating in their presence. Appropriately, it is her δμῶες (1950) to whom she gives the order for the execution.

With Eurystheus' entrance, Alcmene's wrath is given free rein, and in it she becomes an expression of pure hatred and revenge. She greets him with ὦ μῖσος (942; cf. 52) and gloats over her captive (942-44). She reviews his persecution of Heracles in an abbreviated version of his labors and his sacrilegious pursuit of her helpless family: "some old people, others still children" (τοὺς μὲν γέροντας, τοὺς δὲ νηπίους ἔτι, 956). She recognizes only one necessity, and as self-appointed judge herself passes sentence: Eurystheus shall die and suffer in the process (δεῖ σε κατθανεῖν κακῶς, 958; χρῆν γὰρ οὐχ ἅπαξ θνῄσκειν σέ, 959-60; cf. 874-75). Critics are near unanimous in their agreement that Alcmene and her arch-rival ultimately prove to be more alike than different.[20] The fear with which she has lived for years he admits to have been the driving force behind his persecution (cf. 996). He acknowledges himself a σοφιστής (993) and provides a demonstration in the sophistry of his defense: he has acted simply out of policy. The hatred (νεῖκος, 986; δυσμένειαν, 991) for Heracles was a disease (νόσον, 990) Hera visited on him against his will; he has only praise for Heracles; he flatters Athens for its piety and discretion (1012-13). Alcmene counters his speech in the sophistry of the "compromise" by which she wins the unseemly collusion of the chorus (1020-25). He insists that she would behave no differently in his place, and she proceeds as though intent to prove him right.

Where Iolaus was deferential to his Athenian protectors, Alcmene argues her way into a full-blown confrontation with the chorus, and —heedless of Eurystheus' rights — rides roughshod over their objections. Where Iolaus' conduct is guided throughout by what people will say about him (cf. 28-30), and his speech refers frequently to the norms of αἰδώς,[21] Alcmene disregards public opinion. She refuses to be restricted by Athenian νόμος (963, 1010), the will of Athens and its leaders (964, 1019), the apparent agreement of Hyllus (967-68), the proprieties of femininity (978-80) or the blame she will incur (974). So consuming is her anger that she is oblivious to the harm she thereby brings upon her own descendents, to the fact that his death will make her return to Argos a κακὸν...νόστον (1042). When Eurystheus reveals the oracle that will make his death a positive advantage to Athens, Alcmene will brook no delay: τί δῆτα μέλλετ' (1045). She orders her servants to put him to death, and ends with a final burst of spleen against her foe (1051-52).

Children of Heracles presents the reader with an image of the elderly female as not only active but aggressive and even frightening. The pathetic and at times comic old age of Iolaus is ultimately offset by the character of his larger representation — his piety and altruism, commitment to the common good, and strong will — so that in the end he becomes ὁ κλεινὸς Ἰόλεως (859), ὁ...ἐσθλὸς Ἰόλεως (936). Where his piety and loyalty win him a divine reprieve from the laws of nature, Alcmene's hour of vengeance culminates in the image of a spiteful and domineering old woman, devoid of the proper femininity of the young Macaria, closer in character to the man who has been her nemesis. Alcmene's assertiveness and independence are vitiated by her selfishness, skepticism, and fanatical demand for revenge. In a sense, her character involves no less a metamorphosis than that of Iolaus. In her assault on Eurystheus she becomes something other than human, like the hydras and lions and hellhounds she adduces in evidence of *his* inhumanity (949-51), like the dogs to whom she would throw his corpse.

To what extent is this combination of femininity, old age and vengeance anomalous? Although Greek literature presents only partial and occasional images of elderly women, there is evidence to suggest that Alcmene's capacity for vengeance is less in spite of her age than in some sense because of it. The association of old women and bitter expressions of vengeance finds frequent expression later in Euripides. In the *Trojan Women* Hecuba, so crushed by fortune that she is frequently prostrate on the ground with grief and age, is animated only once in the play, at the prospect of winning a revenge on Helen. In the agonistic form of Helen's impromptu trial, Euripides develops the quasi-legal atmosphere of Alcmene's judgement of Eurystheus, and Hecuba's denunciation of Helen is further tempered by the presence of Menelaus. The protagonist of the *Hecuba* identifies herself in her opening words as a helpless γραῦς (59), "wretched for wretched old age" (δειλαία δειλαίου γήρως (156, cf. 203). Her helpless appearance, however, conceals enormous depths of hatred and a capacity for revenge that exceeds Alcmene's, both in its grotesqueness (where we are forced to watch the blinded Polymestor fumble about and serve as his own messenger) and in her unashamed use of deceit to win her revenge. In her future transformation into the "bitch of Cynossema" (κυνός ταλαίνης σῆμα, 1273), Euripides presents at last the literal counterpart to Iolaus' rejuvenation.

Far from being peculiar to Euripides, the image of the vengeful old woman has a tradition going back at least to Homer. At the end of the *Iliad,* in a scene that bears more that a cursory relationship to our play, Hecuba tries unsuccessfully to dissuade Priam from his similarly unexpected decision to go the camp of the Greeks. Like Alcmene, she tells Priam he has "lost his wits": πῇ δή τοι φρένες οἴχονθ' (24.201), she asks him. As Alcmene worries for her future, Hecuba cautions Priam about the danger, and in a savage burst of temper against Achilles wishes that she could "sink teeth into his liver and eat it" as vengeance for Hector's death (τότ' ἂν τιτὰ ἔργα γένοιτο, 24.212-14).[22] Even more striking is the behavior of Eurycleia at the end of the *Odyssey,* in a pair of passages discomforting to modern readers. When she is summoned by Telemachus (she is addressed as γρηὺ παλαιγενές, 22.395) and sees the bloody corpses of the suitors, she is set to cry out in celebration (ἴθυσέν ῥ' ὀλολύξαι, 22.408) until her master forbids her such public expressions of joy and reminds her it would be unholy (οὐχ ὁσίη, 22.412) for her to gloat over the dead. She takes an almost sadistic delight in accusing the faithless servant women, telling them of the punishment that awaits them and leading them to their end. When she finally hobbles upstairs to awaken Penelope, she is described as actually "cackling" or "chuckling" (καγχαλόωσα, 23.1) with pleasure, and is told by Penelope to contain her joy, at least for now (μή πω μέγ' ἐπεύχεο καγχαλόωσα, 23.59).

The theme assumes cosmic proportions in Aeschylus' *Eumenides* in the deities who are the very embodiment of vengeance. In developing the Erinyes as representatives of the "old order" (παλαιοὺς νόμους, 808) Aeschylus makes them part of the earlier generation overthrown by the younger Olympians (οἱ νεώτεροι θεοί, 162). Athena acknowledges them as older (γεραιτέρα, 848) than she, and the Erinyes complain of the insult the upstart Apollo does their antiquity (πρεσβῦτιν, 731). But where divinity is otherwise considered ageless in appearance (deity is almost by definition ἀθάνατος καὶ ἀγήρως) the Erinyes are themselves aged beings, "gray goddesses" (γραίας δαίμονας, 150), or again monstrous hybrids of old age and youth, "repulsive maidens, gray and aged children" (κατάπτυστοι κόραι, γραῖαι παλαιαὶ παῖδες, 68-69; cf. 150). Their lust for blood vengeance and the savage anger they display thus reflect both the antiquity of their mind (they call themselves παλαιόφρονα, 838, 871) and their status as old women. These aged deities threaten to engulf heaven and earth in their anger, yet ironically their vengeance proves less intractable and more open to accommodation than that of Alcmene.[23]

Euripides' representations of old age participate in a tradition of images of vengeful old women, and we need to appreciate the extent to which the poet both draws on and contributes to this literary stereotype. But the images may also have a social dimension, and we may conclude by noting studies that suggest that images of aggressive and even frightening old women reflect larger cultural patterns. The cross-cultural work of David Gutmann notes the frequency of a certain "matriarchal shift" in anthropological studies, in which women in old age assume a higher and more aggressive profile than before. Such increased assertiveness and independence often become a social liability, a perception that elderly women have a particular capacity for evil translated into local and negative stereotypes such as that of the "witch." Gutmann would locate this shift at the level of personality itself, and suggests that in both traditional and modern societies roughly opposite patterns of development obtain for men and women: where older men become increasingly passive and dependent, older women tend to give freer rein to their aggressive and egocentric impulses: "across cultures and with age they seem to become more domineering, more agentic, and less willing to trade submission for security.[24] Margaret Mead, on the other hand, relates these changes to the arena within which power is exercised: "old women are usually more of a power within the household than older men. Older men rule by ascribed and titular authority, but wives and sisters rule by force of personality and knowledge of human nature."[25]

In light of the scanty data available, we can only speculate on the extent to which such "matriarchal shift" was a reality among elderly women in Greece. It may well be the case that old age brought Athenian women, particularly widows, greater freedom of movement in the city as midwives, participants in festivals, and mourners even for those other than close relatives.[26] It was only in the immediate aftermath of widowhood, for instance, that the Greek woman won temporary control over her possessions.[27] But as Philip Slater and others have reminded us, images of female power and authority may be not so much public as domestic in their origin.[28] Elderly widows, their adult sons required by law to care for them, seem most often to have come under their κυρίεια and to have taken up residence with them, so that the *oikos,* perhaps earlier the scene of mother-son antagonism, might also have been the arena for struggle for domestic dominance with his young wife.[29] While nominally under the authority of their κύριος, one wonders if in their personal lives elderly widows did not often behave effectively as their own κυρίαι: in Athenian comedy, to be sure, the feisty, argumentative, and even sexually aggressive old woman becomes a staple, and her behavior may provide a telling if absurd reflection of their domestic profile.[30] At any rate, Euripides' image of Alcmene and the literary stereotype it elaborates provide a tragic version of the disparaging images of elderly women—images that have unfortunately been a part of their history, in literature and in life.

Notes

1. The text is that of Murray's OCT (1902), though without accepting the extent of textual corruption he suggests; translations are my own. An earlier version of this essay was presented at the meeting of the Classical Association of the Middle West and South in April 1987.

2. Burian 1977.15-16 calls the ending "a brief coda that unflinchingly reverses every major theme of the play, reopens every question, challenges every conclusion." Burian's account of the play's dramatic form offers the best reading of the play as a whole and one with which I am largely in agreement, although I would argue that the violence of the play's ending is carefully anticipated in Alcmene's representation throughout.

3. The literature on the play is usefully reviewed in Burian 1977.1-3, and the textual questions reconsidered most recently in Lesky 1977. The best defense of the integrity of the text remains Zuntz 1947. The quote is from Grube 1941.174.

4. See, e.g., Delebecque 1951 ch. 2, Zuntz 1955.33-38 and 81-88, Vellacott 1975.183-86, Burnett 1976, and Taylor and Brooks 1981.5-7 and 15-22.

5. Burnett 1976.4.

6. Iolaus is described or addressed as γέρων or γέραιος at: 39, 75, 80, 86, 129, 166, 333, 343, 466, 501, 548, 572, 584, 630, 636, 653, 793, 796, 956; as πρέσβυς at 461, 560, 574, 843. Alcmene is similarly described at 39, 446, 584, 653, 654, 888, 911, 956. Their age is underscored by the many references in the play to ἥβη, νέος and other words for youth, by Iolaus' rejuvenation, and in staged productions by masks and appropriate gestures. In the elderly chorus (cf. πρέσβυς, 120), Euripides is clearly drawing upon the tradition of the *Marathonomachoi* as representatives of traditional virtues of Athens' past.

On old age in Euripides generally, see de Romilly 1968. 158-71 and Falkner 1985.

7. Cf. πόλιν...Μυκήνας...πολυαίνετον ἀλκᾷ, 761; ἀλκίμου μάχης, 683; ἀλκίμου δορός, 815.

8. Cf. Avery 1971.553-55. Burian 1977.13 n. 36 minimizes the significance of Iolaus' senescence, noting that no one refers to it explicitly in the drama. But Euripides could hardly have emphasized his age more in the play than he does, and while the audience would surely have "granted" him this license, it requires nonetheless an adjustment from the more familiar legends of Heracles.

9. Cf. νῷν 640. The two are spoken of as a pair at 584 and 630-31, and Alcmene refers to them as τοὺς...γέροντας (956). The pairing of Iolaus and Alcmene reflects other instances of doubling in the play: Demophon and Acamas as δισσοὺς...Θησέως παῖδας (35); Hyllus, who offstage leads the older brothers described as οἷσι πρεσβεύει γένος (45), and Macaria who, οὐ ταχθεῖσα πρεσβεύειν γένους (479),

leads the girls within the temple and may well be the eldest among them (her talk of marriage at 523-24, 579-80, and 591-92 implies that she is of marriageable age); the Argive herald Copreus and Eurystheus in their appearances at the beginning and end; and Heracles and Hebe in their capacity as twin deities of youth. Cf. Burnett 1976.5 n.4.

10. Lesky 1977.235 observes that the messenger's entrance halts Iolaus' κάτω ὁδός and turns it toward the coming rejuvenation. Grube 1941.171 suggests that the dark tones of this scene anticipate her vengeance later.

11. On the theme of βία, see Burian 1977.6 and Burnett 1976.23.

12. Lesky 1977.234-37 suggests a discrepancy between Iolaus' position as described at 603-4 and that shown in 633-35, to be explained by the loss of an intervening scene reporting Macaria's death; cf. Cropp 1980.

13. The dialogue repeatedly opposes verbs of doing to expressions of wishing, wanting, and seeming: cf. 692 and 731-37. Zuntz 1955.29 speaks of the passage as "almost Aristophanic ridicule," and Burian 1977.11 labels it "perhaps the most overtly comic in extant tragedy."

14. As Burian 1977.12 n. 33 observes, the relation between Iolaus' onstage weakness and offstage vigor is one of "total contrast."

15. His remarks at 297-303 on the importance of marrying within one's station are somewhat off the point, as is his kind but useless (γενναῖα...ἀλλ' ἀμήχανα, 464) suggestion to Demophon that he be delivered to the enemy (cf. 466-67). Zuntz 1955.28 notes Iolaus' tendency to moralizing generalizations.

16. Zuntz 1955.36 describes her entrance as being "like a chicken in a thunderstorm." Lesky 1977.237 compares the comic character of the drunken Heracles in *Alc.* and Clytemnestra's address to Achilles at *Iph. Aul.* 819 ff.

17. Burnet 1976.8, comparing Creusa and Apollo in *Ion*, notes the comic overtones in the aged Alcmene's complaints of ill-treatment by her lover.

18. So Iolaus, on his knees in formal supplication of Demophon, puts himself totally at his mercy: "be a kinsman to these children, be their friend, father, brother, master (δεσπότης)" (229-30). The word is also used of Athena, who is the city's "mother, guard and δέσποινα" (772).

19. Cf. Burian 1977.16 n. 43. The point is even stronger if we accept the emendation κρατοῦσα in 884.

20. Zuntz 1955.36-37: "how alike they are. . . . The law of lawlessness has

been used against her and she uses it in return when her chance comes."
Fitton 1961.457: "Alcmena...seems spiritually hardly better than her
persecutor." Avery 1971.560: "Alcmene takes on some of the bad
qualities which had been attributed to Eurystheus earlier." Burian
1977.17: "In effect she has become another Eurystheus. She puts into
practice here the same unrelenting hatred of the enemy that he practiced
so long."

21. Iolaus refers to αἰδώς, αἰσχύνη, and behavior that is αἰσχρόν at 6, 43,
    200, 223, 460, 541, 700.

22. The passage recalls Hera's readiness to "eat Priam and Priam's children
    raw" to appease her anger (3.34-36), thereby associating Hecuba's anger
    with the terrible χόλος of Hera.

23. The theme is perhaps implicit in the *Theogony* in the representation of
    Earth, to the extent that she is in a sense "old" by reason of her antiquity
    if not her appearance. It is Earth who initiates the violent revenge
    (τίσιν, 210) on Sky and who later (though the passage may be an
    interpolation) produces Typhoeus, who attempts a kind of last revenge
    on the new order of Zeus.

24. Gutmann 1977.309. Also interesting in light of Gutmann's own
    fieldwork is the frequency with which elderly men achieve heightened
    religious power and/or prestige as priests and mediators between the
    divine and human worlds, qualities Iolaus evinces if not in an official
    capacity in his piety and in the favor the gods show him.

25. M. Mead, "Ethnological Aspects of Aging" (cited in Gutmann 1977.311)
    Cf. de Beauvoir 1972.488, who remarks that old age is often a liberating
    period for women: "all their lives they were subjected to their husbands
    and given over to the care of their children; now at last they can look after
    themselves."

26. On the subject in general, see Bremmer 1985 and Lacey 1968.116-17, 175
    and notes.

27. Cf. Lacey 1968.22 and n.20.

28. On the Greek mother-son relationship as one of conflict and tension, see
    esp. Slater 1968.28 ff.

29. That Plato (*Laws* 775E-776B) recommends against the practice suggests
    his awareness of the ill-will it created.
    Alcmene is necessarily under the κυρίεια of some male whether of
    Hyllus or, if he is to be considered a minor, of Iolaus as his guardian. In
    this context, the anxious exchange between Alcmene and Iolaus (712-

16) also suggests her apprehension for her legal and social status in the event of his death.

30. On the representation of elderly women in Aristophanes, see Henderson 1987.

References

Avery, H.C. 1971. "Euripides' 'Heracleidai'," *AJPh* 92.539-65.

de Beauvior, S. 1972. *The Coming of Age,* tr. Patrick O'Brien. New York.

Bremmer, J.N. 1985. "La Donna Anziana: Liberta e Indipendenza," in *Le Donne in Grecia,* ed. Giampera Arrigoni. Rome. 275-98.

Burian, P. 1977. "Euripides' *Heraclidae:* An Interpretation," *CPh* 72. 1-21.

Burnett, A.P. 1976. "Tribe and City, Custom and Decree in *Children of Heracles,*" *CPh* 71. 4-26.

Cropp, M. 1980. "*Herakleidai* 603-4, 630 ff. and the Question of the Mutilation of the Text," *AJPh* 101. 283-86.

Delebecque, E. 1951. *Euripide et la Guerre du Péloponnese.* Paris.

Falkner, T. 1985. "Euripides and the Stagecraft of Old Age," in *The Many Forms of Drama,* ed. K. Hartigan. Lanham, MD. 41-45.

Fitton, J.W. 1961. "The Suppliant Women and the Herakleidai of Euripides," *Hermes* 89. 430-61.

Grube, G.M.A. 1941. *The Drama of Euripides.* London.

Gutmann, D. 1977. "The Cross-Cultural Perspective: Notes Toward a Comparative Psychology of Aging," in *Handbook of the Psychology of Aging,* eds. J.E. Birren and K.W. Schaie. New York. 302-26.

Henderson, J. 1987. "The Crones of Aristophanes," *TAPhA* 117. 105-29.

Lacey, W.K. 1968. *The Family in Classical Greece.* Ithaca, NY.

Lesky, A. 1977. "On the 'Heraclidae' of Euripides," *YClS* 25. 227-38.

McLean, J.H. 1954. "The *Heraclidae* of Euripides," *AJPh* 55. 197-224.

de Romilly, J. 1968. *Time in Greek Tragedy.* Ithaca, NY.

Slater, P.E. 1968. *The Glory of Hera.* Boston.

Taylor, H. and R.A. Brooks. 1981. "Introduction" to *The Children of Herakles,* Oxford. 3-26.

Vellacott, P. 1975. *Ironic Drama.* Cambridge.

Zuntz, G. 1955. *The Political Plays of Euripides.* Manchester.

_____. 1947. "Is the *Heraclidae* Mutilated?" *CQ* 41. 46-52.

5

"Do Not Go Gently..."
Oedipus at Colonus and the
Psychology of Aging

Thomas Van Nortwick

A stranger arrives, is recognized by certain telltale signs, and dies.
These are hardly unusual plot twists in a Greek tragedy. But the
alien is not a vigorous adventurer defying the dictates of the gods: he is
a very old man, looking only for death in the place assigned to him by
his destiny. In this as in so many other ways, Sophocles' *Oedipus at
Colonus* is an unusual play. Indeed, 'unusual' would be too kind a word
in the view of the work's detractors, who have seen it as a rambling
pastiche, showing the effects of the author's dotage—Sophocles was,
after all, nearly ninety when he completed his last play.[1] But if he was
old enough for us to suspect his powers of intellection, was he not also
in a position to be considered an expert on how it might feel to *be* a
man looking death in the face? My purpose here is to examine the
Oedipus at Colonus in a way that takes this special qualification into
account. Recent work on the psychological effects of aging has
suggested that there may be certain attitudes and perspectives that are
typical for males in certain kinds of societies as they reach old age.[2]
Looking at Sophocles' last version of the tragic hero in the light of
these findings will not solve all the problems scholars have been
grappling with these many centuries, but it will afford a fresh
perspective that tends to support a more positive assessment of the
play.

My approach may seem problematic. The psychology of aging is a
relatively new field — indeed, the influence of Freud's fascination with
infantile states has meant that only fairly recently has attention been
paid to *any* part of adult life from the perspective of developmental

132

psychology.[3] Furthermore, the obvious importance of cultural factors in any assessment of psychological patterns in the aged raises some questions in regard to my purpose here. The risk of anachronism is of course present in any attempt to read a Greek play through the prism of modern theoretical methodology. We do, on the other hand, have some evidence, from fifth-century sources, about typical attitudes toward the aged, evidence against which we can measure our modern models. At the same time, one particular area of modern research, the cross-cultural study of aging, has produced information about psychological patterns in old men which is less likely to be culture-specific.[4] It is this particular area of research that will be especially important for my purposes. There are, it seems, certain attitudes toward the world which characterize old men in a widely diverse group of traditional, sometimes preliterate cultures, western and eastern. Reading the play with these characteristics in mind provides a fresh angle from which to view the remarkable transformation of Oedipus, one that reveals yet again the complexity and profundity of Sophocles' vision. In taking this approach, I make no attempt to offer proof of any particular theory about aging, or indeed of *proving* anything about the play. My aim is to enrich our understanding of a complex work of art by suggesting a dimension of experience as yet unexplored by scholars to which it responds.

David Gutmann, the most prolific student of cross-cultural patterns of aging, has isolated the following common characteristics in the psychological makeup of old men in traditional societies:

First of all, he sees movement from active to passive mastery of the environment.

> . . . we see traces of an autonomous current in human development that urges men in their younger and middle years towards competitiveness, agency and independence, and in later life towards some reversal of these priorities: familism takes priority over agency; a receptive stance, particularly in regard to women, tends to replace independence; passive affiliation with supernatural power tends to replace the control and deployment of human strength.[5]

This affiliation with the supernatural, combined with the obvious fact that the old are closer to the mysteries of death and thus the world of spirits, can make the old man a kind of intermediary between humans and gods:

> But the final paradox of the gerontocrat's power is that it stems as much from weakness as from the particular wisdom or skills that he may have acquired over time. Precisely *because* of their frailty, the aged are moving into the country of the dead; they take on some of the fearsome aura of the corpse that they will soon become. Furthermore, in old age, a strong spirit is revealed in its own terms, no longer masked by the vitality of a young body. Thus, besides intersecting the mythic past, the aged overlap the spirit world which they will soon enter; and as they blend with that world they acquire its essential physiognomy and powers... Clearly, the old traditionalist's power does not depend on his ability to dominate men, but on his ability to influence God.[6]

Gutmann also observes that, on the other hand, longevity seems to be linked to a *resistance* to passivity, to a preservation of some kind of active engagement with the world:

> Integral to active mastery, and perhaps to longevity, is the capacity to externalize aggression, to turn potentially debilitating inner conflicts into external struggles. This author has observed that surviving traditionalists frequently complain about a faceless "someone" who is trying to rob or kill them. In some cases the enemy is clearly a metaphor of death.[7]

In addition, Gutmann found that old men have a fear of being viewed as an *alien, an outsider.* While the power that can accrue as a result of being thought of as somehow closer to the gods can be a source of security and well-being for old men, that power is not, however, according to Gutmann, a sufficient condition in itself of that sense of security:

> This depends on his claim not only to the love of God but also to the love of his children. As de Beauvoir (*The Coming of Age* [New York]) observes, "A surer protection—than magic or religion—is that which their children's love provides their parents.[8]
>
> ...societies that sponsor an egocentric, self-seeking spirit in the population will be lethal to young and old alike. But societies which

sponsor altruism, and the formation of internalized objects, provide security to these vulnerable cohorts. The internal object, an emotionally invested representation abstracted from a long history of shared interaction, has constancy and relates the past to the present. Accordingly, the older person who acquired true object status transcends his immediate condition. His child does not see in the parent a useless, ugly person. Rather, he still relates to the vigorous, sustaining parent that he once knew, as well as the weak person immediately before him. By keeping his object status the older person avoids becoming the *stranger*, and is thereby protected against the fear and revulsion aroused by the "other." There is a much noted tendency for the aged to reminisce, and even to relive their earlier life. Though taken as a sign of egocentricity, this may be an adaptive move to escape the lethal condition of "otherness." As they reminisce, the elders seem to be saying, "See me not as I am, but as a total *history,* and as someone who was once like you."[9]

Although these excerpts cannot do justice to the richness of Gutmann's findings, they will provide a sufficient starting point for looking at the play. To summarize, the move from an active to a passive relationship with the world provides the older man with a new source of power and prestige in the eyes of his fellow citizens. Though he loses some leverage because of his decreased physical strength and vitality, he gains in influence because of the common perception that he is somehow *closer* to the supernatural sources of power in the cosmos. The dark side of this new stance is that a certain pugnacity, an active externalization of internal conflicts, seems to be correlated to longevity. The other significant factor in the old man's level of power and influence, both in his own eyes and in the eyes of his fellows, is the preservation of *object status* as a parent. As long as his children see him as the sum of his past and present, and not as a relic unconnected to his former status, he avoids becoming a useless alien, a stanger in his own home.

It will be objected, quite rightly, that Athenian culture of the fifth century was hardly preliterate or unsophisticated, like the societies Gutmann analyzes. Indeed, the generally negative view of aged men in the Greek literature of the time is consistent with that found by modern researchers in urbanized, Western societies.[10] In these latter studies, the 'human nature' approach, which has transformed the studies of infancy and early childhood, seeing specific types of behavior

135

as expressions of 'genotypes' of human development, has given way to a 'reactive' theory of development, which sees behavior patterns in later life as the result of local economic and social conditions, or age-graded kinship and ideological arrangements of particular societies. Thus, the notion of a genotype for behavior patterns in aged populations has not been explored in cross-national studies of highly developed societies. Gutmann's study of traditional societies aims to correct that imbalance, as he sees it:

> But this socio-centric view of aging personality was formed in those largely urbanized, Western European settings where the great majority of cross-national studies have been carried out. In these complex, impersonal milieux, the aged are in a relatively victimized position: they must react to a fate that they cannot shape. It is not surprising that the "reactive" view of the aged would be persuasive for psychologists who meet them largely on urban and Western ground. However, if there are psychological genotypes, aspects of human nature specific to the aged, these will not be identified in cross-national studies, but more in genuinely cross-cultural studies, particularly those undertaken in traditional, preliterate societies, where the aged tend to have the greatest social power, and the greatest leverage over the conditions of their own nurture.[11]

The reading of the play that follows will focus on the behavior of Oedipus in light of Gutmann's categories. The fit between Sophocles' hero and Gutmann's "traditionalist" will not demonstrate that Athens was really a "traditional" society but quite the reverse—that as usual the Sophoclean hero is defined in part by the ways in which he or she differs from, or transcends, the expected modes of behavior.

The play opens abruptly, with no prologue. Oedipus, aged and dressed in rags, questions Antigone about their whereabouts. In his demeanor, meek and passive, there is no trace of the proud king of Thebes: this looks like a broken man. Antigone's reply affirms this initial impression. She calls him *talaiporos*, "wretched"(14) and gingerly helps him to sit down and rest from the "long journey" (20) he has endured. Here is an apt example of the passivity of old men, whether we are looking from the perspective of modern psychological research, or merely observing the normal state of affairs in Greek tragedy. Oedipus has no demands to make of anyone, humbly asks for *smikron,* "a pittance," (5) is willing to take less. His sufferings, he says, have taught him "acceptance," *stergein* (7). We are far away here both from the vigorous, self-confident ruler of the *Oedipus Rex* and from the angry, abusive father who curses his sons with death later in this play. An acquiescent Oedipus will return at the very end of the action, but one already transfigured by his impending kinship with the gods into something in between mortal and immortal.

Oedipus is meek because he is feeble, but also because he is afraid. As "strangers," *xenoi* (13), he and Antigone are suspect to the local inhabitants, and may be driven out. The first resident they encounter is indeed suspicious, alarmed that the old man has taken a seat in the sacred grove of the Eumenides. After calming this man down and dispatching him to Athens to fetch Theseus, father and daughter hide in the grove to listen in secret to the chorus of elders from Colonus who have been told of a stranger in their midst. Their opening song is not promising for Oedipus:[12]

> ὅρα. τίς ἄρ' ἦν; ποῦ ναίει;
> ποῦ κυρεῖ ἐκτόπιος συθεὶς ὁ πάντων,
> ὁ πάντων ἀκορέστατος;
> προσδέρκου, λεῦσσέ νιν,
> προσπεύθου πανταχῇ.
>   πλανάτας,
> πλανάτας τις ὁ πρέσβυς, οὐδ'
> ἔγχωρος· προσέβα γὰρ οὐκ
> ἂν ποτ' ἀστιβὲς ἄλσος ἐς
> τᾶνδ' ἀμαιμακετᾶν κορᾶν,

> Look for the man! Who is he? where's he hiding?—
> where's he gone, rushed away, where now?
>   That man, of all men on earth
> the most shameless, desperate man alive!
> Look for him, press the search now
> scour every inch of the ground!
>   A wanderer, wandering fugitive
> that old man—no native, a stranger
> else he'd never set foot where none may walk,
> this grove of the Furies, irresistible, overwhelming— (117-127)

These are strong words, reflecting the fear of sacrilege, to be sure, but also the age-old suspicion and fear of anything "alien" within the magic circle marked by boundary lines.[13] Oedipus is bringing danger to

137

the precinct by "transgressing" boundaries: *peras gar/peras*, "you go too far, too far . . ." (155-156). The strong sense of *locality* in the opening scenes of the play has often been noted.[14] There is also an emphasis on physical movement, which becomes symbolic of movement on other levels. A full twenty-five lines are taken up with moving Oedipus out of the sacred precinct, the chorus sounding like a bomb squad defusing a dangerous device (176-201). The rest of the play will chronicle the progressive empowering of Oedipus as he becomes ready and able to reenter the grove, not as an intruding "stranger" but at the invitation of the gods.

These opening scenes portray Oedipus in an ambiguous position from the perspective of the psychology of aging. As a "stranger," unconnected to any enduring status in the place where he hopes to find rest, he is threatening to the locals and may be driven out. On the other hand, his passivity and lack of physical strength are accompanied by an apparently special relationship to the supernatural powers of the grove. He can offer a "gift" to the citizens of Attica, in return for the sanctuary he requires in the sacred precinct:

> ἥκω γὰρ ἱερὸς εὐσεβής τε καὶ φέρων
> ὄνησιν ἀστοῖς τοῖσδ'·

> I come as someone sacred, someone filled
> with piety and power, bearing a great gift
> for all your people

> (287-288)

The exact nature of the gift will not be revealed until later, in the exchange between Oedipus and Theseus (621-623), but Oedipus' potential as an intermediary between gods and mortals is established. That role is, as we have seen, a common one for old men in many cultures. Thus the careful attention to locale in the opening sequence is a vehicle for symbolizing Oedipus' *liminal* status, which has both positive and negative implications for him: as an intruder, he brings danger; as an intermediary between the countries of the living and the dead, he can bestow a gift on the citizens of Athens.[15]

The uncertainties surrounding Oedipus' future relationship to Athens are matched by his equally problematical relationship to his past, to Thebes and to his children.[16] An agonizing recognition scene with the chorus (210-236) establishes that Oedipus has not been healed of the scars from his disastrous kingship. Reminiscing, which might apparently be a source of self-esteem for older men, allowing them to keep their 'object status' alive, is no pleasure for Oedipus: he is effectively cut off from his past by his pollution. With the arrival of Ismene (324), the issue of Oedipus' relationship to his children, again a potential source of nurture, moves briefly into central prominence, and again the ambiguous nature of Oedipus' situation is underscored. This child, like Antigone, has remained faithful to her father, but she brings news of betrayal. In reply to a question about Polyneices and Eteocles, Ismene is at first evasive: εἴσ' οὑπέρ εἰσι δεινὰ τἀν κείνοις τανῦν. "They are — where they are . . . now's their darkest hour" (336). This brings a withering blast from Oedipus, denouncing his sons for doing nothing to help him, while his daughters have carried the burden alone. Ismene then gives details:

πρὶν μὲν γὰρ αὐτοῖς ἦν ἔρως Κρέοντί τε
θρόνους ἐᾶσθαι μηδὲ χραίνεσθαι πόλιν
λόγῳ σκοποῦσι τὴν πάλαι γένους φθοράν,
οἷα κατέσχε τὸν σὸν ἄθλιον δόμον·
νῦν δ' ἐκ θεῶν του κἀλιτηρίου φρενὸς
εἰσῆλθε τοῖν τρὶς ἀθλίοιν ἔρις κακή,
ἀρχῆς λαβέσθαι καὶ κράτους τυραννικοῦ.
χὠ μὲν νεάζων καὶ χρόνῳ μείων γεγὼς
τὸν πρόσθε γεννηθέντα Πολυνείκη θρόνων
ἀποστερίσκει, κἀξελήλακεν πάτρας.
ὁ δ', ὡς καθ' ἡμᾶς ἔσθ' ὁ πληθύων λόγος,
τὸ κοῖλον Ἄργος βὰς φυγάς, προσλαμβάνει
κῆδός τε καινὸν καὶ ξυνασπιστὰς φίλους,
ὡς αὐτίκ' Ἄργος ἢ τὸ Καδμείων πέδον
τιμῆς καθέλξον, ἢ πρὸς οὐρανὸν βιβῶν.

At first they were eager to leave the throne to Creon, not to pollute the
   city any longer:
they saw calmly* how the blight on the race,
ages old, clung to your long-suffering house.
But now some god, some sinister twist of mind
has gripped them both, some fatal, murderous rivalry—
they grab for power, the sceptre and the crown.
Now the younger, like some hot-blooded boy,
strips his elder brother Polyneices,

seizes the throne and drives him from his homeland.
But the exile—a flood of rumors fills our ears—
the exile's fled to Argos ringed in hills,
he embraces new kinsmen, bound by marriage,
and a whole massed army of new friends.
Soon, he tells them, Argos in arms
will drag the plain of Thebes from glory
or lift its name in praises to the stars. (367-381)

A further exchange reveals that there are new oracles, telling of
Oedipus' coming power over Thebes:

Ισ. σὲ τοῖς ἐκεῖ ζητητὸν ἀνθρώποις ποτὲ
    θανόντ' ἔσεσθαι ζῶντά τ' εὐσοίας χάριν.
Οι. τίς δ' ἂν τοιοῦδ' ὑπ' ἀνδρὸς εὖ πράξειεν ἄν;
Ισ. ἐν σοὶ τὰ κείνων φασὶ γίγνεσθαι κράτη.

ISMENE
Soon, soon the men of Thebes will want you greatly
once you are dead, and even while you are alive—
they need you for their welfare, their survival.

OEDIPUS
What good could anyone get from the like of me?

ISMENE
They are in your hands, the oracle says,
their power rests in you. (389-392)

It is a sad thing for a man to hate his sons under any circumstances,
but Oedipus' animus is particularly troubling. As an exile from his city,
Oedipus might still take some solace in the love and support of his
children. This has been possible in the case of Oedipus' daughters, but
the betrayal that he sees in the behavior of his sons causes him to cut
himself off from them, and so from the nurture they might provide.
The dispute between Oedipus and his sons will continue to a climax in
the exchange with Polyneices later in the play. In the meantime,
Ismene's messages serve to link this dispute with the issue of Oedipus'
power to help or harm Thebes. In his first exchange with Theseus,
following Ismene's revelation, the old man foresees the time when his
gift to Athens will come to fruition, helping his adoptive countrymen,
harming his Theban tormentors:

ἵν' οὑμὸς εὕδων καὶ κεκρυμμένος νέκυς
ψυχρός ποτ' αὐτῶν θερμὸν αἷμα πίεται,
εἰ Ζεὺς ἔτι Ζεὺς χὠ Διὸς Φοῖβος σαφής.

some far-off day when my dead body, slumbering, buried
cold in death, will drain their hot blood down,
if Zeus is still Zeus and Apollo the son of god
speaks clear and true. (621-623)

Once again, Oedipus' status is ambiguous. Estranged from the past, he
cannot retain the former status that he held in Thebes, and so is adrift
in a way that makes him vulnerable; at the same time, his position on
the threshold of death allows him to wield a new kind of power, one
aspect of which is the ability to issue potent curses against his
enemies.[17] The first of these is directed against his sons (421-460); the
next will be aimed at Creon. In both cases, the new prophecies about
Oedipus' power embolden him to strike out at the very parts of his past
that might, in other circumstances, have been a source of comfort in his
old age.

The anger displayed against his sons has already made Oedipus
more animated and vigorous than he appeared at the beginning of the
play. The arrival of Creon furthers this transformation. Creon begins
by calling attention to Oedipus' appalling condition and to the
wretched life that Antigone has had to endure in order to take care of
her father (740-752). This sounds at first like a sympathetic gesture,
but it soon becomes apparent that Creon means to shame Oedipus:

ἆρ' ἄθλιον τοὔνειδος, ὦ τάλας ἐγώ,
ὠνείδισ' ἐς σὲ κἀμὲ καὶ τὸ πᾶν γένος;

There, heaven help me,
is that painful enough — the shame I heap on you?
Well, it mortifies me too, and all our people. (753-754)

This unfriendly advance receives a scorching rejoiner:

ὦ πάντα τολμῶν κἀπὸ παντὸς ἂν φέρων
λόγου δικαίου μηχάνημα ποικίλον,
τί ταῦτα πειρᾷ κἀμὲ δεύτερον θέλεις
ἑλεῖν, ἐν οἷς μάλιστ' ἂν ἀλγοίην ἁλούς;

What brazen gall! You'd stop at nothing!
From any appeal at all you'd wring

141

some twisted, ingenious justice of your own!
Why must you attack me so, twice over,
catching me in the traps where I would suffer most? (761-764)

Clearly Theseus' reassurances have given Oedipus a new confidence, and an angry exchange between the two old men ensues. At first, Oedipus stridently denounces the hypocrisy of his brother-in-law's agruments: however, he is soon reduced again to abject terror when Creon reveals that he has taken Ismene captive. Oedipus' sense of security is still fragile, and Creon has struck at the most sensitive place. He renders Oedipus yet more vulnerable by taking custody of Antigone, who has come to be an extension of her father, his link to the world of light:

Οι. ποῦ, τέκνον, εἶ μοι;   Αν. πρὸς βίαν πορεύομαι.
Οι. ὄρεξον, ὦ παῖ, χεῖρας.   Αν. ἀλλ' οὐδὲν σθένω.

OEDIPUS:
Where are you, child? I need you!

ANTIGONE:
—Overwhelming me, dragging me off!

OEDIPUS:
Your hands, dear—touch me.

ANTIGONE:
I can't, I'm helpless. (845-846)

Now alone, stripped of the nurture of his daughters, Oedipus has seemingly lost the newfound power that his liaison with Athens was affording him. Facing deportation himself, he summons that one weapon left to old men who are feeble to protect themselves, a curse:

μὴ γὰρ αἵδε δαίμονες
θεῖέν μ' ἄφωνον τῆσδε τῆς ἀρᾶς ἔτι,
ὅς μ', ὦ κάκιστε, ψιλὸν ὄμμ' ἀποσπάσας
πρὸς ὄμμασιν τοῖς πρόσθεν ἐξοίχῃ βίᾳ.
τοιγὰρ σὲ καὐτὸν καὶ γένος τὸ σὸν θεῶν
ὁ πάντα λεύσσων Ἥλιος δοίη βίον
τοιοῦτον οἷον κἀμὲ γηράναι ποτέ.

No!—

let the powers of this place permit me,
let me break their sacred silence, one more curse.
You, you swine — with my eyes gone, you ripped away
the helpless darling of my eyes, my light in darkness!
So may the great god of the sun, the eye of the day
that sees all things, grant you and your race
a life like mine — blind old age at last! (864-870)

This is Oedipus' last trump, and the Theban thugs begin to take him away. Just at this moment, Theseus arrives (bearing the fragrance of melodrama) to save the old man once more. Troops are dispatched to thwart the abduction of the daughters, and Creon is taken into custody. Now it is Creon who must rely on words alone:

πρὸς ταῦτα πράξεις οἷον ἂν θέλῃς· ἐπεὶ
ἐρημία με, κεἰ δίκαι᾽ ὅμως λέγω,
σμικρὸν τίθησι· πρὸς δὲ τὰς πράξεις ὅμως,
καὶ τηλικόσδ᾽ ὤν, ἀντιδρᾶν πειράσομαι.

So oppose me any way you like. My isolation
leaves me weak, however just my cause.
But opposing you, old as I am,
I'll stop at nothing, match you blow for blow.
A man's anger can never age and fade away,
not until he dies. The dead alone feel no pain. (956-959)

As if to demonstrate this last assertion, Oedipus launches into his most blistering attack yet, calling Creon *O lem' anaides,* "Unctuous, shameless...", and then follows with an extended defense of his past behavior, saying that he committed criminal acts against his will and that the gods have made him suffer because of an ancient grudge against his *genos,* "family": how could he be responsible for things that happened before he was born (960-968)? Whether these remarks are justified or not does not concern me here. It is more important for my purposes to note how Oedipus' *apologiae* have grown increasingly assertive as the play has progressed. The chorus' curiosity prompts two earlier reveries, at 203-291, and 521-548. In both instances, Oedipus is dragged reluctantly into the past, and his attempts at self-justification are minimal. Here, on the other hand, Oedipus himself initiates the review, and his defense of his past acts is much more spirited. He even

143

goes so far as to draw what seems to him to be an unflattering comparison to Creon's own behavior:

ἀλλ' ἓν γὰρ οὖν ἔξοιδα, σὲ μὲν ἑκόντ', ἐμὲ
κείνην τε ταῦτα δυσστομεῖν· ἐγὼ δέ νιν
ἄκων τ' ἔγημα, φθέγγομαί τ' ἄκων τάδε.

> But at least I know one thing:
> you slander her and me of your own free will,
> but I made her my bride against my will (985-987)

Clearly anger has mobilized Oedipus once again. In this instance, his fury toward Creon has allowed him to turn some of the poisonous feelings about his past outward, against his new tormentor. As we have seen, the ability to do just this, to externalize conflicts, seems to be a source of strength for old men. As the play has progressed, Oedipus has moved from a helpless, feeble alien into a much more vigorous old man. Part of this comes from the support that Theseus has provided, and part from the oracles that have predicted great powers for Oedipus in the future; yet another part has been generated, however, by the anger that Oedipus feels toward his sons and toward Creon for their part in his present predicament. The exchange with Polyneices brings this particular aspect of Oedipus' character to its fullest and most vivid expression.

True to his word, Theseus returns with Antigone and Ismene. So great is Oedipus' gratitude that he forgets himself for a moment:

καί μοι χέρ', ὦναξ, δεξιὰν ὄρεξον, ὡς
ψαύσω φιλήσω τ', εἰ θέμις, τὸ σὸν κάρα.
    καίτοι τί φωνῶ; πῶς σ' ἂν ἄθλιος γεγὼς
θιγεῖν θελήσαιμ' ἀνδρὸς ᾧ τίς οὐκ ἔνι
κηλὶς κακῶν ξύνοικος; οὐκ ἔγωγέ σε,
οὐδ' οὖν ἐάσω. τοῖς γὰρ ἐμπείροις βροτῶν
μόνοις οἷόν τε συνταλαιπωρεῖν τάδε.
σὺ δ' αὐτόθεν μοι χαῖρε καὶ τὰ λοιπά μου
μέλου δικαίως, ὥσπερ ἐς τόδ' ἡμέρας.

> Give me your right hand,
> my king, let me touch it, if it's permitted,
> kiss your face... wait —

144

What am I saying?
You touch *me*? How could I ask? So wretched,
a man stained to the core of his existence!
I ask you? Never! I wouldn't let you,
even if you were willing. No, the only ones
who can share my pain are those who've borne it with me.
Theseus, stay where you are and take my thanks!
And give me your loyal care in time to come,
just as you have until this very hour. (1130-1138)

This is one of the most poignant moments in Sophoclean drama. In his wretched old age, Oedipus has had no one outside of his loyal daughters to whom he might reach out in gratitude. Now, presented with this rare occasion for human contact, this opportunity to break the terrible physical isolation he has endured, he must once again draw back into himself. The mention of his daughters, who have shared his suffering as much as they can, sets up the last great confrontation of the play, between Oedipus and Polyneices. Theseus mentions that a stranger has been asking for an interview with Oedipus. The man comes, we discover, as a suppliant, flinging himself on the altar of Poseidon while Theseus tries, once again, to complete a sacrifice. Questioning Theseus about the stranger, Oedipus becomes increasingly animated, until Argos is mentioned:

Θη. ὅρα κατ' Ἄργος εἴ τις ὑμῖν ἐγγενὴς
ἔσθ', ὅστις ἄν σου τοῦτο προσχρῄζοι τυχεῖν.
Οι. ὦ φίλτατε, σχὲς οὗπερ εἶ.   Θη. τί δ' ἔστι σοι;
Οι. μή μου δεηθῇς.   Θη. πράγματος ποίου; λέγε.
Οι. ἔξοιδ' ἀκούων τῶνδ' ὅς ἐσθ' ὁ προστάτης.
Θη. καὶ τίς ποτ' ἐστίν, ὅν γ' ἐγὼ ψέξαιμί τι;
Οι. παῖς οὑμός, ὦναξ, στυγνός, οὗ λόγων ἐγὼ
ἄλγιστ' ἂν ἀνδρῶν ἐξανασχοίμην κλύων.

THESEUS:
See if you have a relative in Argos,
someone who might beg this favor of you.

OEDIPUS:
Friend—stop right there!

145

THESEUS:
What's the matter?

OEDIPUS:
Ask no more.

THESEUS:
About what? Tell me.

OEDIPUS:
Well I know, I can hear it in your words—
I know who the suppliant is.

THESEUS:
Who in the world?
And why should I have any objection to him?

OEDIPUS:
My son, king — the son I hate! His words alone
would cause me the greatest pain of any words,
any man alive (1167-1174)

No episode in the play is more controversial than the scene between Oedipus and his elder son. The plot seems to be moving along toward some kind of happy ending, with Creon and his nefarious henchmen dispatched, the old man and his faithful daughters reunited. Oedipus has had the opportunity to defend his past behavior, so that even if we are not totally convinced of his innocence, at least we feel some greater sense of closure. To bring Polyneices on at this point, retarding the denouement in a plot that has already wandered more than is pleasing to some, seems perverse.

The chorus immediately preceding has given us a view of old age that appears to reflect common ideas about aging in Sophocles' day (1211-1248). The thrust of these lines is that old age is a wretched state, best left as soon as possible, certainly not an invitation to the kind of self-assertion that characterized Oedipus' behavior in the scene to come.[18] Furthermore, the exchange with Polyneices shows us an Oedipus who seems singularly preoccupied with present and past injustices for someone about to pass into some eternity or other. That Polyneices wants to use Oedipus for his own ends is clear enough — in

146

this sense he differs little from Creon. Yet the ugly manner that characterizes Creon's speeches, veering between unctuous flattery and bullying threats, is quite absent here: Polyneices has wronged his father and he admits it (1265-1270); he begs for forgiveness, tells the story of his recent past, and reveals the reason for his supplication: whichever side Oedipus favors in the struggle between himself and his brother will be victorious (1331-1332).

The reply to all of this is at first a stony silence, but finally Oedipus is goaded into replying, and the result is hair-raising, a vitriolic denunciation of both sons, a vicious curse:

σὺ δ' ἔρρ' ἀπόπτυστός τε κἀπάτωρ ἐμοῦ,
κακῶν κάκιστε, τάσδε συλλαβὼν ἀράς,
ἅς σοι καλοῦμαι, μήτε γῆς ἐμφυλίου
δόρει κρατῆσαι μήτε νοστῆσαί ποτε
τὸ κοῖλον Ἄργος, ἀλλὰ συγγενεῖ χερὶ
θανεῖν κτανεῖν θ' ὑφ' οὗπερ ἐξελήλασαι.

You — die!
        Die and be damned!
                I spit on you! Out!
your father cuts you off! Corruption — scum of the earth!—
out!—and pack these curses I call down upon your head:
never to win your mother-country with your spear,
never return to Argos ringed with hills —

                Die!
Die by your own blood brother's hand — die! —
killing the very man who drove you out!
So I curse your life out! (1383-1388)

Attempts have been made to portray Polyneices as a consummate villain who deserves everything he gets, but finally these efforts seem forced. It appears, in fact, that Sophocles tries to make Polyneices as sympathetic as he can be in the circumstances.[19] Oedipus' treatment of his son cannot be justified in any convincing way, as much as we would perhaps like to see a different, more temperate response, reflecting the broad vision of a man who has lived long, felt pain, seen suffering up close. It has been suggested, plausibly enough, that we see in this behavior the signs of Oedipus moving into the status he will occupy after death, a vindictive *daimon* who works from beyond the grave to help his friends and harm his enemies.[20] But if Oedipus' behavior towards Polyneices is proleptic, it is also retrospective, in that there is a definite sense of the settling up of accounts here. Indeed, much of what Oedipus does in the play may be understood in this way—for example, the reviews of his Theban past or the encounter with Creon. The exchange between father and son marks a kind of climax in this particular theme, positioning the old man for that final brisk walk into the grove of the Eumenides.

The key to understanding the scene from my perspective here lies in the fact that Polyneices seems to carry with him, almost to embody, the dreadful curse of his family. Charles Segal has observed that the exchange between Polyneices and Antigone, which follows Oedipus' curse, rehearses a Sophoclean tragedy in miniature.[21] Though fully aware that his father's refusal spells nearly certain doom should he return to fight in Thebes, Polyneices persists in his seemingly wilful act of self-destruction. The passage is worth quoting in full:

Αν. Πολύνεικες, ἱκετεύω σε πεισθῆναί τί μοι.
Πο. ὦ φιλτάτη, τὸ ποῖον, Ἀντιγόνη; λέγε.
Αν. στρέψαι στράτευμ' εἰς Ἄργος ὡς τάχιστά γε,
καὶ μὴ σέ τ' αὐτὸν καὶ πόλιν διεργάσῃ.
Πο. ἀλλ' οὐχ οἷόν τε. πῶς γὰρ αὖθις ἂν πάλιν
στράτευμ' ἄγοιμι ταὐτὸν εἰσάπαξ τρέσας;
Αν. τί δ' αὖθις, ὦ παῖ, δεῖ σε θυμοῦσθαι; τί σοι
πάτραν κατασκάψαντι κέρδος ἔρχεται;
Πο. αἰσχρὸν τὸ φεύγειν, καὶ τὸ πρεσβεύοντ' ἐμὲ
οὕτω γελᾶσθαι τοῦ κασιγνήτου πάρα.
Αν. ὁρᾷς τὰ τοῦδ' οὖν ὡς ἐς ὀρθὸν ἐκφέρεις
μαντεύμαθ', ὃς σφῷν θάνατον ἐξ ἀμφοῖν θροεῖ;
Πο. χρῄζει γάρ· ἡμῖν δ' οὐχὶ συγχωρητέα.
Αν. οἴμοι τάλαινα· τίς δὲ τολμήσει κλύων
τὰ τοῦδ' ἕπεσθαι τἀνδρός, οἷ' ἐθέσπισεν;
Πο. οὐδ' ἀγγελοῦμεν φλαῦρ'· ἐπεὶ στρατηλάτου
χρηστοῦ τὰ κρείσσω μηδὲ τἀνδεᾶ λέγειν.
Αν. οὕτως ἄρ', ὦ παῖ, ταῦτά σοι δεδογμένα;
Πο. καὶ μή μ' ἐπίσχῃς γ'·

ANTIGONE:
Polyneices, listen to me, I beg you,
just one thing.

148

POLYNEICES:
> Dearest, what? Antigone, tell me.

ANTIGONE:
Turn back the armies, back to Argos, quickly!
Don't destroy yourself and Thebes.

POLYNEICES:
> Unthinkable —
how could I ever raise the same force again,
once I flinched in crisis?

ANTIGONE:
> Again? Oh dear boy,
why should your anger ever rise again?
What do you stand to gain,
razing your father-city to the roots?

POLYNEICES:
Exile is humiliating, and I am the elder
and being mocked so brutally by my brother —

ANTIGONE:
> Don't you see?
You carry out father's prophecies to the finish!
Didn't he cry aloud you'd kill each other,
fighting hand-to-hand?

POLYNEICES:
> True,
that's his wish — but I, I can't give up.

ANTIGONE:
Oh no...but who would dare to follow you now,
hearing oracles the man's delivered?

POLYNEICES:
I simply won't report them, not a word.
The good leader repeats the good news,
keeps the worst to himself.

ANTIGONE:
So, my brother, your heart is set on this?

POLYNEICES:
Yes — (1414-1432)

Polyneices, like so many Sophoclean heroes, will persist blindly in his determination to defy what the oracles foretell. He will avoid the curse by not speaking of it, denial being here—as so often in Greek tragedy— the final maneuver of desperate mortals.

Having delivered his last curse, Oedipus stands aside to observe in silence the inexorable workings of divine will. He might be watching himself as a younger man in the *Oedipus Rex,* vigorously defying the dictates of the gods, refusing to listen to the warnings that Tiresias tries to bring him.[22] It is almost as if Oedipus, by cursing his sons, divests himself of the taint of his past behavior, passing the curse on to his sons. In this we can see again the pugnacious old man's impulse to externalize those parts of himself that he somehow perceives as hostile to his own well-being, so that the enemy within becomes an enemy without.

Thunder follows the departure of Polyneices, a sign from the gods that the time has come for Oedipus to find that rest for which he has been searching so long. The old man's confident walk into the grove, leading his younger protector, is one of the most striking moments in Greek theatre. The frailty is all gone now, and so is the anger: Oedipus is certain that the gods want him to be right where he is, doing just what he is doing. Along with this surety comes a return to the attitude of acceptance that characterized his actions in the opening scenes of the drama. Looking at the play as a whole, we might see a tripartite structure, with the beginning and end focused on Oedipus' relationship to the gods and the middle on his relationship to mortals, in particular to his family.[23] At the same time, the opening scenes establish a clear direction for the entire drama, establishing as its goal the realization by Oedipus of his desire to make a good death:

ὦ πότνιαι δεινῶπες, εὖτε νῦν ἕδρας
πρώτων ἐφ' ὑμῶν τῆσδε γῆς ἔκαμψ' ἐγώ,
Φοίβῳ τε κἀμοὶ μὴ γένησθ' ἀγνώμονες,
ὅς μοι, τὰ πόλλ' ἐκεῖν' ὅτ' ἐξέχρη κακά,
ταύτην ἔλεξε παῦλαν ἐν χρόνῳ μακρῷ,

ἐλθόντι χώραν τερμίαν, ὅπου θεῶν
σεμνῶν ἕδραν λάβοιμι καὶ ξενόστασιν·
ἐνταῦθα κάμψειν τὸν ταλαίπωρον βίον,
κέρδη μὲν οἰκήσαντα τοῖς δεδεγμένοις,
ἄτην δὲ τοῖς πέμψασιν, οἵ μ᾽ ἀπήλασαν·
σημεῖα δ᾽ ἥξειν τῶνδέ μοι παρηγγύα,
ἢ σεισμόν, ἢ βροντήν τιν᾽, ἢ Διὸς σέλας.
ἔγνωκα μέν νυν ὥς με τήνδε τὴν ὁδὸν
οὐκ ἔσθ᾽ ὅπως οὐ πιστὸν ἐξ ὑμῶν πτερὸν
                                    ἀλλά μοι, θεαί,
βίου κατ᾽ ὀμφὰς τὰς Ἀπόλλωνος δότε
πέρασιν ἤδη καὶ καταστροφήν τινα,

When the god spoke those lifelong prophecies of doom
he spoke of *this* as well, my promised rest
after hard years weathered —
I will reach my goal, he said, my haven
where I find the grounds of the Awesome Goddesses
and make their home my home. There I will round the last turn
in the torment of my life:
A blessing to the hosts I live among,
disaster to those who sent me, drove me out!
And he warned me signs of all these things will come
in earthquake, thunder perhaps, or the flashing bolt of Zeus...

Now, goddesses, just as Apollo's voice foretold,
grant my life at last some final passage,
some great consummation at the end. (84-95; 101-103)

If we look at the entire drama as a preparation for the final mysterious disappearance and bear in mind the characteristics Gutmann has described as typical for aging men, the overall structure of the play takes on a certain coherence. Oedipus, initially excited by the thought that he may have finally found the place where his sufferings are to cease, is ready to acquiesce in whatever instructions the locals give him to secure permission to let him stay. He is meek in his acceptance of their directions as they move him out of the grove again, and is characterized in general by a *passive* relationship to the world he lives in. He can offer the inhabitants a gift not because he can actively engage with the present world of mortals, but because he is, typically for an old man, simply closer to the world beyond. At this

151

point, he seems to be literally on the threshold of that world, and his liminal status gives him leverage.

The request by the elders for information about his history, however, brings back all the horrors of the past, suddenly putting into jeopardy Oedipus' newfound sense of security, threatening him with the deadly status of "the other." It is all that he and Antigone can do to keep the locals from driving them out once again, from denying to Oedipus the sanctuary of the Goddesses. This brings the first of the three speeches of self-defense from Oedipus, which convinces the men of Colonus to await the decision of their king, Theseus, before driving the polluted alien out. At this juncture, Ismene arrives, bringing news of her brothers, and keeping the family history before us.

From here on until the departure of Polyneices, the issues arising from Oedipus' past history and his relations with his family are constantly in the foreground. As he confronts these issues, Oedipus becomes more and more assertive, until the climactic cursing of his sons at the end of the play. Having been pulled back from the threshold of death, he plunges combatively back into the world of the living and uses those sources of power available to him as an old man: cursing his enemies to keep them at bay and exorcising, in that last terrible scene with Polyneices, his own family curse. Only then, having dealt with his unfinished business, can he put aside his pugnacity and turn once again to look eternity in the face, stepping forth serenely to meet it. If there is any kind of implicit message in this structure, it would seem to be that as much as Oedipus would like to give up his struggle to live on when he first reaches Athens, he may not yet do so because he has not finished his business with this world. He must turn back to face his past once more and somehow rid himself of the pollution before he can cease fighting.

Oedipus' struggles and eventual triumph seem, then, to be structured around those attitudes which modern research would identify as characteristic of old men from traditional societies facing the prospect of death. Whether his behavior is different from that of aging males in the society of fifth-century Athens is difficult to gauge, given the relative lack of information, apart from literary works whose value as historical sources is somewhat problematical. He is certainly different from the usual portrait of old men in Greek tragedy, and especially from those in this play. To what may we attribute these differences?

First of all, it is hardly surprising, as I have said, to find a Sophoclean hero departing from the norm for his society; nor is it surprising, given Sophocles' own situation, to find him conversant with the issue of facing death. If Gutmann is right in seeing possible genotypes for the emotional and spiritual dynamics of aging in his traditional elders (and a final determination of this must await more work in the field), then our findings confirm yet another aspect of Sophocles' genius: the ability to retell an old story in such a way as to make it universally relevant to the human condition. The *Oedipus Rex,* written some twenty or so years earlier, dramatizes the problem, critical to middle age, of the limits of mortals' ability to control the world through their own knowledge. Now, in extreme old age, Sophocles seems to have confronted the question of how an enfeebled, seemingly defenseless old man can be heroic. How, in other words, can such a man face the last and greatest of life's challenges and achieve that measure of *transcendence* that characterizes all Greek heroic figures, while being at the same time wholly reflective of what is most common in the life we lead? That his answers are perhaps disquieting to us, challenging our notions of how elderly people ought to behave, is entirely consistent with the ability of all great works of art to lead us beyond comfort to a deeper truth.[24]

Notes

1. The strongest objections to the episodic nature of the play come from U. von Wilamowitz (cf. T. von Wilamowitz 1917.332, 352). See also Robert 1915.469-70, and Jebb 1900.xliii. Lately critics have been prone to defend the play's integrity. See, e.g., Whitman 1951.196-97, Knox 1966.143-62, Gellie 1972.159-60, Burian 1974.408-10, Winnington-Ingram 1980.248-79, and Segal 1981.362-408. Reinhardt's appraisal of the overall structure of the play (1979.193-24=1933.202-32) is still one of the best treatments.

2. The available data, and these are not yet very extensive, indicate that there are clear differences between the way males and females evolve psychologically in adulthood. See Lowenthal 1975, Levinson et al. 1978.8-9, Gutmann 1977.309 and 1975, and May 1980.71-161.

3. See Gould 1972.521-31, Neugarten 1977.626-49, and Levinson et al. 1978 ix-x.

4. See Gutmann 1977 with extensive bibliography. Gutmann has been a pioneer in the cross-cultural study of aging. His work has involved the analysis and synthesis of massive amounts of field work done by himself and other scholars, and the application to this work of theoretical models from developmental psychology. Thus, though my references are predominantly to Gutmann's work, there lies behind it the research of many other scholars, as his bibliography will attest. For an interesting contrast to Western patterns, see Palmore and Maeda 1985.

5. Gutmann 1977.308.

6. *Ibid.* 314.

7. *Ibid.* 308-9.

8. *Ibid.* 314.

9. *Ibid.* 315-16.

10. For the view of old men in Greek tragedy, see Knox 145 and Falkner 1987. It is interesting to note that Knox singles out Tiresias as an exception to the generally negative view. The Theban prophet epitomizes the "passive mastery" that Gutmann and others have seen as a typical source of power for older men in traditional societies.

11. Gutmann 1977.303.

12. The Greek text is that of A.C. Pearson (Oxford 1928); all translations, with the exception of single words, which I translate, are from Robert Fagles, *Sophocles: The Three Theban Plays* (New York 1984). Fagles has very occasionally adopted different readings of the Greek text, in which cases (marked with an asterisk) I have adapted his translation to fit the Pearson text.

13. Gellie 1972.366.

14. See Jones 1962.222ff., Gellie 1972.160, Gould 1973.90, Winnington-Ingram 1980.249, and Segal 1981.364.

15. See Segal 1981.386ff.

16. See Gellie's interesting remarks (1972.165-66) on the two disparate themes that he sees Sophocles working with in regard to the relationship of Oedipus to his past.

17. On cursing as a weapon of old men see Gutmann 1977.305.

18. See Falkner 1987.

19. E.g., Adams 1957.173-74, Meautis 1957.164, Whitman 1951.211-12, Gellie 1972.177, and Winnington-Ingram 1980.258. Easterling 1967.1-

13 takes a middle ground, finding fault with Polyneices, but also seeing it as Sophocles' intention that we pity Polyneices and be appalled at the curse.

20. See Knox 1966.148, Winnington-Ingram 1980.275ff., and Segal 1981.389.

21. Segal 1981.389

22. On the parallels between this scene and Oedipus' encounter with Tiresias in *Oedipus Rex,* see Seidensticker 1972.268-69.

23. See Reinhardt 1979.195.

24. Thanks are due here to Thomas Falkner and Judith de Luce for their gentle prodding and hard work on my behalf, and to the anonymous reader who gave careful attention to this paper.

References

Adams, S.M. 1957. *Sophocles the Playwright.* Toronto.

Burian, P. 1974. "Suppliant and Savior: Oedipus at Colonus," *Phoenix* 28.408-29.

Easterling, P. 1967. "Oedipus and Polyneices," *PCPhS* 193.1-13.

Falkner, T. 1987. "Strengthless, Friendless, Loveless: The Chorus and the Cultural Construction of Old Age in Sophocles' *Oedipus at Colonus,*" in *From the Bard to Broadway*, Latham, Maryland.

Gellie, G.H. 1972. *Sophocles: A Reading.* Melbourne.

Gould, J. 1973. "Hiketeia," *JHS* 93.74-103.

Gould, R. 1972. "The Phases of Adult Life: A Study in Developmental Psychology," *American Journal of Psychiatry.* 129.521-31.

Gutmann, D. 1975. "Parenthood: Key to the Comparative Psychology of the Life Cycle?" in *Life-Span Developmental Psychology: Normative Life Crises,* eds. N. Datan and L. Ginsberg. New York.

———, 1977. "The Cross-Cultural Perspective: Notes Toward a Comparative Psychology of Aging" in *Handbook of the Psychology of Aging,* eds. J. Birren and K. Schaie. New York.

Jebb, R.C. 1900. *Sophocles: The Plays and Fragments, part II: The Oedipus Coloneus.* Cambridge.

Jones, J. 1962. *On Aristotle and Greek Tragedy.* London.

Knox, B. 1966. *The Heroic Temper.* Berkeley.

Levinson, D. et al. 1978. *The Seasons of a Man's Life.* New York.

Lowenthal, M., M. Thurnher, and D. Chiriboga. 1975. *Four Stages of Life.* San Francisco.

May, R. 1980. *Sex and Fantasy.* New York.

Meautis, G. 1957. *Sophocle, Essai sur le Heros Tragique.* Paris.

Neugarten, B. 1977. "Personality and Aging" in *Handbook of the Psychology of Aging,* eds. J. Birren and K. Schaie. New York.

Palmore, E. and D. Maeda. 1985. *The Honorable Elders Revisited: A Revised Cross-Cultural Analysis of Aging in Japan.* Durham, N.C.

Reinhardt, K. 1979. *Sophocles,* trans. H. Harvey and D. Harvey. New York (orig. publ. Berlin 1933).

Robert, C. 1915. *Oidipus,* vol. 1. Berlin.

Segal, C. 1981. *Tragedy and Civilization: An Interpretation of Sophocles.* Cambridge, Mass.

Seidensticker, B. 1972. "Beziehungen zwischen den beiden Oidipus-dramen des Sophocles," *Hermes* 100.255-74.

Whitman, C. 1951. *Sophocles: A Study in Heroic Humanism,* Cambridge, Mass.

von Wilamowitz, T. 1917. *Die dramatische Technik des Sophokles.* Berlin.

Winnington-Ingram, R.P. 1980. *Sophocles: An Interpretation.* Cambridge.

6

The Ashes and the Flame:
Passion and Aging in Classical Poetry[1]

*Stephen Bertman**

---

*M*illennia after Helen is said to have followed her husband Menelaus from Troy's blazing ruins, the 20th century poet Rupert Brooke pondered what their married life would have afterwards been like. Brooke imagined the sort of sequel a Homer would have refrained from describing.

> How should he behold
> That journey home, the long connubial years?
> He does not tell you how white Helen bears
> Child on legitimate child, becomes a scold,
> Haggard with virtue. Menelaus bold
> Waxed garrulous, and sacked a hundred Troys
> 'Twixt noon and supper. And her golden voice
> Got shrill as he grew deafer. And both were old.
>
> Often he wonders why on earth he went
> Troyward, or why poor Paris ever came.
> Oft she weeps, gummy-eyed and impotent;
> Her dry shanks twitch at Paris' mumbled name.
> So Menelaus nagged; and Helen cried;
> And Paris slept on by Scamander side.[2]

Homer, Brooke implies, was wise to end the tale where he did. Roses are best remembered in bloom rather than in decay, and so is it with *eros:* love is a play that should mercifully spare us its final act — the once-passionate lovers as senior citizens.

Yet Homer, fascinated as he was by the course of wrath, could not have failed to be curious also about the path of love, an emotion just as powerful. So in the third book of the *Iliad* (380-448) he portrays Helen's love for Paris after years have passed, a love turned rancid by time and introspection. And, contrary to Brooke's assertion, Homer *does* let us view an older Menelaus and Helen. In the fourth book of the *Odyssey* we meet the royal couple in Sparta, years after the war. Despite Menelaus' reclaiming of his wayward wife, once home she could bear him no more children (4.3-14). The once sensuous Helen is now compared to virginal Artemis (4.122), and her barrenness is contrasted with the exotic fertility and abundance of Egypt (4.127, 229-232, and 404f.).

This ironic portrait of marital reconciliation prefigures another and more important reunion in the poem: that of Penelope and Odysseus, kept apart by ten years of war and another ten of post-war separation. Because of the passage of twenty years, it is a fortyish Penelope to whom Odysseus will return, a notion Homer plays with as he earlier tempts Odysseus with an offer from Calypso: immortality in exchange for spending his life with *her*. With a combination of factual honesty and tact, Odysseus admits that in physical terms Penelope would be no match for divine Calypso. "I readily acknowledge," he says (5.216f.), "that you surpass prudent Penelope in form and stature, for she is mortal, while you are undying and ageless." Nevertheless Calypso understands how much Odysseus yearns to see his wife, for whom he longs day after day (5.209f.). That yearning, we and Calypso see, is not to be reckoned in "form and stature", but in terms that transcend them.

Even so, Odysseus himself must undergo physical rehabilitation before being reunited with his wife. To prepare Odysseus for his reunion, Eurynome the housekeeper bathes, anoints, and clothes him, and the goddess Athena showers handsomeness upon him, making him taller and more broad-shouldered (23.153-157). The goddess even makes thick, curly hair grow on his (balding?) head (23.157-158).

After Penelope tearfully embraces her long-lost husband, Athena magically lengthens the night of their passionate reunion by holding back the chariot of the Dawn (23.241-348).

Eos, goddess of the Dawn, had herself known the meaning of love, and had learned the effect of aging upon love and passion. When she arose, Homer tells us (*Iliad* 11.1 and *Odyssey* 5.1), she arose "from her bed beside noble Tithonos." The story of Eos and Tithonos is told in the Homeric *Hymn to Aphrodite,* where it is narrated by none other than Aphrodite herself (218-238).

Eos, it seems, had fallen in love with a man named Tithonos, a member of Troy's royal family. Knowing that Tithonos was mortal, Eos asked the king of the gods, Zeus, for a special dispensation, that Tithonos be allowed to live forever in order that she might love him eternally. Zeus granted the goddess' wish, but with results she had not anticipated.

> Poor fool! Queenly Dawn did not think to ask for youth as well and exemption from old age. Now as long as precious youth was his, Tithonos rejoiced in Dawn of the golden throne, the early-born, living with her by the currents of Ocean at the edge of the world. But when the first gray hairs flowed down from his handsome head and noble chin, queenly Dawn abstained from his bed, though cherishing him still in her halls and bestowing upon him food, ambrosia, and fine raiment. Yet when old age finally crushed him and he could not move or lift his limbs, this is the plan that seemed best to her: she laid him down in a room and closed the shining doors. There his voice endlessly babbles, nor is there any vigor such as once stirred in his pliant limbs.

The story of Tithonos weds the themes of love and mortality, reminding us that human beings are not meant to live forever and showing us that such a blessing would soon become a hideous curse without everlasting youth. Speaking to her own mortal lover, to whom she tells the tale, Aphrodite concludes: "Merciless old age will soon enshroud you, remorseless old age which eventually stands beside everyone, deadly, wearying, hateful even to the gods" (243-245).

Such animosity toward aging is reflected also in the traditional epithets for old age found elsewhere in Homeric poetry: στυγερόν, "hateful" (*Iliad* 19.336); λυγρόν, "miserable" (*Iliad* 10.79, 18.434, 23.644; *Odyssey* 24.249-250); and χαλεπόν, "harsh" (*Iliad* 8.103, 23.623; *Odyssey* 11.196). The heroic age measured manhood by the standard of physical prowess, and that is precisely what old age deprived the individual of, for it was a time when "might is undone" (*Iliad* 8.103). The superannuated warrior was consigned to the less than enviable role of watching others fight or offering advice that was often ignored (*Iliad* 3.150-153, 4.321-325, 23.643-645).[3]

In the Archaic Period (the 7th and 6th centuries B.C.) poets continued to address the woes of old age. Theognis complained: "Alas for youth and alas for ruinous old age! The one because it goes; the other because it comes" (1.527-528). Alcaeus bemoaned "incurable decrepitude" (9 & 10.175), while Solon lamented "evil old age approaching" (1.24). Noting the special frustrations of aging, Semonides observed that "old age, which no one wants, overtakes a man before he reaches his goal" (1.1.11-12).

Some dramatists of fifth-century Athens agreed with their poetic predecessors. Echoing Mimnermus (1.2.9-10), the chorus of Sophocles' *Oedipus at Colonus* said not being born is best; but, saving that, it is preferable to make a quick exit before the evils of old age descend —"abhorrent old age, powerless, unsociable, friendless, in which all the worst evils cohabit" (1211ff.). Another elderly chorus in Euripides' *Hercules* declared: "Miserable, murderous old age I hate," viewing it as a form of divine punishment and a burden heavier than the rocks of Mt. Aetna (637ff.). Such comments were not reserved for tragedy alone, as the comic old-men's chorus of Aristophanes' *Wasps* shows when it rhetorically asks: "There certainly are many terrible evils in old age, aren't there?" (443). Indeed, the fact that so many Greek choruses consist of the elderly points up the painful ambiguity of being old: having wisdom but being unable to affect the course of human affairs. The elderly stand by and watch in anguish the unfolding of events they can only observe but not control.

The Greek corollary to this resentment toward aging was the love of youth, a love celebrated for centuries in Greek sculpture, most notably in the statues of young men and women of the Archaic Period and the Classically idealized figures of the Parthenon frieze. Youth was the moment of humankind's biologic perfection, a fact keenly felt by a culture driven by the inner compulsion to excel and recognize excellence in all things. Except for the Hellenistic Period, Greek sculptors habitually eschewed the portrayal of the elderly and the physical deterioration and degeneration they embodied.[4]

Yet even as they affirmed the preciousness of youth, the Greeks realized the bittersweet truth that such preciousness is short-lived. Simonides saw that many failed to appreciate how much they soon would lose:

> As long as a man holds in his hand the beautiful flower of youth, he light-heartedly assumes that many things have no end, not expecting himself to grow old and die, and not anticipating — when healthy —his ever falling ill. How naive are they who think this way, not realizing that for mortals youth and life itself are short. (37)

In a less serious vein, an anonymous Hellenistic poet advised: "Enjoy your prime, for everything will soon decline: one summer turns a kid into a shaggy old goat!" (*The Greek Anthology* 11.51).

It was not simply youth that faded away, however, but the precious beauty that accompanied youth. In this respect, human beings were likened to the natural world surrounding them. Said Mimnermus in the 7th century B.C.:

> We are like the leaves that come into being in flowering springtime, growing rapidly in the rays of the sun, enjoying for a short span the blossom of youth... Soon comes the harvest of youth, as soon as the sun spreads its light upon earth. (1.2.1-8)

A similar lesson was learned by a Latin poet a thousand years later as he strolled through a rose garden and saw one flower blooming while another decayed.

> One moment, all on fire and crimson glowing,
> All pallid now and bare and desolate.
> I marvelled at the flying rape of time;
> But now a rose was born: that rose is old.
> Even as I speak the crimson petals float
> Down drifting, and the crimsoned earth is bright.
> So many lovely things, so rare, so young,
> A day begat them, and a day will end.
> O Earth, to give a flower so brief a grace!
> As long as a day is long, so long the life of a rose.
> The golden sun at morning sees her born,
> And late at eve returning finds her old.
> Yet wise is she that hath so soon to die,
> And lives her life in some succeeding rose.
> O maid, while youth is with the rose and thee,
> Pluck thou the rose: life is as swift for thee.
> (*Appendix to Ausonius*, 2:
> trans. Helen Waddell[5])

161

The realization that lovely roses soon fade did not merely constitute the substance of abstract speculation on the transience of beauty; it had, in fact, profound relevance to the thinker's own condition. Even as it sought to create the beautiful, so was the Greek consciousness viscerally repelled by the ugly. Just as καλός meant "beautiful" and "good", so αἰσχρός meant "ugly" and "shameful"; morality and aesthetics were one. When those aesthetics applied to oneself, the moral component applied as well. Thus to live and age was to be trapped by life itself in an inescapable and progressive process of uglification, with no escape but through death. To become old was to become ugly; to become ugly was to grow physically undesirable to others and offensive even to oneself. No writer ever put these sentiments more succinctly than a 4th century B.C. poet named Crates.

> Time's fingers bend us slowly
> With dubious craftsmanship
> That at last spoils all it forms.
> (18; trans. Kenneth Rexroth[6])

This transformation of the outer self would have been especially and acutely painful to a people like the ancient Greeks, a people so sensitive to beauty, so passionately in love with life.

Such external deterioration had internal implications, for an individual who was no longer physically attractive would have less chance finding sexual fulfillment. The general distress over aging, which we have already encountered, thus acquires an erotic focus. Here the negative aspects of aging (physical debilitation and disfigurement) are looked upon as impediments limiting the capacity of the individual to give love and be desired.

So Anacreon humorously observed that a man's white hair could make a lady turn up her nose (1.15). For Mimnermus, however, the erotic implications of aging were deadly serious, for without love life itself was not worth living.

> What, then, is life if love the golden is gone? What is pleasure?
>   Better to die when the thought of these is lost from my heart:
> the flattery of surrender, the secret embrace in the darkness.
>   These alone are such charming flowers of youth as befall
> women and men. But once old age with its sorrows advances

upon us, it makes a man feeble and ugly alike,
heart worn thin with the hovering expectation of evil,
    lost all joy that comes out of the sight of the sun.
Hateful to boys a man goes then, unfavored of women.
    Such is the thing of sorrow God has made of old age.
        (1.1-3; trans. Richmond Lattimore[7])

It was a Roman poet, however, who penned the most savage indictment of old age and its effect on male sexuality. Snarling at those who naively prayed for longevity, Juvenal said

A long old age is full of continual evils:
Look, first of all, at the face, unshapely, foul, and disgusting,
Unlike its former self, a hide, not a skin, and chopfallen;
Look at the wrinkles too, like those which a mother baboon
Carves on her face in the dark shade of Numidian jungles.
Young people vary a lot; one, you will find, is more handsome,
One more robust, but the old are all alike, and they look it —
Doddering voices and limbs, bald heads, running noses, like children's,
Munching their bread, poor old things, with gums that are utterly toothless,
Such a disgusting sight to themselves, their wives, and their children.
They are even despised by Cossus the legacy-hunter.
Wine is no good anymore, food everlastingly tasteless.
As for the act of love, that long ago was forgotten,
Or if you should try, though you play with it all night long,
You will never rise, you cannot, to meet the occasion.
This is a state of things to pray for, this impotent sickness?
When desire outruns performance, who can be happy?
    (10.190-209; trans. Rolfe Humphries[8])

Over a century earlier, Cicero had praised old age, finding remarkable consolation in the loss of sexual appetite and sensual pleasure (*De Senectute,* 12-14). "What a splendid service aging renders," he declared, "if it takes from us the most depraved aspect of youth" (12.39). Denigrating the "bondage of passion" (3.7), he quoted from Plato (*Republic* 1.329c) an anecdote about the playwright Sophocles who, when asked if he still engaged in sex, is said to have replied: "Heaven forbid! I was only too glad to escape from that thing as I would from a savage and raging master" (14.47). Such sentiments, however, would have little impressed Mimnermus and Juvenal, who raged "against the dying of the light."[9]

According to Aristophanes, the aging process took a heavier toll on women than on men. In wartime, he says in the *Lysistrata,* young women can grow old for want of a groom.

> When a soldier's come home, even if he's gray, he can quickly find himself a young girl to marry. But a woman's time is short, and if she doesn't make the most of it, then no one wants to marry her, and she'll sit at home feeding on empty dreams. (593-597)

To compensate for this decline in marketability, the upstart female legislators in Aristophanes' *Ecclesiazusae* pass a law requiring that men, before marrying young women, sleep with old women first (616-617 and 877-1111, especially 1015-1020).

The reality underlying such humor was plaintively voiced in a stanza attributed to Sappho.

> Down has gone the moon
> and Pleiades, half-gone is
> night, time passes,
> and I lie down alone. (111)

The poet here invokes the Pleiades, a constellation whose setting traditionally told farmers it was time to seed their fertile fields. Identifying herself with the solitary (and feminine) moon, the poet in her barren solitude senses in the passage of the stars her own alienation from the rhythms of earthly fertility. Time passes, and she lies alone.

In later Classical poetry, the woman who lost, or would lose, her beauty and sex appeal became a frequent theme. In such poems the poet assumes the role of a scorned lover who either mocks the woman who scorned him (because she is now old and unattractive to others) or vows that someday such vengeance will be visited upon her. These "I told you so" or "You'll be sorry someday" poems were written in Greek and Latin between the 3rd century B.C. and the 6th century A.D.

Macedonius the Consul, for example, described a once-lovely woman whose waxing moon had waned (*The Greek Anthology* 5.271). Myrinus joked that his former lover could pass for Deucalion's antediluvian grandmother (*The Greek Anthology* 11.67). Rufinus compared his old girlfriend to a neglected tomb (*The Greek Anthology* 5.21), while Horace warned his former lover that she'd become "a hag forlorn in a deserted alley" (*Odes* 1.25.9-12; trans. Charles Edwin Bennett[10]). For Ovid, the threat of aging became a device to coax a woman into showing affection.

> Bronze shines from being handled, and a pretty dress begs to be worn, but houses abandoned by tenants soon sink into ruin. Beauty, unless you offer it, grows old with disuse, but it takes more than a single lover to make things right. (*Amores* 1.8.51-54)

The litany of insults in these poems points to the physical changes an aging woman probably feared. Gray hair is mentioned by Callimachus, Agathias Scholasticus, and Julianus, Prefect of Egypt (*The Greek Anthology* 5.23, 273, and 298), with Agathias terming it "the Nemesis of Desire," because it comes first to those who deserve it most. Rufinus, Macedonius the Consul, and Julianus cite wrinkles (*The Greek Anthology* 5.76, 233, and 298), with Rufinus telling how a once beautiful woman now has "a wrinkled face uglier even than an old monkey's." Agathias Scholasticus names drooping eyebrows and pendulous breasts (*The Greek Anthology* 5.273).

The most brutal attack on failed feminine beauty is found not in Greek but in Latin poetry, in the writings of the 1st century A.D. poet Martial. Except in the verses of Martial's contemporary, Juvenal, its surgical savagery is unmatched anywhere in ancient literature.

> Here you are, Miss Oldlady, having lived through
> the reigns of three hundred consuls, and you have
> three hairs left on your head, and four teeth,
> a chest like a cricket, legs the color of an ant,
> a forehead with more folds in it than a matron's gown
> and breasts that sag like spiderwebs. The mouth
> of a Nile crocodile looks narrow compared with your
> gaping jaw. The croaking frogs of Ravenna prattle
> more melodiously than you, and the Atrian mosquito
> hums a prettier tune. You see about as well
> as an owl at dawn. You smell like rank he-goats,
> you have the rump and tailfeathers of a scrawny old duck.

And your bony cunt could outstare Diogenes,
when the lamp is out and the attendant lets you in
to join the other whores in the cemetery.
In mid-August heat the winter chill grips your bones
but fever can never gain an inch. Now, after two hundred winters,
you have the gall to want to marry, and madly seek a man
to cuddle up to your ashes. It's as if a piece of marble
suddenly started itching. Is someone to call you wife
and hail you as spouse whom old Philomelus recently
referred to as a grandmother? I suppose you will order
your corpse dug up from the grave and stretched out prone
on Anchoris' couch which alone might grace your wedding cry
and as a corpse-burner carry the torch for this new wedding.
Only a torch could enter that scorched cunt you own.
      (3.93; trans. Palmer Bovie[11])

By comparison, Horace's advice to Chloris (*Odes* 3.15) — that she'd best leave amorous adventures to her daughter and retire from them herself to the grave — seems mild, but both Martial and Horace shared the same view, that past a certain age making love (at least for a woman) can be obscene.

For some women, however, the answer to old age was to mask its symptoms. Poets of the 1st and 2nd centuries A.D. both Greek and Latin mention the use of such cosmetic devices as black hair-dye, wigs, and curling irons; eyeshadow, rouge, and white-lead makeup; and even imitation baby-talk as remedies for seeming old (cf. Martial 3.43 and 4.36; and Antiphilus of Byzantium, Myrinus, Lucilius, and Lucian in *The Greek Anthology,* 11.66, 67, 68, and 408). Lucian (*ibid.*) wisely states that rouge and powder will never Hecuba into Helen make.

Some women were singled out as exempt from the ravages of old age, women whose natural beauty or inner radiance endured despite the passage of years. Bassus of Smyrna marveled at the bride-like vitality of aged Cytotaris (*The Greek Anthology* 11.72), while Philodemus(*The Greek Anthology* 5.13) praised a 60-year-old prostitute whose rich hair was still dark, whose skin was unwrinkled, and whose braless breasts stood firm as cones of dazzling white marble. To Agathias Scholasticus (*The Greek Anthology* 5.282), Melite — on the threshhold of old age — had such beauty, grace, and spirit that it showed "time cannot subdue nature." Paulus Silentiarius (*The Greek*

Anthology 5.258), while acknowledging the wrinkles and sagging breasts of Philinna, proclaimed: "Your autumn surpasses another's spring; your winter is warmer than another's summer," declaring he would rather grasp her pendulous breasts in his hands than feel the firm breasts of a younger woman.

Such women were, however — to judge by the testimony of poetry —the exception. In addition, some women, it seems, felt that past a certain age it was time to retire from love. So the courtesan Nicias, over fifty, hung up her sandals, locks of her hair, her mirror, her girdle, and certain unmentionables as farewell offerings to Aphrodite upon retiring from her profession (Philetas of Samos in *The Greek Anthology* 6.210). A similar sentiment appears in an imaginary monologue by Ausonius (*Epigram* 65). There Laïs, famous for her beauty, dedicates her mirror to Venus because she can no longer recognize herself in it and does not wish to see the woman she has now become.

In a similar vein, Propertius found he had to plead with the older woman he loved to accept him despite the discrepancy in their ages (2.18a). The example he adduced was that of aged Tithonos who accepted youthful Eos' love. Yet Propertius' contemporary, Tibullus, admitted that after a certain age lovemaking was no longer seemly (1.1.71-72).

But for some, despite age, the hungers of passion persisted. Bitto, a widow of forty, cast off her loom comb and abandoned a homemaker's skills to turn to love, for "desire is stronger than time" (Antipatros of Sidon in *The Greek Anthology* 6.47). Turning gray, Philodemus yielded to his longing for Xanthippe, proclaiming (at the advanced age of 37) "in my hungry heart the embers still burn" (*The Greek Anthology* 11.41). And the lyric poet Ibycus, falling in love again, felt like "an old race-horse, unwillingly pulling the swift chariot up to the track one more time" (2).

Yet even when caught in the tide of passion, some recognized they could no longer have what might once have been theirs. Knowing this, however, did not keep them from seeking erotic gratification, however short it fell from what once might have been. So Agathias Scholasticus humorously pleads: "When you were an unripe grape, you didn't even look my way; when you became a ripened bunch, you told me to leave; don't begrudge me now a taste of your raisin" (*The Greek Anthology* 5.304). The same theme achieved unmatched power and poignancy in the bittersweet verses of Ausonius.

> I used to tell you, "Frances, we grow old.
> The years fly away. Don't be so private
> With those parts. A chaste maid is an old maid."
> Unnoticed by your disdain, old age crept
> Close to us. Those days are gone past recall.
> And now you come, penitent and crying
> Over your old lack of courage, over
> Your present lack of beauty. It's all right.
> Closed in your arms, we'll share our smashed delights.
> It's give and take now. It's what I wanted,
> If not what I want.
> (*Epigram* 34; cf. Rufinus, *The Greek Anthology* 5.21;
> trans. Kenneth Rexroth[12])

Indeed, with aging a keener edge can come to passion. Sensing the end of life approaching, the poet realizes that for life or love it is now or never. Tibullus would say: "Too late is love and youth recalled, when hoary years have bleached an aged head" (1.8.41-42). But Horace would respond by urging his love Leuconoë to live fiercely for today (*Odes* 1.11).

> Don't ask what's wrong to know, Leuconoë, what end
> The gods will will for you, for me. Don't try
> Astrology.
> Better to take what comes:
> Many storms or (if God choose) that last
> That now breaks down on crumbling cliffs
> The winter sea.
>
> Be wise: drink deep the wine,
> Forget that thing called hope.
> For even as we speak, life leaves.
>
> Take today for all it is,
> Trusting little in tomorrow.

The philosophy of *carpe diem,* born from the realization of one's mortality, was later intensified by the poet Martial, who said: "To live today's too late for us. The wise man lived yesterday" (5.58).

The flame of life, many believed, should burn near its end even more brightly than at its beginning. "Yes, I'm old," says a festive song from the *Anacreontea* (47c), "but I can outdrink the young!" "The closer Death comes, the more it's right for an old man to have fun," says another, inspired by the remarks of ladies at a party that thinning hair should dissuade a man from thoughts of love (*Anacreontea* 7). And as another song says: "If an old man dances, his hair says he's old, but his heart says he's young!" (*Anacreontea* 39).

That old age should not be the end is proclaimed by the elderly chorus of Euripides' *Hercules* (685f.): "Not yet shall we cease from the Muses, who called us to the dance!" To live in spite of life itself, to love in contravention of nature's destructive will, to feel passionately when all else but passion has been stolen, to create, to rejoice, to endure —this is the larger message we hear. Betrayed by time, angry at erotic injustice, the poets of Greece and Rome counterattacked with verse both as an act of vital defiance and as an affirmation not only of life but of the human need to love and be loved. Tasting the bitterness of the ashes, they lived as the flame.

And yet, with all of our listening, we must hear the silences too. It is the voices of women that are missing, almost without exception. We lack their perspective on what it was like to grow old. What relationship did they see between aging and the human capacity to give love and be desired? Did they view old age as a time when erotic passion ends? Did they believe one is ever too old to love? And yes, did they ever laugh at suitors who were balding or fat?

Except for one brief poem attributed to Sappho (111) and two others too fragmentary to trust (42 and "Appendix" 6.118), we lack the literary evidence to know, having only poems written by male authors instead. This may seem to be no different from the problem presented by Classical literature in general, where writers were almost exclusively male; however, it is a far more critical issue here because of the very intimacy of the subject.

Nonetheless, the poems we do have are remarkable in their totality, for they constitute a play within a play. Composed about aging, they themselves comprise an aged body of literature, far older by thousands of years than the lifetimes their verses recall. These poems have survived, transcending time itself by the force of their conviction, by the ardor of the love they contain. On cracked manuscript pages and in fading ink we meet elderly verses whose abiding vigor endures. Among the graying ashes the embers still burn.

Notes

1. Translations used in this essay are my own unless translators' names are given. For the reader's convenience, all references to Classical works follow the divisions and numerations used in the Loeb Classical Library editions published by Harvard University Press, including (for Greek personal poetry) *Elegy and Iambus* (ed. and trans., J.M. Edmonds), *Lyra Graeca* (ed. and trans., J.M. Edmonds), and *The Greek Anthology* (ed. and trans., W.R. Paton).

2. From Rupert Brooke, "Menelaus and Helen".

3. See Querbach 1976.

4. For Hellenistic works, see Pollitt 1986.141ff.

5. Waddell 1947.27-29.

6. Rexroth 1962.44.

7. Lattimore 1960.16-17.

8. Humphries 1958.128-129.

9. From Dylan Thomas, "Do not go gently into that good night".

10. Miller 1909.48.

11. Bovie 1970.153-154.

12. Rexroth 1962.35.

References

Bovie, P., trans. 1970. *Epigrams of Martial.* New York.

Brooke, R. "Menelaus and Helen".

Edmonds, J.M., ed. and trans. 1931-1961. *Elegy and Iambus,* 2 vols. Cambridge, Mass.

————. 1945-1958. *Lyra Graeca,* 3 vols., rev. ed. Cambridge, Mass.

Humphries, R., trans. 1958. *The Satires of Juvenal.* Bloomington.

Lattimore, R., trans. 1960. *Greek Lyrics,* 2nd ed. Chicago.

Miller, M.M., ed. 1909. *Horace and the Satirists* (Vol. 3 of *The Latin Classics*). New York.

Paton, W.R., ed. and trans. 1948-1960. *The Greek Anthology,* 5 vols. Cambridge, Mass.

Pollitt, J.J. 1986. *Art in the Hellenistic Age.* New York.

Querbach, C. 1976. "Conflicts between Young and Old in Homer's *Iliad*", in *The Conflict of Generations in Ancient Greece and Rome,* ed. S. Bertman. Amsterdam. 55-64.

Rexroth, K., trans. 1962. *Poems from the Greek Anthology.* Ann Arbor.

Thomas, D. "Do not go gently into that good night".

Waddell, II. 1947., trans. *Medieval Latin Lyrics,* 4th ed. rev. London.

7

Horace's Old Girls: Evolution of a Topos

Carol Clemeau Esler

*H*orace's three odes to aging women (1.25, 3.15, 4.13) are generally interpreted as mere variations on the theme of the *moecha senescens,* a theme widely attested in poetry both before and after his time. *The Greek Anthology* is liberally sprinkled with epigrams sneering, lamenting or gloating at the decay of beautiful women grown, or growing, or soon to grow old. Some are little more than plays on standard zoological or mythological types of old age: this woman is as old as a crow, or a stag, or Hecuba; she is a contemporary of Nestor, Deucalion, or Rhea.[1] Others elaborate a single metaphor: this woman is like a tomb beside the highway, ignored by passing travelers; or a bramble trying to pass itself off as a rose; or a waning moon; or a battered and leaky ship.[2] Several of these epigrams, not surprisingly, emphasize the contrast between the subject's former beauty and her present ugliness and catalogue the features of one or both phases. Most frequently singled out are the lovely face that is now wrinkled and the beautiful hair now gray, or unkempt, or dyed, or false.[3] Although there are occasional references to other symptoms of physical decay (dull eyes, a quavering voice, sagging breasts),[4] there is a notable avoidance of the more violent forms of denigration: disgusting gastrointestinal sounds, the repulsive appearance and smell of anus and genitals, and so forth. Also noteworthy in the Greek epigrams is the low level of emotional involvement on the part of the poets: pity, anger, even disgust—if expressed at all—are expressed without much heat. Overall, these poems convey the impression of literary exercises, ringing the changes on various aspects of a well-worn poetic convention.

Horace himself had already experimented with the harsher aspects of this topos in Epodes 8 and 12. The former is essentially a catalogue of an old woman's repulsive physical traits (rotten teeth, wrinkled face, gaping anus, sagging breasts and flabby stomach, scrawny thighs and swollen calves), which are poorly calculated to rouse the poet's desire. Epode 12 focuses more on an aging woman's unseemly behavior than on her body: she plies Horace with unwanted gifts, letters, and (above all) reproaches regarding his flagging virility; but here too some attention is paid to such physical details as the woman's repellent body odors and the revolting compound of sweat and cosmetics on her face.

In our odes, Horace dealt freely with these traditional materials, in three rather distinct ways. This paper will analyze the variations in style, tone, imagery and diction which combine to produce three fundamentally different poems; they differ both from each other and from their prototypes and parallels, despite similarities of subject matter.

The ode to Lydia (1.25)[5] catches its subject at a moment somewhere between youth and age, a moment when love has not yet deserted her entirely but is coming less frequently (*minus et minus iam*, 6), and more grudgingly (*parcius*, 1). The Janus-like character of this topic is reflected in certain dualities of style and structure: the first two stanzas, which look back to Lydia's past, are deliberately artificial, even playful: they play wittily on the conventions of amatory poetry,[6] setting up a kind of retrospective *paraklausithuron* whose lovelorn tone is mocked by ambiguities of word order: *parcius* (1), for example, is usually taken as modifying *quatiunt* ("they rattle your shutters less eagerly"), but the adverb first affects *iunctas*, suggesting the secondary sense "and those windows aren't quite so tightly shut as they used to be, either." At the end of the third line, *amatque* dangles for an instant without subject or object, producing an effect something like "and nowadays all the loving that's going on — is between the door and the threshold."

In contrast, the third and fourth stanzas,[7] which look forward to the grim future that awaits Lydia, retain, more than either of the other two odes, something of the *saeva indignatio* of the iambic treatments of this theme: of the street scene in these stanzas, commentators consistently use phrases like "sombre realism," "furchtbarer Realismus," and "truly devastating realism":[8] we see a woman, a thing "of no account" (*levis*, 10),[9] alone in a deserted Catullan *angiportus*, Thracian winds howling around her like Bacchants on a moonless night, maddened by her own unsatisfied lust like a mare in heat — an image worthy of Juvenal himself. Thus Horace mocks the pretty fiction of love that Lydia must soon abandon, with a highly-colored, quasi-satirical picture of the bitterness of approaching old age; the poet sets the elegiac and iambic conventions face to face in ironic comment upon each other.

The imagery in this poem,[10] rather than being mere static elaboration of a single metaphor, evolves in reflection of Lydia's progressive decline: in the third stanza (by implication) she is a Bacchant, the wind that "riots" (*bacchante*, 11) through the deserted alley being the objective correlative of her frustrated lust. In the next metaphor (14) she is compared to a mare in heat — still a living creature, but now bestial rather than human. In the last stanza she has become mere *aridae frondes* (19), inanimate vegetable matter, less alive than the personified door that "loves" the personified threshold in the first stanza. The bitterness of Lydia's fate is further emphasized by the diction, which is dominated by a series of vivid and violent verbs: *perire, bacchare, flagrare, furiare, saevire.*

The Chloris ode (3.15)[11] contrasts sharply with 1.25 on all these levels. By injecting into the old topos of the *moecha senescens* a new element of admonition,[12] suggesting to Chloris not only that her girlish behavior is grotesque but also what she ought to be doing instead, this poem has closer ties with certain of the philosophical odes than with the iambic tradition. Here the theme of untimely sexuality, though still central, is presented in broader and less violent terms than in 1.25, summed up by the verb *ludere* (corresponding to *paizein* in the Greek epigrams). Similarly, the theme of physical decay so conspicuous in Epodes 8 and 12 is even more muted here than in the Lydia ode.

Though the language is sufficiently damning in its implications,[13] the ugly specifics are softened into generalization and metaphor: Chloris is *maturo propior funeri* (4), she is a *nebula* among the *stellae candidae* of youth (6) — but we are spared the sight, sound and smell of her physical repulsiveness. Something of the vigor and vividness of the street-scene in the Lydia ode is echoed here in the third stanza, where Chloris' daughter Pholoe "besieges the houses of young men like a Bacchant;" the comparison of Lydia to a mare in heat is paralleled here

174

by the comparison of Pholoe to a "frolicsome deer" (12). But the tone is entirely different: Pholoe's animal-like behavior, her *ludere* (12), unlike her mother's (5), is *decens,* appropriate to her age and status, and therefore charming rather than revolting or pathetic. The style is less conspicuously mannered than in the Lydia ode. There are only two similes and one metaphor, and they are comparatively simple and conventional; the word order, by Horatian standards, is relatively straightforward and unambiguous. The tone is calm, hortatory but unheated, the verbs (except for those in the description of Pholoe) imperative or equivalent to imperatives; *fige* (2), *desine* (4), *non decet* (7-8), *non decent* (14). In contrast to the Lydia ode, in which auditory images predominate (stones rattling against shutters, wind howling, *exclusus amator* wailing, the old woman weeping and lamenting), here the few images are mostly visual, appealing to the most intellectual of the senses: we see the mist casting its shadow on the stars, the playful deer, the wool with which Chloris ought to be occupying herself, the roses and wine jar with which she ought *not* to be occupying herself. Also in keeping with the hortatory character of the poem, its diction (alone among the three odes) is dominated by words connoting propriety and moderation: *modus, rectius, decet* (twice).

The latest of the three odes, 4.13,[14] is also the longest, the most complex, and in certain respects the most Horatian. It can be read as a kind of synthesis — a characteristically Horatian synthesis — of the various strands of the tradition we have been discussing.

The poem is unique among the three under discussion, and among other treatments of the aging-woman *topos,* in the breadth of its tonal range and the complexity of the attitudes it adopts. From an expected, conventional posture of triumphant scorn in the opening lines, the ode gradually moves toward pity and even identification with its subject,[15] both subsuming and passing beyond the attitudes of the odes to Lydia and Chloris. The vindictive, almost gloating tone of the opening — *Audivere, Lyce, di mea vota, di/ audivere, Lyce* — recalls the harshness of the street scene in 1.25, with its emphasis on the bitterness of age as a richly deserved punishment for the woman's past heartlessness.

But the Lyce ode does not stop here. It moves on to consider, in much the same terms as the Chloris poem, the reasons *why* Lyce's old age is so grim a punishment: what Horace prayed for, his *vota,* was not merely that she should grow old (which was inevitable, with or without his intervention),[16] but that Lyce (like Chloris) should grow old ungracefully — i.e., without a philosophical acceptance of the changes of attitude and behavior that would make her old age dignified and worthy of respect: *fis anus et tamen* ...(2). Like Chloris, Lyce's mistake is that she insists on acting like the girl she no longer is —drinking, flirting, trying futilely to hide the ravages of time; again, like Chloris, she is given a foil, a young and desirable woman for whom *ludere* is appropriate, not *impudens* (4) as it is for Lyce.

At this point, however, the poem again veers away from the line taken by its predecessor. Unlike Chloris, Lyce is not exhorted to accept philosophically the adjustments and retrenchments that time forces upon her: the imperative mood is conspicuously absent from this poem. Rather, the phrase *volucris dies* (16)[17]—"silks and jewels cannot bring back that season which *fleeting time* has shut up, once and for all, in the public archives" — this phrase acts as a kind of trigger that sends the poem off in a new direction: "fleeting time" now suggests to Horace something more than the ludicrous girlishness of an aging woman. Lyce becomes, in the next two stanzas, a symbol not merely of female folly but of mortality in general. And human mortality, to Horace, is no matter for scorn or triumph. The startling outburst of emotion and direct personal involvement in stanza 5 conveys a radically altered reaction to Lyce's misguided efforts to halt (or ignore) the passing of time. Suddenly it is no longer the repulsiveness of her behavior that strikes the poet most forcefully, but its pathos.

This shift in tone and point of view in stanza 5 is reflected in several points of style. The insistent anaphora (of which there is very little in the two earlier poems) of *quo...quo...quo, illius...illius*, and *quae...quae* is as emotional as that of the opening lines (*Audivere, Lyce, di...,/ audivere, Lyce*), but the emotion expressed is very different: longing and regret now, rather than scorn. The exclamation of grief, *heu,* in the middle of line 17, is the only occurrence of such a word in any of the three odes. Most significant of all, in the three odes it is only here and in the opening line that we find first-person pronouns referring unequivocally to the poet himself.[18] It was *his* prayer that Lyce suffer a humiliating old age, and it was *he* who long ago loved the young Lyce whose beauty made his senses reel, *quae me surpuerat mihi* (20).

The diction too reflects the unique orientation of this ode: it is heavy with words and phrases connoting age, time, movement and change: *fieri, anus, lentus, transvolare, refugere, tempus, fasti, volucris dies, breves anni, diu, vetulus.* The imagery referring to Lyce herself follows a progression reminiscent of the series Bacchant-horse-dead-leaves in 1.25: she is first compared to a once-living thing now dead (*aridas quercus,* 9-10), then to an animal emblematic of excessively long life (*cornicis vetulae,* 25), and finally to an inanimate object once warm and bright but now cold and useless (*dilapsam in cineres facem,* 28).

Comparative study of these three odes provides a fascinating glimpse into Horace's mind as he explores the possibilities and implications of a poetic convention. In 1.25 he plays with a variety of literary postures borrowed from elegy, iambic, and satire, keeping a considerable distance between himself and his subject.[19] In 3.15 he adopts something of the tone and diction of the philosophical odes, offering Chloris a kind of *rectius vives*; seriousness of intent here takes precedence over artfulness of manner. In 4.13 we find at last something of the complexity, the doubleness of vision, the shift from mood to antithetical mood which we associate with some of Horace's best and most characteristic work. In the end, it would seem, the aspect of the old *topos* that spoke most poignantly to him was not the repulsive appearance or ludicrous behavior of aging women but the pathos of the passing of time and the losses it brings to women and men alike.

Yet for all his skill and ingenuity in repeatedly reworking various aspects of the aging-women theme and in ultimately molding them into an artefact unmistakably his own, there is one significant limitation on Horace's exploration of these materials. Though he goes further than other poets in accepting his kinship with women in the aging process, he never takes the further step of recommending to them the compensating pleasures and satisfactions he finds appropriate to his own and other men's later years.

The women of the amatory odes — which is to say, the feminine fictions created by Horace, with whatever basis or lack of basis in Roman social history — are party girls. They have turned their backs on the aristocratic ideal of *pietas,* of devotion to the community or to the micro-community of the family. Like some fictitious Roman men (e.g., the *amatores* of elegiac poetry), they have devoted themselves to *voluptas,* their own and others', to self rather than to community, to a kind of vulgarized Epicureanism. They have, in a sense, subscribed to one part of Horace's own philosophy — the *carpe diem* half — of the enjoyment of innocuous sensual pleasures.

They have failed, however, to grasp the other side of Horace's doctrine: that such pleasures, and above all those associated with sex, are (in terms of the metaphor of which the poet himself was so fond) essentially "seasonal" in nature, the prerogative of youth and youth alone. In old age (whatever and whenever that may be) one must turn to other satisfactions: poetry and music and philosophy, occasional decorous intoxication, asexual friendships.

Why do these women fail to understand what Horace sees so clearly? More accurately, why did he never create a fictional woman who is brought (by the irresistible force of his own eloquence and logic, presumably) to see the truth about old age? The answer would seem to be that for them the emotional outlets favored by Horace are unavailable. Which is to say that Horace has given them, in their youth, no attributes or functions that can reasonably (from his point of view) be carried over into old age. Their physical beauty must inevitably deteriorate, and any erotic skills they may possess will therefore become irrelevant. Even drinking wine will become problematic in a woman's later years, because like other Romans Horace distrusts the female's ability to drink in dignified moderation: Chloris' imbibing is painted in satirical colors (*non decent . . . poti vetulam faece tenus cadi,* 3.15.14ff.), and Lyce's is *impudens* (4.13.4).

The only acquired skill (other than those associated with lovemaking and personal adornment) that Horace attributes to a few of these *hetairai* — skill in singing or playing a musical instrument — exists, in Horace's mind, exclusively to attract and delight lovers. One is reminded of the lecherous old woman of Epode 8 who scatters "Stoic pamphlets" on her bed, not because she shares Horace's interest in philosophy but because she thinks (quite wrongly) that a display of *doctrina* will impress lovers. It is apparently beyond Horace's imaginative powers to conceive of a woman, even a fictitious one, who delights in the exercise of intellectual or artistic powers for their own sake and for her own pleasure, even as he himself does. The best he can suggest for an aging woman is that she become *domiseda et lanifica* like Amymone on a monument.[20]

It is unfortunate, as Victor Estevez remarks,[21] that so sensitive and intelligent a man as Horace was unable to see beyond the assumptions of his culture to the possibility of sexual love in old age, for himself or anyone else. It is equally symptomatic of the cultural imperatives within which he worked that he was unable to extend to women the intellectual and emotional satisfactions he recommended, to himself and other men, as viable and appropriate in old age.

Notes

1. Crow, *Anth. Pal.* 11.67 (Myrinus), 11.69 (Lucilius); stag, 11.72 (Bassus); Hecuba, 5.103.4 (Rufinus); Nestor, 11.72.2 (Bassus); Deucalion, 11.67 (Myrinus), 11.71 (Nicharchus); Rhea, 11.69 (Lucilius).

2. Tomb, 5.21.6 (Rufinus); bramble, 5.28.6 (Rufinus); moon, 5.271 (Macedonius); ship, 5.204 (Meleager).

3. Wrinkles, 5.76 (Rufinus), 5.298 (Julianus Prefect of Egypt); hair gray, 5.103 (Rufinus), 5.112 (Philodemus); unkempt, 5.27 (Rufinus); dyed, 11.66 (Antiphilus), 11.67 (Myrinus), 11.68 (Lucilius); false, 5.76 (Rufinus).

4. 5.273 (Agathias Scholasticus).

5. The ode has received more sympathetic readings in recent years than it had from T.E. Page ("It has no merit, and may be omitted with advantage," *Q. Horatii Flacci Carminum Libri IV, Epodon Liber,* London 1895, 189) and N.E. Collinge ("the crudest and nastiest poem in Horace's lyrics," *The Structure of Horace's Odes,* London 1961, 52). See Boyle 1973, Henderson 1973.55-60, Pöschl 1975, Arkins 1983.

6. Henderson 1973.55-60; Pöschl 1975.189 (who characterizes the whole ode as "eine 'klassische' Synthese verschiedener Aspekte des Liebesphänomens und seiner dichterischen Gestaltungen," namely the elegiac, the iambic and the sympotic).

7. The correspondences and contrasts between stanzas 1-2 and stanzas 3-4 have been painstakingly analyzed by Pöschl 1975.188 and Boyle 1973.176-178.

8. Quinn 1980.170, Kiessling-Heinze 1955.111, Henderson 1973.58.

9. Boyle 1973.177 translates *levis* as "trash," which neatly combines the connotations of lifelessness, worthlessness, repulsiveness and profligacy.

10. Boyle 1973.177 has an especially good discussion of the imagery of this ode, which he regards as "perhaps its central strength."

11. This poem has received less individual treatment than 1.25, outside the standard commentaries. Commager 1962.249f. discusses it as an expression of the "morality implicit in time itself. Attempts to hold to the prerogatives of youth presented themselves to [Horace] not as a foible of age but as a cosmic impropriety." Henderson 1973.62f. considers only the "inverted motif" of the *exclusa amatrix* Pholoe in lines 8-10, which he sees as an allusion to the paraklausithyron and a link with 1.25.

12. Syndikus 1973.155: "ganz ungewöhnlich in einem Hohngedicht ist es . . . , dass der angegriffenen Person der richtige Weg aufgezeigt wird."

13. Syndikus 1973.154 (n.4) shows that Horace's characterization of Chloris is "schonungsloser, als es die abmildernden Übersetzungen ahnen lassen": the words *nequitiae* (2) and *famosis laboribus* (3), in particular, are quite harsh in tone and connotation.

14. Discussed by Fraenkel 1957.415f., Commager 1962.299-302, Reckford 1969.129-131, Syndikus 1973.407-412, Putnam 1986.219-235.

15. Despite important differences in theme and imagery, the tonal curve of the Lyce ode is reminiscent of that in the Cleopatra ode (1.37): both open with a shout of triumph at the downfall of a hated woman, move on to scornful vituperation and conclude on a note of sympathetic identification with the erstwhile enemy.

16. I cannot agree with the assertion of Putnam 1986.229 that the poet, who possesses "the ability to spellbind with verses," also "has jurisdiction over the processes of temporality." I would prefer to read the opening lines as a piece of momentary self-delusion on the part of the poet, comparable to Lyce's own: his sense of being in league with the *di* of time is as unrealistic as her sense of having triumphed over them. The truth is that aging poet and aging courtesan are equally powerless to control or influence the processes of time and change. Understood in this way, the opening verses help prepare us for the poet's implied realization, in the last three stanzas, that he (and we) are no more allies of the immortal gods than Lyce or Cinara. The *di* of temporality are not our servants but our common enemy.

17. Horace had used the phrase once before, at 3.28.6, where he exhorts Lyde not to be so slow about making preparations for a party, as if she imagined time was standing still *(veluti stet volucris dies)*. The repetition of the words suggests that both women, though from opposite ends of the age spectrum, are making the same mistake of underestimating the brevity of

life's joys: Lyde imagines that there is no need to hurry to snatch them, Lyce that there is no need to relinquish them once their proper season is past.

18. I agree with Arkins 1983.163 that the *me* at 1.25.7 "is not to be identified with Horace or indeed with his poetic *persona;* rather, [it] should be taken to represent any particular lover at a particular time. . . ." However, the pronoun seems to be taken as referring to the poet by Henderson 1973.57.

19. Arkins 1983.171 finds 1.25 "considerably more objective than either *Carm.* 3.15 or *Carm.* 4.13." Syndikus 1973.247 remarks "wie erstaunlich und wie bezeichnend für diese Ode gerade das Ausklammern eines persönlichen Anlasses, ja fast das Ausklammern der eigenen Person ist."

20. CIL 6.11602: "Hic sita est Amymone Marci optima et pulcherrima, lanifica pia pudica frugi casta domiseda."

21. In the conclusion of an unpublished paper, *"Aridae Frondes, Duri Lumbi:* Aspects of Aging in Catullus and Horace," which he kindly allowed me to read.

References

Arkins, Brian. 1983. "A Reading of Horace, *Carm.* 1.25," *Classica et Mediaevalia* 34.161-175.

Boyle, A. J. 1973. "The Edict of Venus: An Interpretive Essay on Horace's Amatory Odes," *Ramus* 2.163-188.

Commager, Steele. 1962. *The Odes of Horace, A Critical Study.* New Haven.

Fraenkel, Eduard. 1957. *Horace.* Oxford.

Henderson, W. J. 1973. "The Paraklausithuron Motif in Horace's *Odes,"* *Acta Classica* 16.51-67.

Kiessling, A., and R. Heinze. 1955. *Q. Horatius Flaccus Oden und Epoden.* Berlin.

Pöschl, Viktor. 1975. "Horaz C. 1,25," in *Dialogos für Harald Patzer* eds. J. Cobet, R. Leimbach, A. B. Neschke-Hentschke. Wiesbaden. 187-192.

Putnam, Michael C. J. 1976. "Horace Odes 3.15: The Design of Decus," CPh 71.90-96.

_____. 1986. *Artifices of Eternity: Horace's Fourth Book of Odes.* Ithaca, NY.

Quinn, Kenneth. 1980. *Horace: The Odes.* London.

Reckford, Kenneth. 1969. *Horace.* New York.

Syndikus. H.P. 1973. *Die Lyrik des Horaz.* Darmstadt.

8

The Old Man in the Garden: *Georgic* 4. 116-148

Jenny Strauss Clay

*T*he *Georgics* contain a host of vivid, one might even say, seductive tableaux which mutually illuminate each other, first in their immediate context, and then in relation to the work as a whole. Virgil's poem presents both a linear progression, in which each image in turn commands our attention and seems to assert its exclusive validity, and an over-arching architecture, wherein individual sections finally assume their proper configuration within the larger edifice. The complex and delicate interplay of contrasting and balancing images creates both the richness and density, but also the profound ambiguity of the *Georgics.*

This intricate interplay of balanced parts poised in equilibrium can be exemplified by the fourth *Georgic* which, as a whole, offers a counterweight to the dark themes which dominated *Georgic* 3. The terrible sexual passion and mortality which there swept the animal kingdom contrast sharply with the lighter tones of the description of the asexual and seemingly immortal bees which occupies the first half of *Georgic* 4. In turn, the narrative of Aristaeus and Orpheus, which concludes the poem, restates within a mythical framework the themes of human passion, suffering, and death, but also mysterious intimations of immortality through the complex complementarities of the figures of Orpheus and Aristaeus.[1]

Virgil employs similar techniques of framing, counterpointing, and balancing on a smaller scale within the first half of the fourth *Georgic.* The instructions concerning bee-keeping are interrupted by the poet's personal reminiscence (*memini vidisse*) of an old gardener, the *Corycius senex,* whose relation to the context of the bees has, for the most part, been ignored or misunderstood. The digression has been pointedly detached from its surroundings through an elaborate *praeteritio,* both at beginning and end. Had Virgil wished, he could have integrated the vignette of the old gardener easily into his discussion of the care and character of the bees. The necessary links lay ready at hand, for Virgil has just mentioned the bees' need for a garden environment (cf. *horti* 109), and the old Corycian, we are told, tends bees in his Tarentine garden (139-141)[2]. Instead, Virgil seems to go to great lengths to set off the picture of the old man from his main theme and to label it an excursus. This strategy throws the apparently self-contained digression, framed by the bees, into relief and obliges us to question its meaning and relation to its context far more insistently than if the poet had integrated it smoothly into the surrounding material.

> Atque equidem, extremo ni iam sub fine laborum   116
> vela traham et terris festinem advertere proram,
> forsitan et pinguis hortos quae cura colendi
> ornaret, canerem....
> . . . .
> verum haec ipse equidem spatiis exclusus iniquis   147
> praetereo atque aliis post me memoranda relinquo.

> If I were not already drawing in my sails at the
> very end of my labors and hurrying to turn the
> prow to the shore, perhaps I would also sing of
> rich gardens and what cultivation befits them.
> . . . .
> Excluded by the confines of space, I pass over these
> matters and leave them to others after me.

In the first of these lines, Virgil declares for the first time that he is nearing the end of his georgic labors. The poet's indication that his work is drawing to a close encourages his reader to look back on the work thus far and signals him to start to consider the inter-relationships between the parts up to this point. The alerted reader can now begin to notice the subtle alternation of theme and tone which makes up the architecture of the *Georgics*. He may also wonder what relation the topic of gardens has to the georgic themes considered hitherto. It appears that the subject of gardening, however attractive to the poet, cannot properly be treated within the confines of his georgic poem. Virgil has no intention of "sketching the plan of what might have been a fifth Georgic."[3] Gardens and the old gardener are somehow peripheral to the georgic world, perhaps sub-georgic because sub-urban, while the sphere of the poet could be said to lie beyond the world of the *Georgics*.[4]

Be that as it may, our first effort must be to understand the meaning of this "graceful digression," as Conington calls it, in its poetic surroundings, to ascertain why it interrupts the narrative of the bees, and what light man and bees mutually shed upon each other. Critical scrutiny has for the most part focused on either one or the other. Yet failure to understand the function of the old gardener who forms the core of the excursus entails a failure to understand the meaning of the bees. Dahlmann, for example, in his essay on Virgil's bees, completely ignores the presence of the old Corycian embedded in the text he sets out to explicate. This leads to his misreading of the bees as an unambiguous model for human society and for Augustan Rome.[5] Burck's article, on the other hand, focuses on the old gardener and illuminates many interconnections with earlier themes, especially from the second *Georgic*. However, he devotes little attention to the immediate relation between the *senex* and the framing bees. Pointing only to the industriousness which characterizes both, Burck fails to indicate the critical differences in their respective industry.[6] Similarly, Richter is satisfied to consider the bees as a "Bild der naturhaft-glücklichen Gemeinschaft" and the old man as the "naturhaft-glücklichen Einzelmenschen."[7] For Wormell, too, the gardener presents "in many ways the human counterpart of the bees he tends."[8] Surprisingly disappointing on our passage is Klingner,[9] who, while rejecting Burck's view of the close thematic connections between the gardener and the earlier books, seems content to consider the excursus to depend purely on the association of bee-keeping and gardening. Although he does wonder why Virgil should have chosen such a *Grenzfall* to illustrate the topic of gardens, Klingner makes little effort to integrate the digression into any organic relation to its context. For him, it simply continues the light tonality of the whole first half of the fourth *Georgic*. Otis' interpretation of the structure and tone of the passage is likewise insufficient. "The poet," he claims, "wants to mark a break between the introductory section (8-115) and the central panel

(149-227)" and thereby "to prolong, to intensify, to give climax to the joyful mood of the whole section."[10] One can, however, argue with some point that the episode containing the old gardener *is* the central panel of the first half of the poem, with line 228 ff. merely forming a transition to the Aristaeus epyllion. The critical consensus, for the most part—if it perceives the problem at all—tends to view the Corycian gardener as an extension of the positive and idealizing tone of the beginning of *Georgic* 4. Pridik is the only scholar I have come across who states the problem of the relation between bees and old man with some rigor and understands it as an intentional contrast. But the terms of the opposition he discovers are, I believe, false, with the bees as embodiments of life in the golden age and the old man as a representative of the *durum genus,* man in the age of iron.[11] Even those critics who uncover some questionable or disturbing overtones in Virgil's characterization of the bees do not seem to recognize how the old man in the garden provides us with a prism with which to view and evaluate the bees.[12] For Putnam, the digression, while suggesting many oppositions, finally offers "a realm apart, an imaginative garden" and an escape from the "martial impersonal bees."[13] Our task must be to reintegrate the society of the bees and the solitary old man in our interpretation as we find them integrated in Virgil's text. The architecture of the poem demands that we consider them together and explore their interrelationships. Taken as a whole, the portrait of the old Corycian stands as a counter-poise to the bees who, however marvelous (*admiranda*) they may be, can offer only a partial and problematic paradigm for human life.

If God resides in minute detail, so too does the work of interpretation. We must now turn to the details of the description of the Corycian, constantly comparing them to Virgil's bees in order to get a bearing on both. The first thing we learn about the gardener whom Virgil commemorates is that he is old. In a peculiar way, age creates a link to the bees whose most striking characteristic is their asexual nature, granted them by Jupiter, and which exempts them from erotic passion. Old age is likewise free of *amor* and the *furor* which so often accompanies it, as we have learned from the powerful and shattering animal images of *Georgic* 3. There, however, the diminution of sexual energy as well as the loss of physical prowess and ambition (*amor laudum* 3. 112) means exile (*abde domo* 3.96). The senescence of animals is disgraceful and unforgivable (*nec turpi ignosce senectae* 3. 96) and must be dealt with ruthlessly.[14] But the old age of the gardener liberates him from both passion and personal ambition and leads to a humane inner freedom and serenity. The old Corycian presents a human possibility — not, to be sure, always realized[15] — which stands midway between uncontrollable animal passion and the super-human but also inhuman unerotic nature of the bees.

If we may trust Servius, Virgil's *senex* was one of the pirates from Cilicia whom Pompey rewarded for their loyalty by settling them in southern Italy.[16] The Corycian, then, lives far from his native land, is not a Roman, and has no political ties to Rome. On his small plot of seemingly useless land, he lives in what appears to be complete isolation. Virgil mentions neither family nor children to help the old man with his chores.[17] We may compare the emphasis on the family with its clear political implications in Virgil's idealized portrait of the farmer at the end of *Georgic* 2(512 ff.). To call the old man of the fourth *Georgic* the perfect *vir bonus Romanus agricola* as Richter does in his commentary, [18] means to misread and distort Virgil's text and intention. The apolitical solitude of the Cilician gardener transplanted to Tarentum stands in pointed contrast to the extraordinary political and social organization of the bees. To the teeming hive, with its social castes and highly developed division of labor, Virgil opposes this solitary figure who tends his garden.

On his unpromising plot, he grows flowers, fruits, and vegetables amid the thistles. The flowers, at least, are cultivated for their own sake and not for food. But perhaps they indicate a sustenance of another kind: the love of the beautiful for its own sake. The old man, to be sure, is neither a poet nor an artist; for that we shall have to wait for the tragic figure of Orpheus at the end of the poem. But he possesses the human pre-condition for art: *amor florum*. Love of flowers: the expression arises naturally here, although Virgil uses it of his bees (205). There, however, it stands nearly synonymous with the *innatus amor habendi* (177). The bees' love of flowers is equivalent to their instinctual need to produce honey, to what in human terms would be called greed.[19] Through his use of terms properly applicable only to human beings, Virgil, here as elsewhere in his description of the bees, points as much to their essential differences as to their apparent similarities.

The Corycian lives under the shadow of the walls of Tarentum. He, like the rest of the *Georgics,* belongs to the Iron Age,[20] the age of cities. The over-all architecture of the *Georgics* makes this clear; the description of the old man in *Georgic* 4 corresponds exactly with Virgil's account of the genesis of the Iron Age in *Georgic* 1 (4. 125-148; 1. 125-148).[21] If the old gardener indeed supported the cause of Pompey in his youth, then his present existence implies a renunciation of sailing and warfare, both symptoms of the decline from a golden age. Living in apparently voluntary isolation, he avoids commerce with the nearby town. In fact, one of the great sources of his pride are his *dapes inemptae,* his unbought feasts (133). Against the gardener's proud self-sufficiency, we must again set the fragile dependence of the bees as Virgil presents them. While the old man creates out of an unproductive parcel of land an environment of trees and flowers which sustains him both physically and spiritually, the bees depend on the constant attention of the bee-keeper to create appropriate *sedes* for them. The bulk of Virgil's initial instructions (9-115) stresses the critical importance of the proper surrounding for the hive.[22] It must, we hear, contain the right vegetation to attract the bees and must be carefully protected from all noxious influences. Even when all is in order, the bee-keeper must occasionally intervene with greater or lesser force to seduce or compel the *instabiles animi* of the bees to return to their hive.[23] The fragility of the society of the bees is further signalled by their absolute dependence on their king. When the king perishes, the whole social order collapses as the bees tear apart the honey-combs they themselves have built (213-214). The gardener, on the other hand, depends on neither king nor keeper to transform his few acres into a paradise. Rather, he considers himself the equal of kings in his self-sufficiency and inner freedom (*regum aequabat opes animis* 132).

Similarly, while the activities of the bees are precisely regulated by the rhythm of the seasons and even by the times of the day,[24] the old Corycian, through his industry, manages to be ahead of the seasons and not merely subject to them. In spring, he is the first to pick the rose; in autumn, the first with his harvest. While winter still holds all of nature in its icy grasp, the old man is already busily gathering hyacinths; he curses the summer for its lateness and is the first to collect honey from his bees (134-141). Virgil conveys this ability to anticipate the seasons which characterizes the gardener's activity by the repeated *sera, seram, seras* (late) balanced by *primus, primus, iam, iamque* (first, now). Unlike the bees, man has the ability to change or bend the natural order for possibly productive ends.[25] The reward for such industry is the full realization of natural potential; every spring blossom bears autumnal fruit (142-143).

The culmination of the old man's art of gardening is the transplanting, not of seedlings, but of fully-grown trees (*seras ulmos* 144) and grafted plants. In Book 2, the various modes of grafting (2. 22-82) offered wonderful examples of the possibilities of the cooperation of nature and art. That which was by nature sterile could be made to bear fruit through grafting; the spontaneous energy of nature could be made productive. Here in *Georgic* 4, the old man transcends even the wondrous achievements of grafting described earlier through his transplanting of grafted plants and mature trees *in versum.*[26] The purpose of such virtuoso feats of cultivation goes far beyond utility. In the famous theodicy of the first *Georgic*, whose placement corresponds to the digression on gardening, man's slow and painful discovery of the arts is necessitated by Jupiter's suppression of the natural abundance which characterized the Golden Age. Want and scarcity form the first impulse for the art (*duris urgens in rebus egestas*); the arts emerge under the immediate pressure of utility (*varias usus...artis*). The gardening of the old man of Tarentum goes far beyond such beginnings and points to the cultivation of the arts for the sake of the beautiful. In this connection, it is well to remember, as Griffin has noticed, that Virgil's bees are stripped of their traditional affiliation with poetry and the Muses.[27] Their unpoetic nature is closely related to their unerotic nature and points forward to the erotic poet *par excellence,* Orpheus. With his Corycian, Virgil offers no portrait of the artist as an old man, but rather the fact that art — in this case, the cultivation of flowers and the transplanting of trees — transcends both instinct and utility and forms an essential impulse of the human heart.

Virgil's bees have been taken as an encomium to Augustan Rome and as a criticism of Augustan imperialism. Both sides can only be maintained by means of crude over-simplification and the suppression of one or another aspect of the bees. Whether the society of the bees is assessed positively or negatively frequently appears to depend more on the interpreter's political bias than on Virgil's text. Those who are incapable of following the poet's exhortation to marvel at the wonderful microcosm of the bees (*admiranda tibi levium spectacula rerum* 3) also cannot understand its limitations. Virgil transcends both pro- and anti-Augustan propaganda to question the nature and limits of the political in human life. We must finally recognize that Virgil's bees have more in common with Plato's *Republic* than with the Rome of Octavian. Virgil makes clear their philosophic ancestry by his citation (*quidam...dixere* 219-221) of the Platonic-Stoic doctrine of the World-Spirit, without, however, owning his allegiance to such views.

It is against the backdrop of this tradition of political idealism that Virgil sets the portrait of the private, peripheral figure of the old man in the garden. Inhabiting a remote corner of the landscape, a marginal figure between city and country, of no consequence politically, himself insignificant, he enters the poem only on the basis of the poet's memory, which retrieves him from oblivion. λάθε βιώσας: the phrase almost presents itself. Obscure and isolated from political and social organization, the old man who tends his garden presents that aspect of human nature which is strictly private and individual and whose highest embodiment is the poet, or, perhaps, the sage.

The single-mindedness of the super-human bees (*mens omnibus una* 212) and their common labor for the good of the community (*labor omnibus idem* 184) stand in opposition to the universal enslavement to passion which characterizes the animal world (*amor omnibus idem* 3. 244). But only for man is neither *mens,* nor *labor,* nor *amor* one and the same. By juxtaposing the anonymous old man in the garden against the marvelous society of the bees, Virgil indicates the irreconcilable tension between the demands of the political life and the requirements of the human heart. And this, *si parva licet componere magnis,* after all, is the great theme of the *Aeneid.*

Notes

1. For a "whirlwind doxography" of recent opinion on the meaning of the Aristaeus-Orpheus story, see Griffin 1979.61-62 and notes.

2. Klingner 1967.310 claims "dass sich der Garten eines Imkers *wie von selbst* in ein Gartengelände wie das des Alten von Tarent öffnet und

erweitert" [italics mine]. It surely could have, but Virgil carefully marks it off.

3. Conington 1898.350.

4. For the poet's landscape, see *Georgic* 2. 486ff. (*o, ubi campi....*) Cf. Putnam 1979.149 on that passage: "Virgil is imagining the source of his poetry, a landscape that at once quickens the mind and serves as intellectual and emotional retreat. Greece...." See also Perkell 1981.

5. Dahlmann 1954.562 concludes: "...durch das Gleichnis des Bienenstaates gibt der Dichter...die politisch-philosophische Begründung der gottgewollten und natürlichen Berechtigung des Prinzipates." Cf. more recently, Coliero 1971.113-114.

6. Concerning the activity of the gardener, Burck 1956.169-170 remarks: "...gerade dieses *selbstverständliche Tun* ist dem Dichter wesentlich. Denn es ähnelt *überraschend* dem naturhaften Triebe der Bienen zu ihrer Arbeit...." [Italics mine]. What unites man and bees, according to Burck, is the Jovian dispensation of *labor*.

7. Richter 1957.346.

8. Wormell 1971.430. But Wormell recognizes that "there is something uncanny" and "not wholly human" about the bees.

9. Klingner 1967.308-10. Tellingly, Klingner's main discussion is confined to a lengthy footnote.

10. Otis 1963.184; cf. Wilkinson 1969.103.

11. Pridik 1971.118 claims that "Vergil diesen korykischen Greis als einen Menschen des *durum genus* gezeichnet hat, um ihn den Bienen gegenüberzustellen, die noch am Leben der Goldenen Zeit teilhaben." "Uns scheint vielmehr hinter der vergleichenden Darstellung des Menschen- und des Bienenlebens die Sehnsucht des Dichters nach dem Verlorenen und vielleicht die Hoffnung auf Wiederkommendes durchzuscheinen" (119-120).

12. Cf. Otis 1963.183 on the bees: "There is a hollowness, an absence of solid reality in the description here that warn us against taking the bee symbols too seriously. Man, Virgil seems to be saying, is like this but not when he is really human...." Also Segal 1966.310 notes, pointing ahead to the second half of the poem: "...bees are *not* men; the metaphor does not hold." Perhaps to redress the earlier critical bias in favor of the bees, Putnam 1979.236-270 emphasizes their negative aspects. Griffin 1979.62 ff. maintains a fine sense of balance between the admirable and

questionable qualities of the bees, but never mentions the old gardener in his discussion nor does he seem to recognize how his presence in the midst of the bees helps to maintain the necessary equipoise.

13. Putnam 1979.252.

14. This contrast is brought out by Perkell 1981.

15. Consider, above all, the Aristaeus / Orpheus episode which concludes the poem.

16. Cf. Servius on line 127 and Probus *ibid*. At present (1988) I no longer believe in Servius' identification of the *senex* and hope at some point to discuss the question of his identity.

17. The only companionship alluded to in our passage is *potantibus* (146), which suggests neither political nor familial associations, but the company of friends.

18. Richter 1957.348. The un-Roman coloring of the passage is also brought out by the Greek name, Oebalia.

19. Cf. Putnam 1979.258.

20. Attempts to link the *senex* with the *aurea aetas* are misconceived. See, for example, Burck 1956.170. The *Georgics* is an iron age poem in which the golden age is irretrievably lost. Cf. Büchner 1956.1336; and Putnam 1979.107: "The era of gold has long since yielded to the iron age in which men now find themselves."

21. First noticed by Perrett 1952.70.

22. Cf. Klingner 1967.307 and Pridik 1971.113. The whole first section may be subsumed under the rubric *sedes apibus statioque* (4.8).

23. Virgil signals three main interventions on the part of the bee-keeper. First, he must lure the bees to the hives by means of attractive smells and sounds (4. 62-66). Then, he must quash their civil wars by throwing a handful of dust and killing off the inferior king (4. 86-90). Finally, swarming-fever must be suppressed by ripping out the wings of the king so that the bees will remain in their hive (4. 103-108).

24. Putnam 1979.242 notes: "Man can go a long way toward making the bees' surroundings productive. . . . Of external variables, seasonal change alone seems here beyond his capacity to master."

25. Putnam 1979.251 speaks suggestively here of the gardener's "bending of time."

26. Perhaps a playful allusion to that ordering of nature by art which creates poetry?

27. See Griffin 1979.64ff. who correctly stresses the unmusical character of Virgil's bees. Klingner 1967.317-18 notes certain important characteristics of the bees mentioned by Varro, Virgil's main source for apiary lore, but omitted by Virgil: "Gutartigkeit, mit Tapferkeit verbunden; Zugehörigkeit zu den Musen; *ratio atque ars,* Vernunft und Kunstfertigkeit, sind wenigstens nicht ausdrücklich genannt." Klingner, however, draws no conclusions from these striking omissions.

References

Büchner, K. 1956. "P. Vergilius Maro," *RE* 8A. 1201-1486 (=*P. Vergilius Maro. Der Dichter der Romer.* Stuttgart. 1960).

Burck, E. 1956. "Der korykische Greis in Virgils Georgica," *Navicula Chilonensis:* Festschrift F. Jacoby, 156-72. Leiden.

Coliero, E. 1971. "Allegory in the IVth Georgic," in *Vergiliana* (eds. H. Bardon and R. Verdiere), 113-23. Leiden.

Conington, J. and Nettleship, H., eds. 1898. *The Works of Virgil: Vol. I.* 5th ed., revised by F. Haverfield. London.

Dahlmann, H. 1954. "Der Bienenstaat in Virgils Georgica," *Akad. d. Wiss. Mainz, Abh. D. Geistes- u. sozialwis. Kl.* 10.547-62.

Griffin, J. 1979. "The Fourth Georgic, Virgil, and Rome," *G&R* 26.61-80.

Klingner, F. 1967. *Virgil.* Zurich.

Otis, B. 1963. *Virgil, A Study in Civilized Poetry.* Oxford.

Perkell, C. 1981. "On the Corycian Gardener of Vergil's Fourth Georgic." *TAPhA* 111.167-77.

Perret, J. 1952. *Virgile, l'homme et l'oeuvre.* Paris.

Pridik, K.H. 1971. *Vergils Georgica.* Tubingen.

Putnam, M.C.J. 1979. *Virgil's Poem of the Earth.* Princeton, NJ.

Richter, W. 1957. *Virgil: Georgica.* München.

Segal, C.P. 1966. "Orpheus and the Fourth Georgic," *AJPh* 87.307-25.

Servius. 1887. *Commentarii in Vergilii Bucolica et Georgica* (ed. G. Thilo). Leipzig.

Wilkinson, L.P. 1969. *The Georgics of Virgil.* Cambridge.

Wormell, D.E.W. 1971. "Apibus quanta experientia parcis," in *Vergiliana* (eds. H. Bardon and R. Verdiere), 429-35. Leiden.

9

Ovid as an Idiographic Study
of Creativity and Old Age[1]

Judith de Luce

Most discussions of old age and poetry, when they have been undertaken at all, have tended to focus on representations of old age: what it looks like, how it behaves, how it is regarded by those not yet old. In this chapter I want to take a preliminary look at the poetry of aging and the aging poet: does creativity change with age? Do the ways poets look at things change? Do the ways they express those perceptions change over time?

In order to begin looking at the relationship between creativity and old age, I propose to start with a single example. A close reading of the work of one poet cannot possibly produce general principles that would hold true for all ancient authors, but this idiographic study will provide some insight into the method and substance for a study of creativity and old age. In terms of the present chapter, I have compared selected features of the *Tristia* and the *Epistulae ex Ponto* with some of Ovid's earliest poems, the *Amores*.

Ovid recommends himself for such a study for a variety of reasons. We know that he wrote continuously from young adulthood until his death at sixty in A.D.17. In spite of some questions about the date of the *Amores* and the authorship of the *Halieutica,* we are reasonably certain about the order in which Ovid published his poems and of their dates.

Ovid presents some problems, as well, the most significant of which is that he lived in exile from the time he was fifty. Thus reading his final poems requires that at some point we distinguish between the influence of old age[2] and the influence of exile on his poetry, and that we consider whether the two may actually be synonymous in Ovid's mind.[3]

195

Reading Ovid's poetry across his lifespan, I am struck by the quantity and variety of his work, at the same time that I am puzzled by the tendency for his final poems to recall the earlier poems. Ovid wrote the *Tristia* and *Epistulae ex Ponto* when he was in his fifties: these poems generally impress their readers as dreary, repetitive, and tiresome. Even Fränkel, ever the thoughtful and kindly critic, has said of the poems: "...if we read too many poems in a row we feel keenly the heaviness of repetition as far as material content, general ideas and patterns of thought are concerned."[4]

The poet himself acknowledges the repetitiveness, in *Pont.* 3.9.39-40:

> cum totiens eadem dicam, vix audior ulli
>   verbaque profectu dissimulata carent.

> I write so often of the same things that scarce any listen, and my words, which they feign not to understand, are without result.[5]

It is precisely this tendency towards repetition, in a poet who rarely repeated himself[6], which has prompted this chapter. Ovid's final works are not only repetitive among the poems contained in the two collections, they repeat the genre and to some extend the motifs of his earliest poems. We may want to apply to Ovid Lawrence Lipking's observations about how an aging poet might conclude a poetic career. "Poetically, he redeems a series of old phrases, images, ideas, motifs —the stock-in-trade of his poetic career, by arranging them in a new creation."[7] When Lipking wrote this, he had been speaking of Eliot's *Four Quartets:* I suggest that he might as well have been writing about Ovid's exile poetry.

What follows is a preliminary examination of the broader question of creativity in old age. I have limited my discussion to a series of questions: How does old age effect Ovid's productivity? Do his perceptions of old age change as he ages? Do his perceptions of poetry and his poetic career change? What future research agenda do the answers to these questions suggest?

At the outset, we must approach these questions unburdened by assumptions about what occurs in old age as far as creativity is concerned. The lurking suspicion that, in spite of an occasional Grandma Moses or Pablo Casals or I. F. Stone, there is a decline in quality and quantity of creative work is not supported by respectable evidence.[8] Very little is known about the relationship between age and creativity, although a variety of social factors as well as the presence of stimulation and rewards play a part in the creative process. Hendricks and Hendricks have observed that "Whatever declines occur in divergent thinking over the life course can seemingly be offset by increased opportunities to explore new approaches."[9]

With that in mind, we can turn to Ovid. Old age does not seem to impair Ovid's productivity. If the *Amores* were written when he was in his twenties, Ovid wrote consistently and published regularly over a forty year period, producing at least eleven works which are extant, the lost *Medea,* and perhaps the problematic *Halieutica* in the course of that career. Among other lost works may be poems hinted at in the *Tristia* and *Epistulae ex Ponto,* poems involving the emperor or praising military victories. Not only did Ovid write continuously, but the extant works alone represent nearly every genre, from the elegiac to the epistolary to the didactic to the narrative, from the *Amores* and the *Heroides* to the *Ars Amatoria* and the *Remedia Amoris* to the *Metamorphoses* and the *Fasti* and the *Ibis.* Rather than trying his hand at something different in his final poems, however, Ovid actually echoes his earlier works.[10]

This echoing has prompted me to take as a framework for this chapter Robert Butler's theory of the life review. In an article as reliant on psychiatric therapeutic anecdote as on references to literature, Butler has examined the tendency of the elderly to engage in what can be called a life review, a "naturally occurring, universal mental process characterized by the progressive return to consciousness of past experiences, and, particularly, the resurgence of unresolved conflicts."[11] This process is "prompted by the realization of approaching dissolution and death, and the inability to maintain one's sense of personal invulnerability. It is further shaped by contemporaneous experiences and its nature and outcome are affected by the lifelong unfolding of character."[12] "Janus-like,"[13] the review tends to look forward to death and backward to what went before.

The life review may have positive or negative consequences, in part depending upon the personality of the individual undertaking the review. On the positive side, the life review may move the individual toward "personality reorganization," a process that may leave the viewer with a greater sense of meaning in her or his life. This may also account for the serenity or wisdom often attributed to the elderly.[14]

On the negative side, however, the consequences may range from reminiscence and nostalgia to anxiety and depression to the most extreme manifestation with its "obsessive preoccupation of the older person with his past."[15] The most severe consequences may occur in those who engage in this review in isolation, those who have been profoundly affected "by increasing contraction of life attachments and notable psychosocial discontinuities."[16]

The appeal of Butler's theory as a framework within which to study Ovid's exile poetry is irresistible. At fifty Ovid found himself relegated from the urbane, sophisticated, literary world he occupied, separated from his family, friends, and literary colleagues, and banished to Tomis, a community utterly alien to him. Nothing recommended Tomis to Ovid: its savage weather was intolerable, the ever present danger of attack from the neighboring tribes terrified him, the absence of other writers, or critics, or even someone to read his poetry left Ovid even more isolated. The very fact that the inhabitants spoke neither Latin nor Greek meant that this most articulate poet was deprived even of conversation.[17] Surely he was a candidate for the most extreme consequences of life review, according to Butler. But he was not forbidden from writing, and write he did, at least the ninety-six poems that we have and perhaps others as well.

As I observed at the start, an initial reading of the exile poems suggests that Ovid has returned to the genre and a number of the themes of his earliest poems. Yet even as he returns or echoes those earlier efforts, Ovid, like Eliot, makes some changes. Nagle has argued that Ovid returns to his earlier poems precisely because he is writing from exile and is anxious to point up the differences between the conditions under which he wrote as a young man and the conditions under which he now must write.[18] I suggest that while his motive may well have been to attract sympathy and aid in changing the conditions of his exile, his age and the proximity of death play an important part in how he writes.

How does the poet regard old age, and what role does death assume in his poetry? Ovid includes the *Amores* among his *iuvenalia carmina:* old age has no place here, neither does ill health. Here there are no sympathetic representatives of the elderly: the old *lena* Dipsas (1.8), for example, can summon the dead and perhaps even change herself into a bird, but nonetheless thwarts the lover's intentions.[19] Old men fare no better: the young lover is a soldier in 1.9, but an old man can be neither a good soldier nor a good lover. In 1.13, the poet asks why he must pay just because Aurora married an old man whom she detests. Finally, the impotent lover wonders in 3.7 what his old age will be like if he cannot enjoy himself in his youth. As for ill health, in these earlier poems, if the poet becomes thin or suffers from insomnia, or feels despair, it is generally within the context of his disappointment over his treatment at the hands of his mistress, as in 1.2 and 1.6.

If old age had no place in the *Amores,* death had even less. At least, the poet's serious reflection on his own mortality is missing from the earlier poems. The poem written on the death of Tibullus is an exception to this general pattern, and I will return to that poem later.

At this point, we may attribute the absence of old age to a variety of factors. Perhaps it is that as a young man Ovid no more considers the possibility of his own old age or death than any other young person; or that the aged have no place, as far as Roman culture is concerned, in affairs of the heart; or that the genre does not allow for any serious or sympathetic inclusion of old age.

Old age recurs as a motif in the later poems, and this time it is primarily his own old age that Ovid describes. This is not the comfortable old age of a Cephalus in the *Republic* — a time of peace, rich personal associations, opportunities to discuss politics and philosophy and to enjoy the attentions of the young.[20] Neither is it the vigorous old age promised in *De Senectute.* Cicero's Cato proves that reasonable diet, exercise, and challenging occupations for the mind contribute to a pleasant old age that need not be feared as a time when youthful vigor gives way to illness, diminishing mental alertness or reduced sources of pleasure.[21] But Cato was not in exile in Tomis.

In these poems we see a profoundly vulnerable, depressed man, fearful that he will either succumb to illness or to hostile attack by neighboring tribes. In fact, he regards himself as already "dead."[22] *Tristia* 3.3, addressed to his wife, presents most compellingly his equation of exile with death and his very real fear of dying in Tomis.

Ill and too weak to write, he dictates his poem. He cannot endure

Tomis: he cannot stand the climate or the water

> terraque nescio quo non placet ipsa modo 3.3.8

> and even the land, I know not why, pleases me not

He reassures his wife that she should be glad his death will free him from all the misfortunes of his exile:

> cum patriam amisi, tunc me periisse putato:
> et prior et gravior mors fuit illa mihi. 53-54

> When I lost my native land, then must you think that I perished, that was my earlier and harder death.

But death in Tomis presents new horrors to him: he envisions dying alone, without his wife's comfort, without the familiar funeral rites. He even wishes that the soul might perish with the body: otherwise,

> inter Sarmaticas Romana vagabitur umbras,
> perque feros manes hospita semper erit.
> ossa tamen facito parva referantur in urna;
> sic ego non etiam mortuus exul ero. 63-66

> a Roman will wander among Sarmatian shades, a stranger forever among barbarians. But my bones—see that they are carried home in a little urn: so shall I not be an exile even in death.

At the same time that he acknowledges that the most durable memorial for him would be his poetry, Ovid prepares his own epitaph in which he describes himself, after an immensely prolific poetic career, only as *tenerorum lusor amorum* (73). Again he looks from the end of his poetic career directly back to its start.

Tristia 4.8 takes as its theme old age and considers the physical, psychological and social consequences of growing old.

> Iam mea cycneas imitantur tempora plumas,
> inficit et nigras alba senecta comas.
> iam subeunt anni fragiles et inertior aetas,
> iamque parum firmo me mihi ferre grave est. 1-4

> Already my temples are like the plumage of a swan,
> for white old age is bleaching my dark hair.[23]
> Already the years of frailty and life's inactive time

are stealing upon me, and already 'tis hard for me in
my weakness to bear up.

What a younger Ovid had expected old age would be like does not
correspond with what his old age is like in fact:

nunc erat, ut posito deberem fine laborum
    vivere, me nullo sollicitante metu,
quaeque meae semper placuerunt otia menti
    carpere et in studiis molliter esse meis,
et parvam celebrare domum veteresque Penates
    et quae nunc domino rura paterna carent,
inque sinu dominae carisque sodalibus inque
    securus patria consenuisse mea. 5-12

Now 'twere time that I should of right cease my toils and live with no
harassing fears, to enjoy the leisure that always pleased my taste,
comfortably engaged in my pursuits, devoting myself to my humble
house and its old Penates, the paternal fields that are now bereft of their
master, peacefully growing old in my lady's embrace, among my dear
comrades and in my native land.

He describes old age as *parte...vitae deteriore,* in the midst of
which he is overwhelmed by hardship. Exile has aged him more
thoroughly than the passage of time, as the poet tells his wife:

Iam mihi deterior canis aspergitur aetas,
    iamque meos vultus ruga senilis arat:
Iam vigor et quasso languent in corpore vires....
    Pont. 1.4.1-3

Now is the worse period of life upon me with its sprinkling of white
hairs, now the wrinkles of age are furrowing my face, now energy and
strength are weakening my shattered frame.

He assures his wife that she would not recognize him, were she to
come upon him suddenly. So aged is he by *anxietas animi continuusque
labor* (8) that if anyone counted his years by his hardships, they would
think him older than Nestor. Like overcultivated land or a horse raced
too often

me quoque debilitat series inmensa malorum,
    ante meum tempus cogit et esse senem. 19-20

201

I too am weakened by the measureless series of my woes and am perforce an old man before my time.

His sentiments recall another couple to whom he refers a number of times in his exile poems.[24] Penelope had said as much when, after their interview, she ordered Eurykleia to bathe the disguised Odysseus:

> Come here, stand by me, faithful Eurykleia,
> and bathe—and bathe your master, I almost said,
> for they are of an age, and now Odysseus'
> feet and hands would be enseamed like his.
> Men grow old soon in hardship.
> *Od.* 19.357-60

In the exile poems, Ovid assumes the perspective of advanced age as he looks back on his life. In the *Tristia,* Ovid settles old scores and repays some debts as Butler would expect him to do: he also writes his autobiography (*Tristia* 4.10). Interest in this poem has often focused on the details of Ovid's life, and I will leave it to others to discuss the poem at any length. His account of why he became a poet reminds us of his earlier poems.

With his brother already embarked on a career in oratory, his father would ask Ovid why he pursued so profitless an occupation as writing. Ovid, taking his advice, attempted to give it up, but no matter how hard he tried,

> quod temptabam scribere versus erat

> whatever I tried to write was a verse. 26

This is the same poet who still cannot refrain from writing, whether he is enroute to Tomis, fending off an attack or dreading celebrating his birthday in exile.

This is the same poet who had challenged the claims of *livor edax* (*Amores* 1.15) that in the vigor of young manhood he should heed the call to the soldier's life or the lawyer's or the orator's. Refusing to follow the recommended *cursus,* Ovid chooses to write poetry instead because:

> Mortale est, quos quaeris, opus. mihi fama perennis
> quaeritus, in toto semper ut orbe canar. 7-8

It is but mortal, the work you ask of me; but my quest is glory through all
the years, to be ever known in song throughout the world.

If 4.10 looks at his life as a whole, *Tristia* 2 to Augustus becomes
Ovid's resume—part apologia, part reflection on the poetic life. After
marveling that he could write at all, since poetry got him into trouble in
the first place, Ovid speaks of his *carmen et error* (207), reviews the
kind of poetry he wrote and reports that others wrote of love, too, but
only he suffered for it.

He excuses himself for not having written weightier poems,

> at si iubeas domitos Iovis igne Gigantes
>   dicere, conantem debilitabit onus
> divitis ingenii est immania Caesaris acta
>   condere, materia ne superetur opus. 333-36

But if thou shouldst bid me sing of the Giants conquered by Jove's
lightning, the burden will weaken me in the attempt. Only a rich mind
can tell the tale of Caesar's mighty deeds if the theme is not to surpass the
work.

Ovid had written of the Giants once before, but in a far different
spirit. In *Amores* 2.1, Ovid defends his writing *levia carmina* by
claiming that he could not write anything else. There was a time when
he had dared to attempt writing of the battle of the gods and the giants,

> in manibus nimbos et cum Iove fulmen habebam,
>   quod bene pro caelo mitteret ille suo—
> Clausit amica fores! ego cum Iove fulmen omisi;
>   excidit ingenio Iuppiter ipse meo.
> Iuppiter, ignoscas! nil me tua tela iuvabant;
>   clausa tuo maius ianua fulmen habet. 15-20

I had in hand the thunder-clouds, and Jove with the lightning he was to
hurl to save his own heaven. My beloved closed her door! I—let fall Jove
with his lightning; Jove's very self dropped from my thoughts. The bolts
could not serve me; that door she closed was a thunderbolt greater than
thine.

This lies well within the traditon of the *recusatio*. Ovid uses the
repetition of *cum Iove fulmen* and *Iuppiter* to undercut any serious

defense of his poetry.[25] In fact, throughout the *Amores,* Ovid justifies his choice of genre with a similar lightheartedness. In 1.1 he insists that he has been preparing to write *arma gravi numero* (1):

> risisse Cupido
> dicitur atque unum surripuisse pedem. 3-4

—but Cupid, they say, with a laugh stole away one
foot.

Unable to persuade Cupid to leave him alone, the poet finally gives up:

> ferrea cum vestris bella valete modis! 28

Ye iron wars, with your measures, fare ye well!

Writing to his friend Macer (*Am.*2.18) Ovid claims that he took up weightier themes, but *risit Amor* (15).

In 3.1., Ovid reports that while he was considering what he ought to write, Elegy and Tragedy appeared before him. Tragedy argued that Ovid's earlier poetry was perfectly appropriate for a young man:

> quod teneras cantent, lusit tua Musa, puellae,
>   primaque per numeros acta iuventa suos. 27-28

Thy Muse has been but playing—with matter for tender maiden's song—
and thy first youth has been given to numbers that belong to youth.

Now it was time for him to turn to more mature themes. In the end, Ovid returns to writing Elegy.

In contrast to these poems, Ovid reports a dream in *Pont.* 3.3 in which Amor appeared to him: this is an Amor quite unrecognizable in the world of the *Amores*:

> stabat Amor, vultu non quo prius esse solebat,
>   fulcra tenens laeva tristis acerna manu,
> nec torquem collo, nec habens crinale capillo,
>   nec bene dispositus comptus, ut ante, comas. 13-16

There stood love, not with the face he used to have,
sadly resting his left hand upon the maple post, no
necklace on his throat, no ornament in his hair, his
locks not carefully arranged as of old.

This Amor has no reason to laugh.

While Butler's life review has informed much of this chapter, it does not provide adequate insight into the creation of art in old age. For that I return to Lipking. In *The Life of a Poet: Beginning and Ending Poetic Careers* Lipking presents Virgil as a model, certainly for Eliot, perhaps for all poets, of the problem "What is involved in husbanding a career?"[26] Lipking provides some answers: managing a canon (with the result that the poet will never want to leave anything "unfinished"); making use of other poets; and "progress, successive improvement."[27] Lipking ties Virgil's poetic career to his age, saying of the *Aeneid*, ". . . as old age comes on, he gathers all his powers for a mighty effort that epitomizes the collective wisdom of his civilization, the world as it has been and should be."[28] The conclusion of a poetic career can take many forms: at one time, only the epic was regarded as prestigious enough to conclude a career.[29] Ovid did not follow that course, however—perhaps because he had already written the *Metamorphoses*, perhaps because the effect of exile suggested a different route for him, a route that would take him back to his start. It remains to be considered, then, how Ovid felt about writing poetry.

Even as he continues to write, Ovid argues that his poetry must be excused for its appearance. In *Tristia* 1.1, for example, he excuses his poems because they were not written, as their predecessors had been, in the peace of his garden.[30] In fact, he regards the conditions under which he must write utterly uncongenial to poetry: in Tomis he has no audience, no critics, no books, no stimulation, no other poets with whom to talk or exchange poems.

But even if the conditions were conducive, would he be able to write? In *Tristia* 1.6 he assures his wife that he would make her immortal in his poetry, if only he could manage it:

> ei mihi, non magnas quod habent mea carmina vires,
> > nostraque sunt meritis ora minora tuis!
> siquid et in nobis vivi fuit ante vigoris,
> > extinctum longis occidit omne malis! 29-32

> Alas that great power lies not in my song and my lips cannot match thy merits — if ever in former times I had aught of quickening vigour, all has been extinguished by my long sorrows!

In *Pont.* 1.5, Ovid complains:

> et mihi siquis erat ducendi carminis usus,
>   deficit estque minor factus inerte situ.7-8

For me, too, whatever skill I had in shaping song is
failing, diminished by inactive sloth.

> haec. . .scribimus in vita vixque coacta manu. 9-10

Even this. . .I write forcing it with difficulty from an unwilling hand.

Even if he can manage to write, he does not revise as he once would
have:

> cum relego, scripsisse pudet, quia plurima cerno
>   me quoque, qui feci, iudice digna lini.
> nec tamen emendo. labor hic quam scribere maior,
>   mensque pati durum sustinet aegra nihil. 15-18

When I read it over I am ashamed of my work because I note many a thing
that even in my own, the maker's judgment, deserves to be erased. Yet I
do not correct it. This is a greater labour than the writing, and my sick
mind has not the power to endure anything hard.

Whether or not his poetic powers are failing, Ovid keeps writing
even when doing so reopens old wounds. Like Juvenal, but for different
reasons, he cannot not write; he recognizes that in spite of the fact that
it was his Muse that got him into this fix, he cannot live without her.
Besides, writing occupies his time, keeps his mind active and
sometimes allows him respite from his grief. I find the most poignant
reason he gives for writing not the need for distraction or solace but the
need to speak: (in *Pont.*2.6)

> exulis haec vox est: praebet mihi littera linguam,
>   et si non liceat scribere, mutus ero. 3-4

An exile's voice is this: letters furnish me a tongue, and if I may not write,
I shall be dumb.

Writing poetry gives Ovid a voice, allows him to speak in a
situation in which he must otherwise remain silent—perhaps, by using

that voice, he can come to terms with who he is, where he is, what has happened, and what the future holds. In David Malouf's reconstruction of Ovid's years in exile, *An Imaginary Life,* the poet actually finds his twin in a feral child, as unable to communicate with other humans as Ovid claims to be with the other inhabitants of Tomis.

There is another reason for him to write, however—a reason which has not changed since he was a young man, yet one which acquires a whole new importance in his old age. Ovid still claims for poetry its power to bestow immortality on its author. The difference now, of course, is that in the face of his own death, Ovid's claims for the power of song are that much more compelling.

In that same poem in which Ovid had refused *mortale opus* (*Amores* 1.15), the poet announces that he is striving for eternal fame (7-8). He proceeds to cite poets from Homer to Sophocles to Ennius and Gallus, all of whom will survive because their works will be read.

Ergo, cum silices, cum dens patientis aratri
    depereant aevo, carmina morte carent. 31-32

Though hard rocks and though the tooth of the enduring ploughshare perish with passing time, song is untouched by death.

ergo etiam cum me supremus adederit ignis,
    vivam, parsque mei multa superstes erit. 41-42

I, too, when the final fires have eaten up my frame, shall still live on, and the great part of me survive my death.

It is impossible to forget that he would end the *Metamorphoses* with lines which echo the *Amores*:

Iamque opus exegi, quid me nec Iovis ira nec ignis
nec poterit ferrum nec edax abolere vetustas. 15.871-72

And now my work is done, which neither the wrath of Jove, nor fire, nor sword, nor the gnawing tooth of time shall ever be able to undo.

parte tamen meliore mei super alta perennis
astra ferar, nomenque erit indelebile nostrum. 15.875-76

Still in my better part I shall be borne immortal far beyond the lofty stars and I shall have an undying name.

Amores 3.9 on the death of Tibullus not only continues this traditional claim but contrasts poignantly with Ovid's later claims to immortality through poetry. In many ways, the poem is a pastiche of commonplaces: the poet as *sacer vates* (17), the inexorability of death, the mythological exemplum of grief (Venus and Adonis, 15), the litany of famous singers (Orpheus, Linus, Homer) all of whom died. The singer may not be able to escape physical extinction, but

defugiunt avidos carmina sola rogos. 28

'Tis song alone escapes the greedy pyre.

At least Tibullus died at home, where his mother and sister could be with him and provide the funeral rites; this is a luxury which Ovid in exile will not be able to claim. Finally, Ovid envisions Tibullus in Elysium with Catullus, Calvus and Gallus.

At the end of his career, Ovid is as insistent on the power of poetry as he was at the start. From the perspective of exile, or perhaps of old age, he may even have come to doubt the talent he had shown as a young man, but in his letter to Perilla (*Tristia* 3.7) Ovid as poet is at his most convincing. It is not surprising to find a poet giving lessons to those who will come after, but in this case Ovid is not simply writing to his artistic progeny: Perilla may be his stepdaughter.[31] While he never denies his grief, Ovid announces that he is returning to his Muses *quamvis docuere* (9).

Asking if she is still writing, Ovid recalls how he nurtured Perilla's earliest efforts (*utque pater natae duxque comesque fui* 18). He used to read her verse and act as critic, and she returned the favor. Always, he urged her to keep writing. Now he is afraid, however, that the example of his punishment will frighten her away from writing.

ergo desidiae remove, doctissima, causas,
    inque bonas artes et tua sacra redi. 31-32

So put aside the causes of sloth, accomplished girl, return to a noble art and thy sacred offerings.

He warns her to keep at her writing because she will not be a lovely young woman forever: there will come a day when reminders of her former loveliness will reduce her to tears.

> ista decens facies longis vitiabitur annis,
>   rugaque in antiqua fronte senilis erit,
> inicietque manum formae damnosa senectus....33-35

That fair face will be marred by the long years, the wrinkles of age will come in time upon thy brow. Ruinous age...will lay her hand upon thy beauty....

Things change—youth and beauty give way to the ravages of old age; the rich become poor. But some things do not change:

> singula ne referam, nil non mortale tenemus
>   pectoris exceptis ingeniique bonis. 43-44

In brief, we possess nothing that is not mortal except the blessings of heart and mind.

Ovid sees himself, exiled, deprived of family and companions, yet he does not betray the depression we find in many of the exile poems. Instead, he claims the immortality of his poetry as vigorously as he did at the end of the *Metamorphoses,* when he wrote:

> quaque patet domitis Romana potentia terris,
> ore legar populi, perque omnia saecula fama,
> siquid habent veri vatum praesagia, vivam! 15.877-79

Wherever Rome's power extends over the conquered world, I shall have mention on men's lips, and, if the prophecies of bards have any truth, through all the ages shall I live in fame.

So to Perilla Ovid declares:

> ingenio tamen ipse meo comitorque fruorque:
>   Caesar in hoc potuit iuris habere nihil.
> quilibet hanc saevo vitam mihi finiat ense,
>   me tamen extincto fama superstes erit,
> dumque suis victrix omnem de montibus orbem
>   prospiciet domitum Martia Roma, legar.
> tu quoque ...
>   effuge venturos, qua potes, usque rogos! 47-54

My mind is nevertheless my comrade and my joy; over this Caesar could have no right. Let any you will end this life with cruel sword, yet when I am dead my fame shall survive. As long as Martian Rome shall gaze forth victorious from her hills over the conquered world, I shall be read. Do thou too . . . ever shun what way thou canst the coming pyre!

In a sense, writing poetry had always been a way to challenge the inexorable mortality of human affairs; in the exile poems, where death seems close at hand, this constant writing is not simply a cry for help but an affirmation of his liveliness and his very self. In the end, the young man who could write nothing but verse becomes the old man who can only write verse.

It is at this point that we most want to know whether Ovid wrote the *Halieutica*. If he did, I could end this chapter gracefully with the following argument. Exiled at fifty, Ovid engages in the life review that Butler describes, and does so in isolation without the support of family or friends. His reaction to the review is an extreme one, with depression, bouts of anxiety, persistent and repeated reflections upon the past. In spite of the threat to his confidence and his sense of identity, however, Ovid weathers more than the winters at Tomis and emerges from this review not only still writing, but writing something new. No longer reverting back to the poetry of his youth, either because he had given up trying to get help or because he had somehow made peace with his situation, Ovid has turned in a new direction when death overtakes him.

However, we do not know whether the *Halieutica* is his. In the end I find that I have raised more questions than I have answered, but I can suggest an agenda for further study of creativity across Ovid's lifespan. In fact, we should expand the question beyond Ovid to ask: What can we discover about the development of other poets throughout their lives? Although the current volume does include efforts to read literature within the context of the poets' lives, scholars in general have displayed a persistent reluctance to look carefully at the connection between a poet's age and that poet's writing. This reluctance strikes me as ironic, considering the number of authors, Greek and Latin, who kept writing well into old age.[32] Aeschylus wrote the *Oresteia* two years before his death at sixty-nine; Sophocles' final play, *Oedipus at*

Colonus, was not performed until 401, four years after his death at ninety. Euripides died in something of a self-imposed exile in 406, at the age of seventy-nine; one of the last plays he wrote was the *Bacchae,* which was performed posthumously.

In addition to a steady stream of speeches, Cicero published the *De Finibus Bonorum et Malorum, Tusculanae Disputationes, De Natura Deorum, De Divinatione,* and *De Officiis* in the last two years of his life, before his death at sixty-four. Horace wrote the fourth book of *Odes* towards the end of his life: he died at fifty-seven. Pliny the Elder wrote the *Naturalis Historia* two years before his death at fifty-six. The list goes on.

The question remains; how best to approach the study of a poet across her or his lifespan? I suggest that the application of a content analysis program, one which would allow a close examination of word choice, metaphor, and repetition and would do so within the context of the actual lines offers the most provocative possibilities.[33] Content analysis would provide insight, for example, into the question of how Ovid's poetry changes and responds to the events of his life or to the social and political events of his day. Content analysis would also provide a fresh perspective on the poet's use of metaphor and allusion. Ovid repeats mythological exempla throughout these poems, but to what end? Why retell the story of Perillus and Phalaris? Why continue to tell of Iphigenia at Tauris encountering her brother Orestes? Are the references to Jason and Medea only prompted by Ovid's presence in Tomis?

How does Ovid compare with other poets writing in old age, particularly Horace? How can we distinguish between the salience of exile and the salience of old age in affecting Ovid's writing?

At this stage there are relatively few conclusions that we can safely draw. My point was not to reinterpret the exile poems, nor was it to propose any theory about what happens to Ovid the poet across his lifespan. Rather, I chose to examine the tendency of his later poems to recall his earlier one, to consider at what points we find continuity and at what points change, and to begin to reflect upon the relationship between old age and creativity. Butler has observed that therapists and other caregivers sometimes find it hard to listen to the elderly, particularly as they reminisce, "but for those who will listen there are rewards."[34] The same can be said for listening to Ovid at sixty.

Notes

1. An expanded version of this thesis was presented orally as "Representations of Old Age in Ovid" at the 1988 symposium "Aging and the Life Cycle in the Renaissance: The Interaction Between Representation and Experience." Parts of the chapter were included in papers presented at the Ohio Classical Conference (1985) and the American Philological Association (1986).

2. Although I realize that Ovid is 'old' in other ways as well, I have tended to limit my discussion to chronological old age, and by ancient standards he was an old man at fifty. Traditionally, women are regarded as 'old' some 10-15 years earlier than their male contemporaries. If a woman is 'old' when she has reached menopause, and if in antiquity it was generally believed that menopause occurred at forty (de Luce 1985), then a man could be regarded as old at fifty. But see Aulus Gellius (*Noctes Atticae* 10.28), where the author cites Tubero who in turn refers to Servius Tullius' determination that after age forty-six, one is *senior.*

3. Thibault 1964 and Green 1982 provide useful and sober reviews of the evidence for Ovid's *crimen et error* and his relegation to Tomis. I am not the first to suggest that exile might operate as a metaphor for old age, but Fitton Brown 1985 has gone even further to propose that Ovid did not go into exile at all. For a rebuttal, see Holleman 1985.

    Even Fränkel 1969.210 questions whether Ovid's exile was as harsh as he describes and suggests that "It is not the business of poetry to cater to the historian's legitimate curiosity and to satisfy his fastidious greed for more and ever more clean, raw, wholesome facts. But if we allow the facts to remain in the background where they belong, and pay more attention to the poet's reactions to them, then, I feel, we can fairly well trust him."

4. Fränkel 1969. 141.

5. I have adopted the Loeb texts for both Latin and translation.

6. For one perspective on Ovid's use of repetition, see de Luce 1977.

7. Lipking 1981.74.

8. The earliest scholarship (Lehman 1953, Dennis 1966, and Taylor, 1974) contributed significantly to the study of creativity and old age, but such work was not without its flaws. See Atchley 1983. 62-63.

9. Hendricks and Hendricks 1986.220.

10. For a full analysis of the exilic poetry, which recognizes these echoes and

is both lucid and humane, see Nagle 1980. Evans 1983 includes useful comments on Ovid as an old man. Other recent scholarship that contributes to a new appreciation of these poems includes Bews 1984, Block 1982, Davisson 1982, 1985, Hinds 1985, Nisbet 1982.

11. Butler 1963.66.

12. Butler 1963.66.

13. Butler 1963.67.

14. Butler 1963.69.

15. Butler 1963.68.

16. Butler 1963.69.

17. Ovid's descriptions of Tomis appear in such poems as *Tr.* 3.3.7, 3.10, 3.12, 5.10, *Pont.* 1.3, 1.8, 1.10, 4.14.

18. Nagle 1980.

19. This *lena* recalls another from the elegiac tradition, Propertius' Acanthis in 4.5. In each case the old woman incurs the hostility of the lover because of her interference in the affair.

20. See Cephalus' discussion of old age in the first book of the *Republic*.

21. Cato reflects upon old age throughout the *De Senectute:* particularly appropriate for a discussion of Ovid's old age would be 3.7-8, 6.16, 6.21, 10.32 and 18.62. Cato even claims to have learned Greek late (8.26), not unlike I. F. Stone.

22. Various poems equate exile with death, e.g. *Tr.* 1.7, 5.1.47, 5.7.23, *Pont.* 1.7.9, 2.3.3, 3.5.33, 4.12.44.

23. These lines inevitably recall Horace's infamous transformation into a bird in *Carm.* 2.20, where that poet, writing in comparative comfort, could manipulate the transformation motif to claim for himself the traditional immortality of the *vates.* Ovid's situation contrasts painfully with that of Horace.

24. The translation is that of Fitzgerald. I am indebted to Thomas Falkner for calling these lines to my attention.

25. I have discussed Ovid's use of repetition to undercut ostensibly serious moments before; see de Luce 1983.

26. Lipking 1981.77.

27. Lipking 1981.78.

28. Lipking 1981.78.

29. Lipking 1981.68.

30. Fränkel 1969.116 comments on the Roman tendency to assume that poetry can only be written under the gentlest conditions.

31. The identity of Perilla is not without controversy, although she has been identified by Wheeler, the translator of the Loeb *Tristia,* as the poet's stepdaughter (page 505).

32. Ancient sources also comment on creativity in old age, as does Cato in *De Senectute* 5.13 and 7.22-23.

33. In a private conversation, Donald McTavish (Sociology, University of Minnesota) described to me the content analysis program which he has developed. This program is most subtle and offers exciting opportunities to study the development of a poet over time by collecting data far beyond what we can obtain from a word count.

34. Butler 1963.72.

References

Atchley, R.C. 1983. *Aging: Continuity and Change.* Belmont, CA.

Bews, J.P. 1984. "The Metamorphosis of Virgil in the *Tristia* of Ovid," *BICS* 31.51-60

Block, E. 1982. "Poetics in Exile: An Analysis of *Epistulae ex Pont.* 3.9," *ClAnt* 1.18-27.

Butler, R.N. 1963. "The Life Review: An Interpretation of Reminiscence in the Aged," *Psychiatry* 26.65-76.

Davisson, M.T. 1982. "*Duritia* and Creativity in Exile. *Epistulae ex Ponto* 4.10," *ClAnt* 1.28-42.

_____. 1985. "*Tristia* 5.13 and Ovid's Use of Epistolary Form and Content," *CJ* 80.238-46.

de Luce, J. 1977. "Cygnus: Diversity and Unity in Ovid's *Metamorphoses,*" *CO* 54.52-54. (published under de Luce More, J.)

_____. 1983. "Iterative Strategies in Ovid." Unpublished paper, presented at the annual meeting of the Classical Association of the Middle West and South.

_____. 1985. "Life Spans and Poetry: Ovid as Test Case." Unpublished paper presented at the annual meeting of the Ohio Classical Conference.

_____. 1985. "Fact, Fiction, and Old Women in Rome." Unpublished paper presented at the annual meeting of the Classical Association of the Middle West and South.

Dennis, W. 1966. "Creative Productivity Between the Ages of 20 and 80 Years," *Journal of Gerontology* 21, 1.1-8.

Evans, H.B. 1983. *Publica Carmina: Ovid's Books from Exile.* Lincoln, NE.

Fitton Brown, A.D. 1985. "The Unreality of Ovid's Tomitian Exile," *LCM* 10. 19-22.

Fränkel, H. 1969 (1945). *Ovid: A Poet Between Two Worlds.* Berkeley.

Green, P. 1982. "Carmen et error. πρόφασις and αἰτία in the Matter of Ovid's Exile," *ClAnt* 1.202-220.

Hendricks, J. and Hendricks, C.D. 1986. *Aging in Mass Society: Myths and Realities.* Boston.

Hinds, S. 1985. "Booking the Return Trip: Ovid and *Tristia 1,*" *PCPhS* 31.13-32.

Holleman, A.W.J. 1985. "Ovid's Exile." *LCM* 10. 48.

Homer. *The Odyssey,* tr. R. Fitzgerald. 1963 (1961). New York.

Lehman, H.C. 1953. *Age and Achievement.* Princeton.

Lipking, L. 1981. *The Life of the Poet: Beginning and Ending Poetic Careers.* Chicago.

Malouf, D. 1978. *An Imaginary Life.* New York.

Nagle, B.R. 1980. *The Poetics of Exile: Program and Polemic in the Tristia and Epistulae ex Ponto of Ovid.* Brussels.

Nisbet, R.G.M. 1982. "Great and Lesser Bear (Ovid *Tristia* 3.4)" *JRS* 82.49-56.

Taylor, I.A. 1974. "Patterns of Creativity and Aging" in E. Pfeiffer, ed. *Successful Aging.* Durham, NC.

Thibault, J.C. 1964. *The Mystery of Ovid's Exile.* Berkeley.

Afterword

When Fields Collide or
A View From Gerontology

Mildred M. Seltzer

---

*T*his chapter is divided into four parts. First, we examine the important relationship between the humanities and gerontology, go on to the issues in obtaining information for its mutual use by those in the two disciplines and then explore the importance of this information for both disciplines. The fourth section contains sources of gerontological information. As will be obvious in the chapter, I am writing this from the viewpoint of a gerontologist from the social and behavioral sciences, a creature somewhat like the proverbial purple cow: many would rather see than be one.

At the risk of criticism from the more precise, I am omitting specific definitions of social gerotology and of the humanities except for a few general and possibly debatable comments. I use Atchley's definition of social gerontology — the scientific study of the nonphysical aspects of aging[1]. The humanities is an inclusive term for the many fields and disciplines that deal with the creative arts, values and meanings of life and death. The alliance between the humanities and gerontology is not new. Moody, in his "Humanities and the Arts" review in *The Enclyclopedia of Aging*, comments on the contributions the arts and humanities have made since the 1970s, particularly in "...history, literary criticism, philosophy, and comparative religion."[2] He identifies four major ways in which the humanities can contribute to gerontology: (1) playing an heuristic role, generating new hypotheses and questions; (2) enabling reflections on issues of time and aging; (3) educating practitioners through the analysis of values; and (4) helping us to understand the meaning and potential meaningfulness of the last stage of life.[3]

While the relationship between gerontology and the humanities has grown and strengthened since the 1970s, the alliance between social or behavioral sciences and the humanities is not new. Its rich history includes McClelland's 1961 work on the achievement motivation in which he traced, by examining Greek pottery and children's literature among other things, the development in Western society of the need to achieve.[4] I remember, when I first became involved in gerontology, reading two articles that made an indelible impression on me: "The supposedly golden age for the aged in ancient Greece: A study of literary concept of old age"[5] (1962) and its duplicate, "A supposedly golden age for the aged in ancient Rome: A study of the literary concept of old age".[6] I have since been informed by classicists that both papers could have been more accurate. Those articles are a quarter of a century old.

While others have written about how aging is depicted in literature of the past and present[7] and even how it might be in the future (e.g., science fiction), publications were relatively few and sporadic. The real impetus toward gerontological humanities or humanistic gerontology (really two different fields), specifically the relationship between classicists and gerontologists, has been quite recent and limited to a fairly small, albeit growing, group of people.

In the introduction to their book *Aging and the Elderly*, Spicker, Woodward and Van Tassel explain, in part, the reason for the recent surge of mutual interest between gerontologists and those in the humanities. They point out (whether aptly or not depends upon your viewpoint) that "aging is too vast a subject to be left solely to social and physical scientists."[8] They go on to write that "the last to realize that aging was an important twentieth-century phenomenon in the west were the academic humanists; and the last to realize that the humanists have important insights to offer to the study of old age were the professional gerontologists."[9]

Such pointed remarks remind us that there are many ways of knowing, discovering and describing the realities around us. To paraphrase an ancient author, there are many disciplines in the academic mansion. It is intellectually arrogant to believe that a single academic discipline, as old as it may be or as rigorous as its claimants believe it to be, has all of the answers. We increase our understanding when we draw from many sources and resources. For example,

218

material in this volume adds to our knowledge about how aging has been viewed in the past. Such knowledge can help in discovering and explaining some sources of current attitudes and beliefs about aging. It can help us to learn what concepts might be universal images of aging across time and place. We can learn, too, not only what other societies have believed about aging and thought about old age and old people, but how they have dealt with aging-related issues. Learning about the past can, it is to be hoped, help us with the present and future. Not only are schools of psychotherapy based on this assumption, those seeking solutions to social problems also believe the past can inform the present. It is, then, no wonder that those in the humanities and those in gerontology can and do benefit from the sharing of information and perspectives about the very human experiences of aging.

There are, however, problems as well as pleasures involved in multidisciplinary endeavors. The problems are sufficiently familiar to anyone who has been involved in multidisciplinary programs in colleges and universities. They do not bear repeating here except to note that aside from academic disciplinary ethnocentricism, there are other important concerns. How, for example, can one become well enough informed in another field to be able to differentiate between good and bad literature in that field? How long does it take to become familiar with disciplinary vocabulary and nuances of language? Having read various chapters in this book, I am only too aware of limitations to my classsical education and of marked differences in vocabularies and approaches. Even when the words are the same, their meanings are often vastly different. Not only are there differences in meaning, but we tend often to make invidious comments about these differences. A colleague who is a classicist refers to my disciplinary language as jargon, I to hers as condescendingly esoteric.

Having set this stage, it is obvious that the comments to follow are those of a social gerontologist. These comments will focus next on research issues considered relevant to those undertaking the kind of research published in this book. Following this discussion, there will be a brief review of the kinds of information gleaned from such research. A final section describes, for those interested in learning more about aging, where to go for eveything they have ever wanted to know but didn't know whom to ask. These specific topics are dictated both by personal choice and editorial recommendations.

Issues of Research Method

In order to provide a framework for remarks about research I will examine a quartet of issues: (a) the use of unobtrusive methods to obtain data, specifically content analysis; (b) idiographic as compared with nomothetic research; (c) the value of qualitative as well as quantitative methods of research particularly when the latter are unavailable; and (d) research design. The four are interrelated but discussed separately.

Unobtrusive Measures

Unobtrusive measures involve examining that which most scientists do not typically consider data — the *in vivo* results and evidences of human behavior: analyzing signatures on library cards to measure the popularity of books and reading patterns of individuals; examining contents of garbage cans to learn about the eating habits and life styles of people; analyses of art products, literature, gravestone inscriptions and other human creations to learn about the values of a society, mortality patterns, social class or other sociocultural phenomena. An analysis of the contents of human products and activities tells us much about a society — and, to some degree. about given individuals.

As a research tool, content analysis is used in many academic disciplines, including sociology, psychology, political sicience, women's studies and certainly, gerontology, in literary criticism and in the analysis of mass communications such as advertising. It is used in the humanities and in Talmudic and Biblical scholarship. An example of its use in social gerontology includes an examination of children's literature to learn how aging has been described and what these descriptions imply.[10] Others have analyzed humor to learn something about the nature of peoples' attitudes, stereotypes and concerns related to aging and old age.[11] Sohngen examines the experience of old age in contemporary novels[12] while Francher analyzed the content of television ads.[13] This kind of research is based on the assumption that a society's attitudes and beliefs are reflected in its media. Those who would learn about a society and individuals who consititute that society can gain some understanding through analyzing contents of creative products.

Laurel Porter, who defines "humanistic gerontology" as "...the application of research in the humanities to the study of aging; literature, history, philosophy, religion, and art as they inform our understanding of human aging"[14] points out specifically how the study of literature can contribute to understanding any human issue.[15] She reiterates Freud's advice that those who would understand human nature should "turn to the poets."[16]

An analysis of literature provides us, then, with samples of how others have viewed any human condition, including that very human phenomenon of aging. Statistical data can tell us what life expectancy probably was in 400 B.C., 17 A.D. or other specific periods of time. Demographers and epidemiologists can tell us some common causes of death, incidence and prevalence of diseases and other quantitative facts at various times in history. Such statistical data cannot tell us, however, how people felt about illness and death, what they believed, how they described other people. An analysis of literature can help to provide answers to questions about these issues and to illuminate these answers. Content analysis provides a rich source of data to supplement quantitative information.

We assume that specific literature survives because it 'speaks to' people about important issues and concerns. Any literature informs about the times in which it was written, the society that produced it, the values which that society held. As Porter points out: "...each deeply personal literary creation does not derive from popularly-held values alone, but is also shaped by social context, esthetic preference, the constraints of tradition, and the integrity of each other's ideas and personality, which is reflected among other ways, by his or her choice of literary genre."[17]

The importance of the individual author or poet leads to the next methodological problem — to what extent are we examining idiosyncratic ideas and beliefs and to what extent are we learning about societal ideas and beliefs?

Idiographic vs. Nomothetic Approaches

From the social and behavioral scientist's point of view (at least that of this one's) the problem is not whether the analysis of an individual author's books adds to our knowledge about aging (in this instance), but rather how to disentangle what is idiosyncratic about the work and what societal. To what extent can we generalize from a single case study (idiographic approach) as compared with generalizing based on a sample of events or people (nomothetic approach)? Analysis of a single poet's or author's works forces us to ask whether the experiences, beliefs, values, described were unique to that individual or commonly shared. How much is idiosyncratic and how much commonly held? Does the poet's work reflect only his or her personal views and experiences, or are there also reflections of societal ones? Can an intensive examination of one tell us about the many? Would not a study of a number of people be more accurate, more amenable to extrapolation? We tell our students that an *N* of one is not sufficient for many purposes. Can one be enough in the kinds of analyses found in this book? Heuristically, a sample of one is valuable if only to generate hypotheses for further research.

The next research issue has to do with the kind of research that can be generated.

Qualitative and Quantitative Research

The differences between qualitative and quantitative research are familiar ones. The former refers to a nonstatistical research. It does not involve experimental design with its concurrent experimental manipulation. Some kinds of research lend themselves more easily to a qualitative research approach. If we want to learn more about the quality of feelings, peoples' world views, their lives as they are lived, then qualitative research is to be preferred. It is, properly conducted, as rigorous as quantitative research. The papers in this book are illustrative of a non-counting, non-experimental qualitative approach.

Research Design

Cross sectional, longitudinal, or some combination thereof

It is important to decide whether one wants a photograph taken at a particular point in time or a movie taken over a long period of time. Cross-sectional research provides a picture of a particular moment. This picture can be compared with other pictures. From this comparison we can draw some conclusions about differences. If, on the other hand, we want to learn more about changes over time, longitudinal research will help us to achieve this goal. We can learn about age differences from cross-sectional research, more about age changes from longitudinal research. If we really want to be more sophisticated, to isolate whether what we find may be age changes, a reflection of the period of history, or some other variable, we can combine the two methods in various ways. An analysis of one author's work over his or her lifetime may be more useful in helping us to learn about age-related changes than the examination of a single work.

In all of the research designs and issues, one of the most important things to define is — what is old? What the contents of this book reinforces for us is that the definition of old age depends upon more than chronology.

Given these research caveats, what can we learn from books such as this one?

The Gleaning of Information

As we move across centuries and sociocultural environments, we learn about earlier views of aging and how these views have changed over time. If, over time, we find similarities in images of aging, these may tell us something about the universal aspects of aging. The fact that aging is not described consistently suggests that in the past, as now, aging was viewed both extremely positively and extremely negatively. Atchley, in his book *Social Forces and Aging*, describes the bipolarity of our views of aging[18], a phenomenon I have described as the Janus-view of old age. Some view old age in three "d" terms — dismal, decremental and deleterious. It is to be avoided at all costs. Others view aging in more positive terms, a time of freedom, wisdom, patience. In reality, aging and old age have elements of both and it is impossible to predict the balance of positive and negative for specific individuals. Luck, hubris, the fates, the gods (and goddesses) have a hand — or perhaps a finger — in influencing or determining which it shall be for any individual.

Our vision of old age and aging is shaped by an individual's social class, gender, health. The experience of aging is filtered through social, psychological and biological phenomena. The positions an individual occupies in the social system shape others' expectations of her or him.

Positions are units of social structure (e.g., mothers, warriors, fathers, nurses, widows, priestesses, priests) while the roles are the behaviors associated with occupying these positions. How a specific individual behaves in the positions he or she occupies is influenced by others' expectations as well as by the idiosyncratic aspects of that person's behavior. One's age, as well as others' expectations of people that age, influence acccess to positions and role behavior.

We learn from writings such as these how current views of old age and human development are rooted in the past. Conceptions of historical, social, individual times, their interrelationships, and their influence on human behavior are not so modern as some believe. Current developmental models are reinforced by earlier conceptions of the life cycle. Simultaneously, the writings of the past can be reinterpreted in terms of current understandings of human development and old age. We learn, too, of how stages of life have been viewed; often, these views are not dissimilar to current ones. Some of the classic Greek and Roman authors saw life as a Gaussian curve, with middle age at the apex and old age on its downside, both socially and individually. For a few authors, there seemed to have been no redeeming qualities to old age.

For the social and behavioral gerontologist, material such as is in this book reminds us that there is both continuity and change in visions and versions of growing and being old. There is no single way in which all societies view aging — thus, the fallacies of stereotypes are once again revealed.

Sources of Information

For those stimulated by books such as this one, excited by the prospect of engaging in multidisciplinary endeavors and of relating specifically to social and behavioral gerontology, where does one go to learn about aging? As noted earlier, a major barrier in becoming involved in multidisciplinary work is in learning how to become informed about the other disciplines in the multi-complex. Where do you go for accurate data? How can you evaluate its accuracy? Who are the 'good' authors? These are crucial questions to ask about any academic discipline or area of activity, particularly newly emerging ones such as gerontology. Gerontology is still a field whose existence some question. Others complain about "instant gerontologists," those individuals who have read a textbook and learned some demographic data.[19] Currently, there is no Ph.D. in gerontology.[20] The fact that someone teaches a course in social gerontology is not, at present, *prima facie* evidence of professional qualifications.

At the risk of answering unasked questions and giving unsolicited advice, let me suggest a few sources of information. There are two national professional membership organizations in the field: The Gerontological Society of America and the American Society on Aging. In addition, the Association for Gerontology in Higher Education, an organization of institutional membership, has a membership of over 250 colleges and universities offering courses and programs in gerontology. All three organizations can provide information. Several publish bibliographies or course syllabi focusing specifically on the humanities and aging. The Gerontological Society of America, a scientific, multidisciplinary organization, has an active Arts and Humanities Committee.

In addition to bibliographies and syllabi, these organizations often have information services and can provide names of specific individuals, schools or books that would be useful. There are a number of introductory gerontology textbooks — far too many to mention by name because of possible unintentional omissions. Such an academic sin should be avoided. Similarly, there are a number of authors who hve written from the perspective of the humanities, some quoted earlier in this chapter. The Gerontological Society of America has announced the publication by Polisar, Donna, Larry Wyant, Thomas Cole and Cielo Perdomo, *Where Do We Come From? What Are We? Where Are We Going? An Annotated Bibliography of Aging and the Humanities.* As is true in many fields, there is also an encyclopedia, *The Encyclopedia of Aging.*[21]

Of journals there are many. The Gerontological Society of America publishes the *Journals of Gerontology* (there are four of these) and *The Gerontologist.* The American Society on Aging publishes *Generations.* Other journals include *The International Journal of Aging and Human Development, Aging Research, Gerontology and Geriatrics Education, Educational Gerontology,* and a host of others focused on specific areas (religion, activities, long term care). I have not mentioned the many mass membership organizations, the local, state and federal agencies involved in aging, nor the vast array of other sources of information and assistance.

The field of aging has grown in quantum leaps in the past twenty years. From a field in which there were so few books one could put them all on one or two shelves, it has grown to one in which an organization is contemplating a journal of book reviews.

If I were to give unsolicited advice to someone entering the exciting morass of gerontology I would probably say the following:

1. Be your usual rigorous self in your work — poor research is poor research regardless of the field.
2. Be not taken in by stereotypes about aging and old people.
3. Consider that old age is neither all good nor all bad — no stage in life is.
4. Be aware that the definition of a gerontologist — what constitutes credentials in gerontology, and the parameters of the field — is not yet established and probably will not be for a while.
5. Remind yourself that colleges and universities are balkanized on the basis of disciplines. Enter multidisciplinary activities at your peril; however, it is worth it. Few intellectual activities are more fun and more satisfying; many are more stultifying.

Conclusions

I have only touched on some of the richness in this book. It has taken me on a fascinating journey of discovery, raising many questions, some unanswerable and some eventually answerable. The kind of material found here provides us with useful information about common themes in aging — themes that seem to bridge time. These include conflicting and often dramatically opposing views of aging, freedom from normative constraints permitted by age, persistence of age and sex norms. Implicit in some of the material are theoretical themes; one wonders about the extent to which scientists are influenced by these themes (e.g. evolution of societies from simple and carefree to complex and burdensome, or stages of life that are qualitatively different from one another) or whether the descriptions of artists and scientists reflect reality. In either or both events, this book reminds us of the pleasures of learning and acquiring knowledge for its own sake and of satisfying our intellectual curiosity for the sake of our essential humanness.

The anthropologist Myerhoff's description of "Homo narrans" tells us that "... the culture in general — specific cultures, and the fabric of meaning that constitutes any single human existence — is the "story" we tell about ourselves."[22] Victor Turner's introductory comments to Myerhoff's book, *Number Our Days,* writes that Myerhoff shows how people "...weave meaning and identity out of their memories and experiences".[23] So, too, do we learn from this book about individuals, societies and ourselves.

Notes

1. Atchley, 1988. 1.
2. Moody in Maddox et al, 1987. 339.
3. Moody in Maddox et al, 1987. 340.
4. McClelland 1961.
5. Haynes 1962.
6. Haynes 1963.
7. Seltzer and Atchley, 1971.
8. Spicker, Woodward and Van Tassel 1978.vii.
9. Spicker, Woodward and Van Tassel 1978.vii.
10. Seltzer and Atchley 1971; Ansello 1977; Robin 1977.
11. Palmore 1971; Palmore 1986; Palmore 1987; Richman 1977; Seltzer 1986.
12. Sohngen 1977.
13. Francher 1973.
14. Porter and Porter 1984.1.
15. Porter and Porter 1984.2.
16. Porter and Porter 1984.2.
17. Porter and Porter 1984.3.
18. Atchley 1988.5.
19. Corbett 1979; Loeb 1979; Seltzer 1979.

20. At this writing several joint degrees are pending — e.g., Gerontology and social policy.

21. Maddox, et al. 1986.

22. Myerhoff 1978.xi.

23. Myerhoff 1978.xi.

References

Ansello, E.F. 1977a. Age and ageism in children's first literature. *Educational Gerontology* 2.255-74.

Ansello, E.F. 1977b. Old age and literature: An overview. *Educational Gerontology* 2.211-18.

Atchley, R.C. 1988. *Social Forces and Aging.* Belmont, CA.

Corbett, S. 1979. The phenomenon of the instant gerontologist: How to maintain quality education in gerontology. In Sterns, Harvey L., E.F. Ansello, B.M. Sprouse, R. Layfield-Faux, eds. *Gerontology in Higher Education; Developing Institutional and Community Strength.* Belmont, CA.

Francher, J.S. 1973. It's the Pepsi generation. . . : Accelerated aging and the TV commercial. *The International Journal of Aging and Human Development* 4.245-55.

Haynes, M. 1962. The supposedly golden age for the aged in ancient Greece (A study of the literary concept of old age). *The Gerontologist* 2.93-98.

Haynes, M. 1963. The supposedly golden age for the aged in ancient Rome (A study of the literary concept of old age). *The Gerontologist* 3.26-35.

Loeb, M.B. 1979. Gerontology is not a profession — the oldest or the youngest. In Sterns, Harvey L., E.F. Ansello, B.M. Sprouse, R. Layfield-Faux, eds. *Gerontology in Higher Education; Developing Institutional and Community Strength.* Belmont, CA.

McClelland, D. 1961. *The Achieving Society.* New York.

Moody, H.R. 1987. Humanities and the arts. In Maddox, G. et al. *Encyclopedia of Aging.* New York.

Myerhoff, B. 1978. *Number Our Days.* New York.

Nahemow, L., K.A. McCluskey-Fawcett, P.E. McGhee (eds.) 1986. *Humor and Aging.* Orlando, FL.

Palmore, E.B. 1971. Attitudes toward aging as shown by humor. *The Gerontologist* 11.181.

Palmore, E.B. 1986. Attitudes toward aging shown by humor: A review. In Nahemow, L., K.A. McCluskey-Fawcett, Paul E. McGhee (eds.) *Humor and Aging.* Orlando, FL.

Palmore, E.B. 1987. "Humor". In Maddox, G. et al. *Encyclopedia of Aging.* New York.

Porter, L. and L.M. Porter (eds.) 1984. *Aging in Literature.* Troy, MI.

Richman, J. 1977. The foolishness and wisdom of old age: Attitudes toward the elderly as reflected in jokes. *The Gerontologist* 17.210-19.

Robin, E.P. 1977. Old age in elementary school readers. *Educational Gerontology* 2.275-92.

Seltzer, M.M. 1986. Timing the significant common variable in both humor and aging. In Nahemow, L. et al (eds.), *Humor and Aging.* Orlando, FL.

Seltzer, M.M. 1979. Reflections on the phenomenon of the instant gerontologist. In Sterns, Harvey L., E.F. Ansello, B.M. Sprouse, R. Layfield-Faux, (eds.) *Gerontology in Higher Education; Developing Institutional and Community Strength.* Belmont, CA.

Seltzer, M.M. and R.C. Atchley. 1971. The concept of old: Changing attitudes and stereotypes. *The Gerontologist* 11.226-30.

Sohngen, M. 1977. The experience of old age as depicted in contemporary novels. *The Gerontologist* 17.70-78.

Spicker, S.F., K.M. Woodward, and D.D. Van Tassel. 1978. *Aging and the Elderly: Humanistic Perspectives in Gerontology.* Atlantic Highlands, NJ.

Bibliography

Old Age in Greco-Roman Antiquity and Early Christianity: An Annotated Select Bibliography

Emiel Eyben

Tout comme le sexe, l'âge est une dimension fondamentale de l'existence humaine. Au même titre que les relations entre les sexes, le rapport entre les catégories d' âge et les générations détermine la structure d'une société.

— L. Rosenmayr, *Communications* 37 (1938) 89.

Introduction

There have been old people in every age. The current world record in longevity is probably not much higher in our day than in either recent or distant past. The percentage of people, however, who do reach a more or less "venerable" old age is much higher today than in the past. One of the consequences of this evolution has been a growing interest in the phenomenon of old age shown by such disciplines as medicine, psychology and even history. Indeed, in every age historians have tended to inquire into the past with the specific questions of their own time in mind, furnishing insight into contemporary society and contributing in a sense to the solution of present day problems. Compared with studies on women or children in a historical perspective, such studies on old age were once relatively uncommon. The situation has recently changed, however, perhaps partly under the influence of de Beauvoir 1970, especially the book's historical chapter, just as the scientific research of Ariès[1] on the history of childhood stimulated interest in the opposite pole of human life. It is no accident, therefore, that we are currently witnessing the publication of a number of important studies in this area: a special number of *Saeculum* (1979) devoted to the study of old age in a number of ancient cultures (including, e.g., Scharbert and Maier on Judaism); the proceedings of the 1986 congress at the Université de Provence on old age and aging in the Middle Ages, edited by Subrenat; an article by Welti (1987) on old age in the Medieval and early modern periods; and a collection of essays on the subject of old age in various literatures, including ancient literature (Croon 1981). In short, the present volume appears at a time when there is a worldwide interest in the subject.

Before reviewing the modern literature, it is important to make one observation. The view advanced particularly under the influence of Ariès, that the distinction of childhood and youth as separate 'ages of man' was the product of romanticism and the industrial revolution[2] is paralleled by the view that there was no perception of old age as such, or as a distinct way of life, in the past (cf. Van Hooff 1983; Philibert 1984). This is not an appropriate place to discuss the matter in detail — suffice it to say that this is a view we cannot support. There are countless occasions in ancient literature where old age is compared to other ages in the human life span, where specific characteristics —moral, intellectual, and psychological — are ascribed to it, and where certain kinds of activity are recommended to the elderly or denied them. Several ancient authors discuss the topic at length: Aristotle's three-fold division of the life span, Horace's distinction of the four ages of man, Juvenal's and Maximian's description of the unhappiness of old age,[3] not to mention the book-length treatments of old age in Cicero's *Cato Maior de Senectute* and Plutarch's *Whether an old man should engage in public affairs*. Nor should we forget that a whole series of tracts on the subject — by Theophrastus, Demetrius of Phaleron, Ariston of Ceos, Varro, Juncus, Diogenes of Oenoanda, Favorinus of Arles, and others — have been lost.[4] There was certainly, in antiquity, no lack of interest in the subject of old age.

Old Age: Part of the Human Life Span

Let us begin by situating old age in the whole of the human life span. In a doctoral dissertation, Philibert 1968 discusses the 'ages of man' in a broader and largely philosophical perspective. Antiquity and old age are mentioned only incidentally in this study, but they are central to the article published by Boll in 1913 on the categorization of the different ages (especially as viewed by the ancient Greeks), a fundamental study which shows how such divisions are influenced by nature (e.g., four ages paralleling the four seasons) or the cosmos (e.g., seven ages and the seven planets). The Latin terminology of the life course is studied from a philological and etymological point of view by Sluşanschi 1974. The same scholar, in 1973, discussed the schema suggested by Varro, with five ages of fifteen years each and *senectus* commencing, as is often the case, at sixty. Eyben 1973a and 1973b discusses the age divisions in Roman and early Christian times from a more sociological perspective, and allows the ancients to comment on the lifespan in their own words. Those anxious to investigate the age divisions in Latin, early Christian and medieval sources can do worse than consult Hofmeister 1926, de Ghellinck 1948, Sears 1986, and Burrow 1986.

The simplest division of age is that which distinguishes only young and old. The tensions between young and old are nicely illustrated in the articles included in Bertman 1976 on generational conflict in Greece and Rome: ancient authors studied in the volume include Homer (Querbach), Aeschylus (Freyman), Euripides (Mench), Aristophanes (Reckford), Thucydides (Wassermann), Catullus and Horace (Broege), Virgil (Bertman) and Persius (Young).[5] Young and old are not always cast in a pitched battle, however. Cicero suggests that it is both possible and desirable for an old man to preserve something of the dynamism of youth (*Sen.* 11.38), and that a young man or even a child can adopt the mentality of an adult or, better still, a man of venerable age. The motif of the "puer-senex" (compare Hes. *Erga* 181 and Virg. *Aen.* 11.311) became very common in late profane and especially Christian antiquity. Gnilka 1972 studies the phenomenon in his book on "spiritual" age, less a literary commonplace than an idea and ideal deeply anchored in the contemporary vision of humanity: a person's age is itself irrelevant, and a child or young man can overcome the limitations of his real age and its characteristic vices.

General Overviews

Aside from a few summary articles (e.g., Finley 1981, with which this collection opens), there are only two major studies which provide a global picture of old age in antiquity and early Christianity and which are of recent date. Minois 1987 studies old age from antiquity to the Renaissance. First, he examines the Greek world under the heading "sad old age," where classical Greece, with its admiration for physical beauty, condemns old age to a subordinate role, a situation which improved a little during the Hellenistic period from about 300 B.C. on; then the Roman period, under the heading "Greatness and decadence of the old man," in which he discusses the power the *paterfamilias* wielded in the family *(patria potestas)* and in the state (e.g., the *senatus* as a council of *senes),* a power which gradually diminished through antiquity; and finally early Christianity, in which 'authentic' old age, and only this, is held in high esteem because it is characterized by 'authentic' wisdom. Still more exhaustive is Gnilka 1983 in the *Reallexikon für Antike und Christentum.* Though the volume stresses early Christianity, secular antiquity is treated at length (col. 997-1043): after an earlier section on terminology, the demarcation of old age and life expectancy, old age is described as it appears in different literary genres, art and medicine. In Judaism (col. 1043-52), old age was conceived as a norm of happiness, a reward for a devout life, even if not everyone saw it as such. Christianity (col. 1052-93) usually viewed old age as the crowning of human existence, emphasized its virtues (wisdom, liberation from the passions), its obligations (e.g., education of the young), its contribution to the Church and the respect due to age, though not without noting that not all old people behaved as expected. Besides, as noted above, age was a relative concept, with youth capable of maturity beyond its years.

Specific Studies

Greek Antiquity

There are some studies which specifically address themselves to the subject of old age in Greek antiquity. Despite its shortcomings[6] and its own relatively old age, Richardson 1933 (reprinted 1969) is still useful. Drawing on a wide variety of sources — literary, epigraphical, iconographical — the author treats, not always very critically, subjects such as the physical aspects of senescence, the mental and emotional endowments of old age, the duties and interests of elderly citizens (in public life, warfare, religion, private life) and the attitude of the Greeks toward the aged. She also deals with old age in art, devotes a chapter to outstanding examples of longevity and tries, on the basis of inscriptional evidence, to reconstruct the average duration of life among the Greeks (her result: 29.43 years), a hazardous undertaking in which a number of scholars have ventured tentative if not satisfactory conclusions (Clauss 1973, with bibliography).

Most of the studies on old age in the Greek and Roman world confine themselves to literary sources, a period in literature, a particular genre, or a given author. Preisshofen 1977 studies the way old age was presented in early Greek poetry. After a treatment of old age among the gods, there follows a study of Homer, Hesiod and the lyric poets. The author devotes particular attention to the peculiar characteristics of each individual author, the laws of the genre, the spirit of the times and the interpretation of each poem taken as a unit, and takes a stand against the widespread opinion that the ancient Greeks unanimously conceived of old age as a complete disaster. The same period is studied, albeit less thoroughly, in Schweingruber 1918, who also explores old age in tragedy (Aeschylus, Sophocles, Euripides), comedy (Aristophanes) and prose (Plato and Aristotle). Also worth mentioning are the more synthetic articles by Schadewaldt 1933, Kirk 1971, and Van Hooff 1983. The last of these suggests that in classical Greece, senescence was not assigned specific psychic and intellectual qualities (an opinion discussed above), and that old people were not marginalized. Kirk treats the transformation of attitudes vis-à-vis old age, especially taking into account questions of creativity and non-creativity. Schadewaldt, for his part, emphasizes the importance of Solon, who sees life as a meaningful, understandable development that progresses in seven year stages, and who adopts a new, positive attitude to old age, thus propounding a new vision of man — body and soul are no longer seen as unity; the soul has its own value, independent of the body and inalterable, and thanks to this philosophy old age receives its true value.

Discussion of the subject of old age in selected Greek authors is to be found in several modern studies. Especially noteworthy are Byl's wide-ranging studies: in 1976 on Homer and the lyric poets, who are seen as having had a generally pessimistic view of things and as having (with the exception of Solon) cursed old age; in 1974 on Plato and Aristotle, who in the author's opinion shared essentially the same vision of old age; in 1975 on tragic literature, where "gray hairs" occasionally (although certainly not always) inspired respect but were often, especially in Euripides, a cause for lamentation; in 1977 (a) on Aristophanes, who viewed old age with contempt and ridicule (on Aristophanes see also the essay by Hubbard in the present collection); in 1977 (b) on Plutarch, who believed that elderly people, with their wide experience and preference for moderation, could play an important role in the management of the state and the education of the young; and in 1978 on Lucian, who laced his observations on old age with sarcasm and irony, except where he himself was concerned.

Some of the authors have been studied by other scholars. Old age in the epics of Homer was the subject of a monograph by Jungclaussen as early as 1870 and is discussed from a sociological point of view in Ulf 1987. On Homer see also (in the present collection) Falkner, who has also written in 1989 (a) on Hesiod's description of old age in the 'myth of the five races', and in 1989 (b) on Solon's 'ten ages of man.' Some Greek lyrics have received special attention, for example, Mimnermus in Schmiel 1974, Anacreon in Woodbury 1979, and especially Solon, whose positive vision of old age is stressed in Schadewaldt 1933 (see above) and Steinhagen 1972. Worthy of mention in this context is the detailed and comprehensive study Vilchez 1983 devoted to the 'ages of man' and their distinctive features in Greek lyric and tragedy.

Vilchez provides a link between archaic lyric and classical tragedy. On tragedy in general, see de Romilly 1968.127-50. In studies on tragedy, particular attention has been devoted to Euripides, for instance in Hohnen's 1953 dissertation on the lamentation of old age in the *Heracles,* which includes an extensive survey of the opinions of other Greek authors, as well as in Harbsmeier 1968, who examines one by one all the old people (Pheres, Peleus, Thetis, and so forth) who appear in Euripides' plays. Several articles by Falkner deal with various aspects of old age in Greek tragedy: 1985 (a) on old age in the *Medea* and 1985 (b) on Euripides' development of a stagecraft of old age (cf. also the essay on the *Children of Heracles* included in this collection). Also noteworthy is Falkner 1987 on Sophocles' last play, *Oedipus at Colonus,* which relates old age and the literary imagination, the work of art and the place of the artist in the human life cycle—see also the essay by Van Nortwick in the present collection.

Besides the tragedians, the Greek philosophers, especially Plato and Aristotle, have stimulated scientific research. The characteristics of the different phases of human life as seen by Plato, including old age, are treated by Stein 1966 in a German doctoral thesis. The author provides extensive materials and, like Clota 1954, highlights Plato's positive attitude toward old age: human life is like a staircase, a man grows step by step to a higher level, and only the senior citizen can be a true philosopher. His pupil Aristotle has a different view of things.[7] Working on the principle that the "via media" is best, he distinguishes three ages *(Rhet.* 2.12-14), with maturity as a middle between youth (which he depicts in a fairly positive light) and old age (which is a time of physical, intellectual, psychological and moral decline). His views of the last period of life are explored in Dyroff 1939.15-34, Gigon 1968 and, from a social point of view, Koumakis 1974.

Plato and Aristotle were certainly not the only philosophers who reflected on old age. Worth noting is the "laughing philosopher" and atomist Democritus, who died at the age of 104(!)[8] and who, as Herter 1975 shows, inspired by his principle of "euthymia" or cheerfulness, adopted a very positive attitude to old age; the epicurist Diogenes of Oenoanda, who also took up the defense of the last age of man (cf. Irigoin 1971) and the peripatetics Ariston of Ceos and Juncus, whose views on the disadvantages and (especially) advantages of old age have been examined by Dyroff 1939.35-45. The writings of the afore-mentioned ancient authors have largely been lost, but Plutarch's tract *Whether an old man should engage in public affairs* has been preserved. Although Byl 1977 (b) (noted above) discusses his views on old age, attention has been focused almost entirely on the sources of this tract — cf. Fornara 1966.

Roman Antiquity

So much for Greek literature. Menander has not been forgotten; he will be discussed below in the company of his later Latin colleagues. The only general survey of the *senex* in Latin antiquity is an unpublished thesis by Berelson, dating from 1934 and dealing with the divisions of life and the beginning of old age (4-7), the feelings of the Romans toward old age (8-25), the *senex* in Roman private and public life (26-52), legislation affecting the aged (53-58), the personification of *senectus* (59-63), longevity and the duration of life (64-88). The studies presently being prepared by Parker and Suder will doubtless fill an important gap in the scientific literature on the project.

The number of Latin authors in whom old age is studied as a separate theme is not great. Those who spring immediately to mind are the comedians Plautus and Terence, together with their Greek models, especially Menander. Important is Oeri 1948, who also deals with the typology of old age in ancient comedy, its origins and later influence. Old people are also discussed in general works, such as Duckworth 1952.242-49. Roth 1913 treats the relationship between the young and old, a relationship often characterized by opposition and even rivalry. Conca 1970 demonstrates that, as can be expected, Menander and Terence give a much more sober picture of the 'old lover' than does Plautus. McCary 1971 describes the different types of elderly persons appearing in Menander's comedies. In the case of Plautus, the old man attracts attention not only as a lover (Cody 1976, Walker 1980) but also as a spouse (Estevez 1966); the names of old and young men in his comedies are studied by Seaman 1969. In Terence the old man is generally portrayed as the loyal husband and the understanding father. Demea and Micio, the severe and the indulgent fathers respectively in *The Brothers,* are studied by Tränkle 1972, whereas Maltby 1979 shows that old men in Terence generally do not speak the same Latin as other people: they use archaisms, elevated lexical features, long-winded expressions and so forth and are characterized as older in subtle ways.

The Latin author whose views on old age have received the most scholarly attention is undoubtedly Cicero. He wrote his *Cato the Elder on Old Age* when he was himself a *senex.* In this plea *pro domo,* the ex-consul refutes the objections to the twilight years (e.g., that the elderly could no longer be active, that they were in physical decline, that they could no longer enjoy themselves, that they lived in the shadow of death) and advances his belief, perhaps mistaking his wishes for reality, that the management of the affairs of state and the education of the young were the specific tasks of those advanced in years. Different aspects of this remarkable tract have been studied in detail. Allen 1907 studies the problem of its date, Wilhelm 1911 and Dyroff 1939.46-79 study its sources, Wuilleumier 1930 traces its Nachleben. Venini 1960 investigates, among other things, the age Cicero had in mind when he wrote his tract (60 in theory, 45 in practice); de Saint-Denis 1956 shows how Cicero 'humanized' the elder Cato; Novara 1980 treats the bucolic joys that are the privilege of the old man; Castelli 1972 discusses the influence on Cicero of the (lost) *Logistorici* (esp. the "Tithonus περὶ γήρως") of his contemporary Varro, who was possessed by the same ideal of humanity; Schröder 1971 sees the tract as a mirror of true "romanitas." Other scholars deal with Cicero from a gerontological point of view: Chandler 1948, Carp 1955, Huebner 1957, Twigg-Porter 1962, Jarcho 1971. One certainly cannot overlook the articles of Alfonsi on the *De Senectute:* 1955 (a) on Cicero's sources (in his view of the peripatetic philosopher Ariston of Ceos); 1955 (b) on the tract's well structured composition; and on Cicero's *Weltanschauung* as it can be distilled from his treatise, which offers the reader a sort of "Lebenssynthese" (1971).

Of the poets who were active under Augustus, Horace and Virgil must be discussed. Generational conflict as depicted by Virgil is studied in Bertman 1976 (see above) and Pavlovskis 1976. For the relation between fathers and sons in the *Aeneid,* one can consult Lee 1979, whereas a separate study is devoted to Anchises, the father of Aeneas, in Lloyd 1957, to "the old man in the garden" in Clay 1981 (included in the present collection) and to "the old man from Tarentum" (a personage from the *Bucolics*) in Wuilleumier 1930.

In his *Ars Poetica* 153-78, Horace describes the ages of man (childhood, youth, adulthood, old age) with their varying character-istics and views the last phase of life in a hostile light. This famous text, discussed only cursorily in Colmant 1956, deserves to have received more scholarly attention. The poet's vision of old age had great influence on later literature and provides, as Harcum 1914 and especially Coffman 1934 demonstrate, an interesting chapter in the history of medieval culture. We should also mention here Hohnen-Pulheim 1988, which discusses how Horace experiences his own (not too advanced) old age. On Horace's representation of old women, see Esler in the present collection. On Ovid's reflections on old age, see de Luce in this volume.

The theme of old age in the literature dating from the Empire has to date received little attention from philologists and historians: Seneca, for instance, whose writings contain much information about old age, is considered from this point of view only by Crisafulli 1953. The younger Pliny has been more fortunate: his views are discussed in

Kebric 1983. Linn 1933-34 offers an anthology of some texts from Persius, Juvenal and Jerome, whereas Neuberger 1947 and more recently Ratkowitsch 1986.75-87 discuss the elegy in which Maximian at the close of antiquity mourned the misery of old age.

Early Christianity

Those looking for information on the theme of old age in Christian authors will be obliged to turn mainly to the general studies of Gnilka 1983 and Minois 1987 mentioned above. Schneider 1954.651-93 furnishes a discussion on age and sex. Old age in Augustine is treated in Sizoo 1955, while Jerome's views are to be found in the studies of Antin 1971 and Hamblenne 1969. For Ambrose we can refer to Bambeck 1972, which treats the problem of the "puer-puella senex" in this Church father's writings, and Lamirande 1982, which discusses the Bishop of Milan's age classification.

It is evident that further research needs to be done in this area. Pioneering scholarly research, however, has already been carried out by Gnilka. In addition to the studies of 1972 and 1983 (as well as the article "Altersversorgung," which will be discussed below), there are three other publications by this German scholar which deserve mention. In an article dating from 1971 he establishes the link between the lamentation of the elderly and their longing for the next world; a second article, dating from 1980, discusses what the Christians understood as a venerable old age; a third written in 1977 shows how the age-old belief that advancing from one age to another involves a sort of death liberates man from the fear of death, for death only involves a migration to a new and better life.

Other Aspects

So much for this survey of old age in different periods of antiquity. Finally, we will bring up some aspects of this subject which have not, or only in passing, been mentioned in the foregoing pages.

For the etymology of words such as *senex,* γέρων or πρέσβυς one can consult a number of articles, e.g., Ernout 1940 and Porzig 1954. Regarding the age at which old age was considered to begin in Roman antiquity (and the Middle Ages), Suder 1978 and 1987 should be mentioned. Concerning longevity, we can refer to McCartney 1925, which deals with this aspect (as well as with rejuvenation) in ancient folklore. On the legendary Tithonos, who received immortality but not eternal youth from Zeus (and so became a cicada), one can read King 1986 (reprinted in this collection). On old age and sexuality in Greek and Latin poetry, see Bertman in this volume: on old age and sex in Greece see Houdijk and Vanderbroeck 1987.

Unfortunately, very few scholars have dealt with old(er) women. According to Bremmer 1984 and 1987, old women in antiquity didn't arouse the interest of men, enjoyed greater freedom than younger women, were active out of doors (e.g., as merchants or midwives), played a role in some cults and were often characterized (in words and in stone!) as addicted to wine — cf. Musso 1968. For the age of menopause we refer to Amundson and Diers 1970.

In spite of all the eulogies of old age, old people certainly did not have an easy life in antiquity (Haynes 1962 and 1963). On the care of the elderly there is the study of Gnilka 1985. They were lucky when they had some money, and children (in Rome, freedmen too) were the best old-age pension. The state intervened only indirectly — for instance, by obliging children to support their elders or by freeing the elderly from the payment of taxes. The situation improved in Christian times, when widows over sixty were supported by the Christian communities and sheltered accommodations arose.

Ancient medicine was aware of the fact that elderly people had their specific diseases and needed specific treatments. For geriatrics in antiquity we can refer to the studies of Orth 1963 and Godderis 1988. The relevant opinions of medical authors such as Aretaeus, Celsus and Galen are treated by Howell 1971 and 1986, and Byl 1988.

People in antiquity certainly did not always have the respect for old people one might expect. The liquidation of old people is a widespread phenomenon, with known examples from the ancient world (Dumézil 1950), both from Greece (Schmidt 1903) and Rome (Néraudau 1978, Guarino 1979).

Finally there is the problem of whether the elderly (men of course) played a role in the management of the state. Although the *gerontes* were important in the Homeric world (Ulf 1987), in Sparta and in some Greek towns of Asia Minor in Hellenistic and Roman times as members of the Gerusia (Oliver 1941), it can not be said that ancient

Greece and Rome were gerontocracies (Roussel 1951). In Rome, for instance, the senate was filled with people from age twenty five to thirty and upwards, and at least from the time of Claudius on senators retired at the age of sixty (McAlindon 1957), the beginning of *senectus*. In Christian times age gave elderly people some prestige, but ecclesiastical offices were certainly not reserved only for them. These never involved an upper age limit, but when a minimum age is required, it is (despite the name πρεσβύτερος) mostly thirty (the *perfecta aetas,* at which age Jesus began his mission) for a priest, fifty (often thirty) for a bishop (Blokscha 1931). The examples of Jesus himself and of the apostles John and Timothy, as well as the 'puer-senex' ideal described above, meant that even important ecclesiastical offices were never the monopoly of the elders (Gnilka 1983, col. 1079 ff.).

Notes

I am indebted to Patrick Daly for the translation from the Dutch and to Ineke Croux for material help.

1. P. Ariès 1960.

2. See, however, his 1983 article, p. 48: "Mais l'enfance existe: ne disons pas comme on me l'a fait souvent dire qu'il n'y avait pas d'enfance et qu'il n'y avait pas du tout de sollicitude à l'égard de l'enfant, autrement nous ne serions pas ici, ni vous, ni moi. Mais l'enfance avait une place, qui n'était pas primordiale et qui confinait parfois à une certaine indifférence. Et bien c'est la même chose pour le vieillard."

3. Arist. *Rh.* 2.12-14, Hor. *Ars P.* 153-78, Juv. 10.188-255, Maxim. *Eleg.* 1.

4. Cf. Gnilka 1983 col. 1021-24. On Diogenes, Clay, in press.

5. Cf. for example also Forrest 1975, and Bonnefand 1982. For a general bibliography, see Esler 1984.

6. See e.g. Schmid in *Gnomon* 10 (1934) 529-32.

7. See Byl 1974.

8. Thus Lucian *Macr.* 18.

References

Alfonsi, L. 1955 (a). "Sulle fonti del De Senectute," *PP* 41.121-29.

―――. 1955 (b). "La composizione del De Senectute ciceroniano," *SicGymn* 8.429-54.

―――. 1971. "Das ciceronische Denken in 'De Senectute'," *Das neue Cicerobild,* ed. K. Büchner. Darmstadt. 208-28.

Allen, K. 1907. "The Date of Cicero's Cato Maior de senectute," *AJPh* 28.297-300.

Amundsen, B. W. and C. J. Diers. 1970. "The Age of Menopause in Classical Greece and Rome," *Human Biology* 42.79-86.

Antin, P. 1971. "La vieillesse chez S. Jérôme," *REAug* 17.43-54.

Ariès, P. 1960. *L'enfant et la vie familiale sous l'ancien regime.* Paris.

―――. 1983. "Une histoire de la vieillesse?" *Communications* 37.47-54.

Bambeck, M. 1972. "Puer et puella senes bei Ambrosius von Mailand. Zur altchristlichen Vorgeschichte eines literarischen Topos," *RomForsch* 84.257-313.

Berelson, L. 1934. *Old Age in Ancient Rome.* Diss. Charlottesville.

Bertman, S., ed. 1976. *The Conflict of Generations in Ancient Greece and Rome.* Amsterdam.

Blokscha, J. 1931. "Die Altersvorschriften für die höheren Weihen im ersten Jahrtausend," *Kirchenrecht Archiv für katholisches* 111.31-83.

Boll, F. 1913. "Die Lebensalter. Ein Beitrag zur antiken Ethologie und zur Geschichte der Zahlen," *Neue Jahrbücher für das klass. Altertum,* 31.89-145.

Bonnefand, M. 1982. "Le sénat républicain et les conflits de générations," *MEFRA* 94.175-225.

Bremmer, J. N. 1984. "Oude vrouwen in Griekenland en Rome," *Lampas* 17.96-113.

————. 1987. "The Old Women of Ancient Greece," in *Sexual Asymmetry. Studies in Ancient Society,* ed. J. Blok and P. Mason. Amsterdam. 191-215.

Burrow, J. A. 1986. *The Ages of Man. A Study in Medieval Writing and Thought.* Oxford.

Byl, S. 1974. "Platon et Aristotle ont-ils professé des vues contradictoires sur la vieillesse?," *LEC* 42.113-26.

————. 1975. "Lamentations sur la vieillesse dans la tragédie grecque," in *Le monde grec. Hommages à C. Préaux.* Brussels. 130-39.

————. 1976. "Lamentations sur la vieillesse chez Homère et les poètes lyriques des VIIe et VIe siècles," *LEC* 44.234-44.

————. 1977 (a). "Le vieillard dans les comédies d'Aristophane," *AC* 46.52-73.

————. 1977 (b). "Plutarque et la vieillesse," *LEC* 45.107-23.

————. 1978. "Lucien et la vieillesse," *LEC* 46.317-25.

————. 1988. "La gérontologie de Galien," in *History and Philosophy of the Life Sciences.* Naples. 73-94.

Carp, L. 1955. "Cicero Speaks on Old Age," *Geriatrics* 10.43-45.

Castelli, G. 1972. "Il Cato Maior de Senectute come 'Ηρακλείδειον,'" *RSC* 20.5-12.

Chandler, A. R. 1948. "Cicero's Ideal Old Man," *JG* 3.285-89.

Clauss, M. 1973. "Probleme der Lebensalterstatistiken aufgrund römischer Grabinschriften," *Chiron* 3.395-417.

Clay, D. in press. "The Philosophical Inscription of Diogenes of Oenoanda: The New Discoveries," *ANRW* 2:36.

Clay, J. Strauss. 1981. "The Old Man in the Garden. *Georgic* 4.116-,148," *Arethusa* 14.57-65.

Clota, J. A. 1954. Platon y la vejez," *Helmantica* 5.61-69.

Cody, J. M. 1976. "The *senex amator* in Plautus' Casina," *Hermes* 104.433-76.

Coffman, G. R. 1934. "Old Age from Horace to Chaucer. Some Literary Affinities and Adventures of an Idea," *Speculum* 9.249-77.

Colmant, P. 1956. "Les quatre âges de la vie (Horace, *Art poétique*)," *LEC* 24.58-63.

Conca, F. 1970. "Il motivo del vecchio inamorato in Menandro, Plauto e Terenzio," *Acme* 23.81-90.

Crisafulli, N. 1953. "L'idea della vecchiezza in Seneca," *Longevità* 2.9-10.

Croon, J. H. et al. 1981. *De lastige ouderdom. De senex in de literatuur.* Muiderberg.

de Beauvoir, S. 1970. *La vieillesse.* Paris.

de Ghellinck, J. 1948. "Juventus, gravitas, senectus," in *Studia R. J. Martin.* Brugge. 39-59.

de Romilly, J. 1968. Time in Greek Tragedy. Ithaca, NY.

de Saint-Denis, E. 1956. "Caton l'Ancien vu par Cicéron," *IL* 8.93-100.

Duckworth, G. E. 1952. *The Nature of Roman Comedy.* Princeton. 242-49.

Dumézil, G. 1950. "Quelques cas anciens de liquidation des vieillards. Histoire et survivances," in *Mélanges de Visscher.* Vol. 3. Paris. 447-54.

Dyroff, A. 1937. "Junkus und Ariston von Keos über das Greisenalter," *RhM* 86.241-69.

———. 1939. *Der Peripatos über das Greisenalter.* Paderborn.

Ernout A. 1940. "Senex et les formations en -k- du Latin," *BSL* 41.92-128.

Esler, A. 1984. *The Generation Gap in Society and History. A Select Bibliography.* Monticello, IL.

Estevez, V. A. 1966. "Senex as Spouse in Plautus and Terence," *CB* 42.73-76.

Eyben, E. 1973 (a). "Die Einteilung des menschlichen Lebens im römischen Altertum," *RhM* 116.150-90.

———. 1973 (b). "Roman Notes on the Course of Life," *AncSoc* 4.213-38.

Falkner, T. 1985 (a). "Old age in Euripides' *Medea*," *CB* 61.76-78.

———. 1985 (b). "Euripides and the Stagecraft of Old Age," in *The Many Forms of Drama*, ed. K. Hartigan. Lanham, MD. 41-49.

———. 1987. "Strengthless, Friendless, Loveless: the Chorus and the Cultural Construction of Old Age in Sophocles' *Oedipus at Colonus*," in *From the Bard to Broadway*, ed. K. Hartigan. Lanham, MD. 51-59.

———. 1989 (a). "Slouching Towards Boeotia: Age and Age-Grading in the Hesiodic Myth of the Five Races," *ClAnt* 8.41-59.

———. 1989 (b). "The Politics and the Poetics of Time in Solon's 'Ten Ages'," *CJ* (in press).

Finley, M. I. 1981. "The Elderly in Classical Antiquity," *G&R* 28.156-71.

Fornara, C. W. 1966. "Sources of Plutarch's 'An seni sit gerenda res publica'," *Philologus* 110.119-27.

Forrest, W. G. 1975. "An Athenian Generation Gap," *YClS* 24.37-52.

Gigon, O. 1968. "Jugend und Alter in der Ethik des Aristotles," in *Antiquitas Graeco-Romana ac tempora nostra*, ed. J. Burian. Prague. 188-122.

Gnilka, C. 1971. "Altersklage und Jenseitssehnsucht," *JbAC.* 5-23.

———. 1972. *Aetas spiritualis. Die Überwindung der naturlichen Altersstufen als Ideal frühchristlichen Lebens*. Cologne and Bonn.

———. 1977. "Neues Alter, neues Leben. Eine antike Weisheit und ihre christliche Nutzung," *JbAC* 20.5-38.

———. 1980. "Καλόγηρος. Die Idee des 'guten Alters' bei den Christen," *JbAC* 23.5-21.

———. 1983. "Greisenalter," *RAC* 12. col. 995-1094.

————. 1985. "Altersversorgung," *RAC Suppl.*, Lief. 1/2, col. 266-289.

Godderis, J. 1989. "ΠΕΡΙ ΓΗΡΩΣ. De antieke geneeskunde over de lichamelijke en psychische kwalen van de oude dag," *Kleio* 18.51-66.

Guarino, A. 1979. "Depontani senes," *AAN* 90.535-39.

Hamblenne, P. 1969. "La longévité de Jérome. Prosper avait-il raison?," *Latomus* 28.1081-1119.

Harbsmeier, D. G. 1968. *Die alten Menschen bei Euripides. Mit einem Anhang über Menelaos und Helena bei Euripides.* Diss. Göttingen.

Harcum, C. G. 1914. "The Ages of Man: a Study Suggested by Horace, Ars Poetica," *CW* 7.114-18.

Haynes, M. S. 1962. "The Supposedly Golden Age for the Aged in Ancient Greece (A study of literary concepts of old age)," *The Gerontologist* 2.93-98.

————. 1963. "The Supposedly Golden Age for the Aged in Ancient Rome (A study of literary concepts of old age)," *The Gerontologist* 3.26-35.

Herter, H. 1975. "Demokrit über das Alter," *WJA* N.F. 1.83-92.

Hofmeister, A. 1926. "Puer, iuvenis, senex. Zum Verständis der mittelalterlichen Altersbezeichnungen," in *Papsstum und Kaisertum,* ed. A. Brackmann. Munich. 287-316.

Hohnen, P. 1953. *Die Altersklage im "Herakles" des Euripides und die Wertschätzung des Greisenalters bei den Griechen.* Diss. Bonn.

Hohnen-Pulheim, P. 1988. "Zeugnisse der Altersreflexion bei Horaz," *Gymnasium* 95.154-72.

Houdijk, L. and P. Vanderbroeck. 1987. "Old Age and Sex in the Ancient Greek World," *WZRostock* 36.57-61.

Huebner, E. 1957. "Cicero's De Senectute in gerontologischer Schau," *Altertum* 3.46-52.

Irigoin, J. 1971. "Le De Senectute de Diogène d' Oinoanda. Principes d'une reconstition," in *Studi V. De Falco.* Napoli. 475-85.

Jarcho, S. 1971. "Cicero's Essay on Old Age," in *Bull NY Acad Med*, 47.1440-45.

Jungclaussen, W. 1870. *Ueber das Greisenalter bei Homer*. Flensburg.

Kebric, R. B. 1983. "Aging in Pliny's Letters: a View from the Second Century A.D.," *The Gerontologist* 23.538-45.

King, H. 1986. "Tithonos and the Tettix," *Arethusa* 19.15-35.

Kirk, G. S. 1971. "Old age and maturity in ancient Greece," *Eranos-Jb* 40.123-58.

Koumakis, G. 1974. "Aristotle's Opinions on Old Age from a Social Point of View," *Philosophia* 4.274-85.

Lamirande, E. 1982. "Les âges de l'homme d'après Saint Ambroise de Milan," *CEA* 14.227-33.

Lee, M. O. 1979. *Fathers and Sons in Virgil's Aeneid*. Albany.

Linn, H. W. 1933-34. "Persius, Juvenal and St. Jerome on old age," *CB* 10.49-50.

Lloyd, R. B. 1957. "The Character of Anchises in the Aeneid," *TAPhA* 88.44-55.

Maier, J. 1979. "Die Wertung des Alters in der jüdischen Ueberlieferung der Spätantike und des frühes Mittelalters," *Saeculum* 30.355-64.

Maltby, R. 1979. "Linguistic Characterization of Old Men in Terence," *CPh* 74.136-47.

McAlindon, D. 1957. "The Senator's Retiring Age: 65 or 60?" *CR* 7.108.

McCartney, E. S. 1925. "Longevity and Rejuvenation in Greek and Roman Folklore," *PMASAL* 5.37-72.

McCary, T. 1971. "Menander's old men," *TAPhA* 102.301-25.

Minois, G. 1985. "La vieillesse dans la littérature du haut Moyen Age," *ABPO* 92.389-401.

―――. 1987. *Histoire de la vieillesse en occident de l'Antiquité à la Renaissance*. Paris.

Musso, O. 1968. "Anus ebria," *A&R* 13.29-31.

Néraudau, J.P. 1978. "Sexagenarii de ponte. Réflexions sur la genèse d'un proverbe," *REL* 56.158-74.

Neuberger, M. 1947. "The Latin Poet Maximianus on the Miseries of Old Age," *BHM* 21.113-19.

Novara, A. 1980. "Le vieux Caton 'aux champs' ou le plaisir exceptionnel de l'agriculture pour un sage vieillard (A propos de Cic., Cato Maior, 51-56)," in *Mélanges P. Wuilleumier.* Paris. 261-68.

Oeri, G. 1948. *Der Typ der komischen Alten in der griechischen Komödie. Seine Nachwirkungen und seine Herkunft.* Diss. Basel.

Oliver, J. H. 1941. "The sacred Gerusia," *Hesperia* suppl. 6.

Orth, H. 1963. "ΔΙΑΙΤΑ ΓΕΡΟΝΤΩΝ. Die Geriatrie der griechischen Antike," *Centaurus* 8.19-47.

Pavlovskis, Z. 1976. "Aeneid V: the Old and the Young," *CJ* 71.193-205.

Philibert, M. 1968. *Les échelles d'âge dans la philosophie, la science et la société. De leur renversement et des conditions de leur redressement.* Paris.

————. 1984. "Le statut de la personne âgée dans les sociétés antiques et préindustrielles," *Sociologie et sociétés* 16.15-27.

Porzig, W. 1954. "Alt und Jung," in *Sprachgeschichte und Wortbedeutung,* Bern. 343-49.

Preisshofen, F. 1977. *Untersuchungen zur Darstellung des Greisenalters in der frühgriechischen Dichtung.* Wiesbaden.

Ratkowitsch, Ch. 1986. *Maximianus amat. Zu Datierung und Interpretation des Elegikers Maximian.* Vienna.

Richardson, B. E. 1969 (1933). *Old Age Among the Ancient Greeks. The Greek Portrayal of Old Age in Literature, Art and Inscriptions. With a study of the Duration of Life among the Ancient Greeks on the Basis of Inscriptional Evidence.* New York.

Roth, E. 1913. *Novae comoediae adulescentes amatores, senes, servi quomodo congruant cum Julii Pollucis personis.* Diss. Leipzig.

Roussel, M.P. 1951. "Etude sur le principe de l'ancienneté dans le monde héllenique du Ve siècle av. J-C. à l'époque romaine," *MAI* 43. 123-227.

Schadewaldt, W. 1933. "Lebenszeit und Greisenalter im frühen Griechentum," *Ant* 9.282-302.

Scharbert, J. 1979. "Das Alter und die Alten in der Bibel," *Saeculum* 30.338-54.

Schmidt, B. 1903. "Der Selbstmord der Greise von Keos," *NJKA* 11.617-28.

Schmiel, R. 1974. "Youth and Age: Mimnermus 1 and 2," *RFIC* 102.283-89.

Schneider, C. 1954. *Geistesgeschichte des antiken Christentums,* vol. 1. Munich. 651-93.

Schröder, R. A. 1971. "Marcus Tullius Cicero: Cato der Altere über das Greisenalter," in *Das neue Cicerobild,* ed. K. Büchner. Darmstadt. 1-9.

Schweingruber, F. 1918. *Jugend und Alter in der griechischen Literatur von Homer bis Aristotles.* Diss. Zurich.

Seaman, W. N. 1969. "On the Names of Old and Young Men in Plautus," in *Classical Studies Presented to B. E. Perry.* 114-22.

Sears, E. 1986. *The Ages of Man. Medieval Interpretations of the Life Cycle.* Princeton.

Sizoo, A. 1955. "Augustinus de senectute," in *Ut pictura poesis. Studia latina P. I. Enk septuagenario oblata.* Leiden. 184-88.

Sluşanschi, D. 1973. "Varron et les gradus aetatum," *AUR, Limbi clasice si orientale.* 22.103-9.

_____. 1974. "Le vocabulaire latin des gradus aetatum," *RRL* 19.104-21, 267-96, 345-69, 437-51, 564-78.

Stein, A. 1966. *Platons Charakteristik der menschlichen Altersstufen.* Diss. Bonn.

Steinhagen, H. 1972. "Solons Lebensalter Elegie (Fr. 19 D): Eine Interpretation," in *Die Griechische Elegie,* ed. G. Pfohl. Darmstadt. 263-81.

Subrenat, J., ed. 1987. *Vieillesse et vieillissement au Moyen-Age.* Aix-en-Provence.

Suder, W. 1978. "On Age Classification in Roman Imperial Literature," *CB* 55.5-9.

———. 1987. "L' initium senectutis nell' impero romano e medio evo," in *Actes du 110e congrès national des sociétés savantes.* Paris. 65-79.

Tränkle, H. 1972. "Micio und Demea in den terenzischen Adelphen," *MH* 29.241-255.

Twigg-Porter, G. 1962. "Cicero, Classic Gerontologist," *CB* 39.231-33.

Ulf, C. 1987. *Das Lebensalter als Kriterium sozialer Bewertung.* Habil. Innsbruck.

Van Hooff, A. J. L. 1983. "Oud-zijn in het oude Hellas," *TG* 14.141-48.

Venini, P. 1960. "La vecchiaia nel *De senectute* di Cicerone," *Athenaeum* 38.98-117.

Vilchez, M. 1983. "Sobre los periodos de la vida humana en la lirica arcaica y la tragedia griega," *Emerita* 51.63-95, 215-53.

Walker, S. L. 1980. *The senex amator in Plautus. A study in development.* Diss. Chapel Hill.

Welti, M. 1987. "Das Altern im Mittelalter und in der frühen Neuzeit," *Schweizerische Zeitschrift für Geschichte,* 37.1-31.

Wilhelm, F. 1911. *Die Schrift des Juncus* Περὶ γήρως *und ihr Verhältnis zu Ciceros Cato Maior.* Breslau.

Woodbury, L. 1979. "Gold Hair and Grey, or the Game of Love. Anacreon Fr. 13.358.PMG, 13 Gentili," *TAPhA* 109.277-87.

Wuilleumier, P. 1930. "Virgile et le vieillard de Tarente," *REL* 8.325-40.

———. 1940. "L'influence du Cato Maior," in *Mélanges A. Ernout.* Paris. 383-88.

Notes on Contributors

Stephen Bertman is Professor of Classical and Modern Languages, Literatures, and Civilizations at the University of Windsor, Ontario. He is the author of *Art and the Romans* (Lawrence 1975) and *Doorways Through Time, The Romance of Archeology* (Los Angeles and New York 1987), as well as the editor of *The Conflict of Generations in Ancient Greece and Rome* (Amsterdam 1976).

Jenny Strauss Clay is Associate Professor of Classics at the University of Virginia and the author of *The Wrath of Athena* (Princeton 1983) and *The Politics of Olympus* (Princeton 1989) as well as articles on Greek and Latin poetry.

Judith de Luce is Associate Professor and Chair of Classics and an Affiliate in Women's Studies at Miami University. Her research has included work on old women in Greece and Rome, feminist revisions of classical mythology, and rhetorical technique in Cicero and Ovid. She is coeditor, with Hugh T. Wilder, of *Language in Primates: Perspectives and Implications* (New York 1983).

Carol Clemeau Esler has taught most recently at Wheaton College. In addition to articles on the *Odes* of Horace, her work includes *Roman Voices: Everyday Latin in Ancient Rome* (Detroit 1974) and *Public Voices and Private Lives*. She is the author of the mystery novel *The Ariadne Clue* (New York 1982).

Emiel Eyben teaches at the Catholic University of Louvain (K.U. Leuven) in Belgium and is Research Associate of the National Fund for Scientific Research, with specializations in Latin literature and the history of mentalities in Greco-Roman antiquity. He has published on a range of subjects related to the human life span in antiquity and early Christianity.

Thomas M. Falkner is Associate Professor of Classical Studies at the College of Wooster in Ohio. He has published essays on Greek and Latin poetry, a grammatical commentary on Euripides' *Orestes,* and a number of articles on aging and old age in Greek literature.

Sir **M. I. Finley,** before his death in 1986, was Master of Darwin College and Professor Emeritus of ancient history at Cambridge University. Well known among his many books are *The World of Odysseus* (New York 1954), *Aspects of Antiquity* (New York 1968), *The Ancient Economy* (London 1973), *The Olympic Games: The First Thousand Years* (New York 1976), and *Ancient Slavery and Modern Ideology* (New York 1980).

Thomas K. Hubbard is Assistant Professor of Classics at the University of Texas at Austin. He is author of *The Pindaric Mind: A Study of Logical Structure in Early Greek Poetry* and articles on Greek and Roman poetry. He is currently writing a book on Aristophanes and the intertextual parabasis.

Helen King is Lecturer in History at S. Katharine's College, Liverpool Institute of Higher Education. She has published articles on ancient myth and medicine, and is currently working on the uses of Hippocratic gynaecology in sixteenth and seventeenth century disease categories. She will be a contributor to *History of Hysteria* (forthcoming, University of California).

Mildred M. Seltzer is Director of Education and Training at the Scripps Gerontology Center and Professor of Sociology at Miami University. Her research has dealt with academic gerontology programs, timing, humor and aging, old women, aging as depicted in children's literature, early retirement incentive programs in academia, reunions, and expected life history.

Thomas Van Nortwick is Associate Professor of Classics at Oberlin College. He has published articles on early Greek epic poetry and Augustan Latin poetry.

Index

Includes references to subjects and authors cited in the text, though not generally the notes. For the modern literature, consult the bibliography and notes for each chapter.

255